More Praise for
Small Business Taxes Made Easy

"Failing to plan is planning to fail. Ignoring The TaxMama = Epic Fail."

—Brent Clanton, CPO, Clanton Communications, LLS, and host of CBS Radio's *Talk650 Morning Show*, Houston, Texas

"TaxMama provides a comprehensive overview of small business accounting and taxation issues in a fun and easy-to-read format."

—Michael T. Hanley, CPA–Managing Partner of Merl & Hanley, LLP, and author of *Effective Tax Planning for the MicroBusiness*

"TaxMama's book provides not only a bit of laughter but also a lot of straightforward information about operating a small business within the guidelines set by the IRS."

—Jan Zobel, EA, author of *Minding Her Own Business*

"As a business owner you must have this book. If you're a work-at-home mother or an Internet marketer or a bricks-and-mortar business owner, this book has answers and instructions presented in TaxMama's irreverent, entertaining, and fun (yes, I said fun) style."

—Stephanie L. Watson, Virtual Assistant Moms

"Every U.S. business owner will benefit from Rosenberg's clear, well-written explanations of complex, arcane tax concepts. You'll run your business more effectively and you'll stay out of trouble with the IRS. Buy this book."

—Shel Horowitz, author of *Principled Profit: Marketing That Puts People First* and owner of frugalmarketing.com

"Here is a book that is short on theory and long on practical, plain-spoken advice. From how to buy office supplies to how to deal with the IRS, Rosenberg taps decades of business savvy to walk readers through the minefields of new business ownership."

—Al Tompkins, author, teacher, consultant

"When I started my career as a CPA, one of the most valuable lessons I learned was to simplify and explain the basics. Eva has managed to take a complex subject and simplify it for all."

—Ken Leebow, The Incredible Internet Guy, www.incredibleinternetguy.com

"From the very beginning, this excellent book clearly sets itself apart from other tax books. As the title implies, Eva's book gives the small business person a good handle on tax issues, and the checklists make it easy to follow through on what you learn. This is a must-have book for every small business person and anyone wanting to start his or her own small business."

—Dennis Gaskill, BoogieJack.com

"Eva Rosenberg counsels new entrepreneurs that they'll need a business plan if they want to succeed. *Small Business Taxes Made Easy* should be the first step in that plan."

—Kay Bell, tax editor at Bankrate.com

Small Business Taxes Made Easy, Second Edition

EVA ROSENBERG, EA

New York   Chicago   San Francisco   Lisbon   London   Madrid   Mexico City
Milan   New Delhi   San Juan   Seoul   Singapore   Sydney   Toronto

The **McGraw·Hill** *Companies*

7 8 9 1   DOC/DOC   1 9 8 7 6

ISBN 978-0-07-174327-3

MHID 0-07-174327-8

This book is intended to be a guide to familiarize the reader with tax and business concepts. It is not intended to provide legal or tax advice. No mere book is a substitute for advice from your own tax professionals, who have a picture of your personal financial and business situation. Also, at the time this book was written, all information was current. Tax laws change quickly, so some information may be outdated by the time you read it.

TaxMama® is a registered service mark of Eva Rosenberg and may not be used without written permission.

McGraw-Hill books are available at special quantity discounts to use as premiums and sales promotions or for use in corporate training programs. To contact a representative, please e-mail us at bulksales@mcgraw-hill.com.

This book is printed on acid-free paper.

This book is dedicated to the three people who take good care of me—my husband, Rick; my right hand, Lourdes Rodriguez; and my technical guru and dancing boy, Andrew McCluskey. You bring sunshine and laughter to my days.

CONTENTS

ACKNOWLEDGMENTS

This book was first conceived by the original editor Donya Dickerson, who called me out of the blue. Michele R. Wells initiated this update, then went off to the world of pictures at Penguin. Mary Therese Church brought this edition to fruition.

When it comes to taxes, nothing happens in a vacuum. It's impossible for any one person to know it all. TaxMama relies on many people to keep me in the loop. Key among them are the hardworking public relations firms for all the top tax software, tax preparation, and publishing companies. They are generous with information, resources, and experts, often on a moment's notice. You make my job look easy.

I want to thank the entire family at TaxMama.com and Team TaxMama. Everyone who asks a question, or answers it, contributes to experiences that shaped this book. All my friends on the Internet, around the world, in a variety of fields tell me their stories, help me build and improve my Web sites, and become the source of stories and cases you're about to enjoy.

I'd like to thank Steven Kerch and Andrea Coombes, two special people from Dow Jones www.MarketWatch.com, who, with their great patience and despite my pushing deadlines, have helped me shape my writing skills.

My thanks also go to Roger B. Adams, an enrolled agent in Lisbon, Portugal, who has become my international tax expert, an instructor at TaxMama's EA Exam Review Course, and my very dear friend. He's an excellent sounding board for all kinds of tax strategies.

Thanks to the wealth of talented, passionate tax professionals who have been part of my advisory team for the past decade—Bruce Drooks, JD; Lucie Sample, EA; Blakely Sanford, EA; Mel Kreger, EA/LLM; Doug Thorburn, EA; Kris Hix, EA; Sharoj Sharma, EA; Rita Lewis, EA; Fred Daily, tax attorney; David L. Mellem, EA; Tom Blair, EA; Linda Dorfmont, EA; Jim Banks, EA; Jan Zobel, EA; . . . and countless others who inspire me or bring me laughter each day.

I especially want to thank all the folks at the IRS and the Taxpayers Advocate Service who are always so generous to me with their time and humor—both personally and on the job. My gratitude also goes to the team at the D.C. Press Office who put up with questions no one else asks, and to the D.C. and Los Angeles Stakeholder Relations teams who work long hours to keep people informed, fix errors when we find them, and do it all with grace and good spirit. Thanks also to those special, dedicated folks at the IRS who actually go out of their way to help complete strangers solve their problems. They prove that a tax system can be administered fairly.

Special thanks to FLOYD T. GREENMAN, EA, in memoriam.
Floyd, a former IRS agent, was the source of many Money Funnies over the years and also of wisdom and valuable advice at our SFV CSEA breakfast meetings.

INTRODUCTION

A Letter from Eva Rosenberg to You, the Business Owner

Dear Entrepreneur,

(Yes, *you*. If you're starting a business, please start thinking of yourself right now as an *entrepreneur*.)

Since this book was first published in 2004, TaxMama has received many letters from business owners with two themes:

1. I wish I had read this book before starting my business. It would have saved me a fortune in time, money, taxes—and errors.
2. Even though I've been in business for many years, this book has helped me cut my taxes and increase my profits. It's my new business bible.

Why are people saying things like that? Because *Small Business Taxes Made Easy* is a book you can use on a day-to-day basis to keep your business on a path to profits and success.

Many books on the market tell you how to organize your business records, prepare your tax returns, even how to make decisions or choices. Some are excellent.

So why does the world need yet another book on small business taxes? Because even the best books focus primarily on the record-keeping or legal aspects of small business taxes. For your business to succeed, you must *also* understand how the reporting requirements can be used to improve your business management, provide better decision-making tools, and increase your profits. Providing that information is what makes this book different.

With all the resentment and resistance toward paying taxes and toward the flood of reporting requirements, you've got to see what's in it for you. What do *you* get from your investment of time and money? It doesn't only benefit the IRS and your state and local governments.

While each chapter of this book explains tax concepts and responsibilities, it also helps you understand how you benefit from following those guidelines.

You're not in business to supply a flood of paperwork to the government. Nor are you sweating blood trying to meet your business, financial, and family obligations in order to buy your tax pro a new BMW.

You're in business to have more control of your life and time; to earn more money than you could on a job; and to build a future—and a legacy—for your family and future generations.

Otherwise, why work so hard? Just go back to your traditional nine-to-five job. Seriously, there's more to running a business than appears on the surface. Some people make it appear effortless—and they often go out of business quickly as a result. Others make it seem a gargantuan burden—and they end up hating every minute of it. They destroy their family and relationships in the process, blaming everyone else for their failures.

Then there are those people who start up, and everything goes right. Life is good. Family and social relationships remain solid, and they maintain balance in their lives. That's what I want for you.

Listening to the news, you often hear when large businesses fail. You're probably still shaking your head over the whole dot-com bust, wondering how all those businesses failed after raising millions of dollars in venture capital or through their initial public offering.

The businesses that failed went wrong in one, or all, of three ways:

1. They didn't have a realistic business plan.
2. They didn't plan for success.
3. They were run by immature and inexperienced people who simply blew all the money without looking for reasonable returns on their spending.

You're buying this book to avoid all those mistakes. Use this book to learn from others' failures and successes. Please, make a commitment to devote all the time and resources needed to make your business work.

Otherwise, put this book back on the shelf. It's not for you.

Using This Book

I didn't write this book to bore you, bully you, or enable your failure.

If you can't make a serious commitment to create your business plan, set up and use a proper accounting system, and be ethical in tax reporting—please don't start the business. You'll earn much more, with less effort, less stress, and less risk, with a job working for someone else. Really, you will.

Take into account how much you could earn on a job or on the money you're investing to get this business going. Even if you borrow the money, think of how many hours of work it will take to pay it back.

Those are called "opportunity costs." It's important to understand what you're giving up to start your business. When I started my business, I knew what I was getting into. I relish the independence and the lack of office politics. I love my clients, the people I work with, and the people whom I consult. Despite being constantly behind in my workload, I rejoice in the flood of new work and fresh ideas that comes pouring in each day from friends and readers.

Here are the two most important things I want you to know going in:

- Love what you do.
- Don't delude yourself into thinking your goal is to pay the least amount of tax possible. Your real goal is to end up with the *highest disposable income possible*—and to be in great physical and mental health when you get there.

That's what I'd like to help you achieve.

You're about to learn how following the IRS's rules for small business owners will make you richer, happier, and less stressed.

TaxMama's warning: Although I can make changes at the IRS, I can't change grammatical rules. So wherever you see URLs in this book that seem to have colons, commas, or periods as the last character, ignore that final character when typing them into your browser.

Comparing a Job and a Business

Be sure to understand these distinctions between a job and a business. People starting out on their own rarely realize just how many things they've taken for granted on a job. These are the things that just happened invisibly, in the background, taken care of by your employer's infrastructure. Even if you felt as though you were doing most of it for him or her, when you're on your own, the sidebar will show you just how many more things you'll need to oversee—things that will drain your time, patience, and resources.

One of the biggest complaints from people working for others is that they do not have control over their income. Their bosses can cut their commissions, territories, or bonuses at will—and often do. When you're in business for yourself, if you earn it, *you* reap the rewards.

When You Have a Traditional Job

THE *GOOD* THINGS

- Your boss ensures there's money coming in, that it gets into the bank, and that your payroll is covered.
- Your boss pays your payroll taxes, your workers compensation insurance, your vacations, and sick pay.
- Your boss, or staff paid by your boss, gets the customers; orders and pays for the supplies you use, buys and sets up your computer, telephone, and the other tools you take for granted every day.
- Your boss arranges to take care of all the billing, the administrative paperwork, all the day-to-day trivia needed to run a business. All you have to do is show up and do your job—you get your paycheck, leave and don't have to think about things once you're off the clock.

THE *BAD* THINGS

But what if you want to leave? Just suppose . . .
- You've got a doctor's appointment.
- Your kids have a recital.
- You're not feeling well.
- Just don't feel like working.
- You have to ask permission—which you sometimes don't get. Or you have to lie.
- You hate a customer or client—you're stuck dealing with them if they're important to your boss.
- You don't like a business practice or policy? If you want to keep your job, you've got to do it their way.
- Your boss assigns the workload. How many times have they dumped stuff on you at the last minute that's been sitting there for weeks? You have to work overtime you hadn't anticipated.

When You Have a Business

THE *BAD* THINGS

- You have to take the time to do all those things listed under "When Your Have a Traditional Job."
- Or, you have to pay people to do all those things. You must generate enough extra income to cover their compensation.
- Trying to do it all yourself, won't give you time to sell and build your customer or client base.
- Or, if you do have the time, you won't have time to do the work.
- So you'll need to learn the most cost-effective use of your time. You'll want to learn what to outsource, or hire staff to do, and what is worth doing yourself.
- Or, you'll need to create a solid budget and business plan to determine how much money you'll need to raise to cover your operating costs until your business starts to turn a profit.
- Remember, while being in business for yourself does mean you work your own hours; it could mean you work all of them. Expect to put in 50%–75% more hours than you worked doing the same job.

THE *GOOD* THINGS

- You can take time off anytime that suits you—no excuses or lies needed.
- You don't have to keep clients or customers that treat you without respect. (Or you can charge them lots more to make it worth your while.)
- You set the policies. You never have to do anything against your morals or ethics.
- *You get to enjoy your life!*

Be sure to read the sidebars to understand the additional demands that owning a business places on you—and your family. Think deeply how all the extra time you spend working will affect your relationships with you parents, spouse, children, and friends. Will you miss the important moments in your children's lives? Or will your business give you the freedom to be present? Before you tackle a new business, visualize how your life will look and feel once you've embarked on this challenge.[1]

---

1. Robert McPhee, *Manifesting for Non-Gurus*, 2010.

Remember to use the worksheets at http://www.YourBusinessBible.com to help you stay focused and organized.

If you're still prepared to go forward, if I can't talk you out of it, if you're getting really excited about your business—then let's get to work. You're going to do great!

Join me for your adventure in building a business.

Best wishes,
Eva Rosenberg
Your TaxMama

LIGHTEN UP

You're about to venture into dangerous and terrifying territory—the World of Taxes.

It's not as bad as you think. Get comfortable with the humor and ironies in this ever-shifting world. It will make all the onerous rules easier to bear.

Believe it or not, these quotes come to you courtesy of the Internal Revenue Service and other fine folks. Come back to this page any time your spirits need a boost of humor.

Did you ever notice that when you put the words "The" and "IRS" together, it spells "THEIRS?"

—Unknown

He who gets his tax advice out of a Cracker Jack box doesn't always get cracker jack advice.[1]

—LINDA DORFMONT, Enrolled Agent

I like to pay taxes. With them I buy civilization.

—OLIVER WENDELL HOLMES JR., U.S. Supreme Court Justice

---

1. Cracker Jack™ is a registered trademark of Frito-Lay.

The government who robs Peter to pay Paul can always depend on the support of Paul.

—GEORGE BERNARD SHAW, Irish
playwright

Taxes are indeed very heavy, and if those laid on by the government were the only ones we had to pay, we might more easily discharge them; but we have many others, and much more grievous to some of us. We are taxed twice as much by our idleness, three times as much by our pride, and four times as much by our folly.

—BENJAMIN FRANKLIN, *Poor Richard's
Almanac*

Alexander Hamilton started the U.S. Treasury with nothing, and that was the closest our country has ever been to being even.

—WILL ROGERS, writer and humorist

The only difference between a tax man and a taxidermist is that the taxidermist leaves the skin.

—MARK TWAIN, writer and humorist

Excellence is a good habit. But do not strive for perfection—it will prevent you from ever finishing anything.

—EVA ROSENBERG, Your TaxMama

The seven deadly sins . . . food, clothing, firing, rent, taxes, respectability, and children. Nothing can lift those seven millstones from man's neck but money; and the spirit cannot soar until the millstones are lifted.

—GEORGE BERNARD SHAW, Irish
playwright

The hardest thing in the world to understand is the income tax.

—ALBERT EINSTEIN, physicist

The only thing that hurts more than paying an income tax is not having to pay an income tax.

—THOMAS DEWAR, First Baron Dewar

A good tax return is like a good mystery novel. You follow the clues, make deductions, and arrive at a profitable conclusion.

—EVA ROSENBERG, Your TaxMama

Visit TaxMama.com for more humor in the weekly Money Funnies column http://taxmama.com/category/asktaxmama/money-funnies. Please feel free to submit your clean jokes, too.

HOW TO USE THIS BOOK

At the beginning of each chapter, you will find a To-Do List and Questionnaire. Read the list and keep it in mind while you read the chapter. As you go along, perform the tasks on the list. If you put everything you do into this book, it will become your business bible. In fact, you can pick up a complete set of worksheets at www.YourBusinessBible.com.

- Enter the dates you complete the tasks.
- Enter the dates you schedule the meetings.
- Set the deadlines.
- Enter the answers to the questions.
- Fill out the forms.
- Enter the relevant ID numbers as you apply for the licenses or government IDs and programs.
- Make copies of all relevant documents and place them behind the To-Do List page.
- Use the resources at the end of each chapter to help you save taxes, operate your business, and increase your profits.

Note about Links in This Book
You will notice that many links in the book have been shortened, especially links to IRS sites. That's because IRS, and other sites, often change their URLs. Using my

Viral URL tool, I can correct the underlying links. That will keep the links in this book up-to-date.

There are many free link shorteners on the market, such as bit.ly and snurl. com. I use Viral URL, which is also free, because it gives me some additional options, including commissions on sales of their other marketing services—http://vur.me/ taxmama.

Small Business Taxes Made Easy

✔ CHAPTER 1   SMALL BUSINESS CHECKLIST
To-Do List and Questionnaire

Fill in this worksheet as you work your way through the book. Each chapter will contribute information to help you complete this. This will be your master summary of the key information related to your business. Consider using an expandable file with A–Z pockets for this purpose. The files come in paper or plastic for under $15.

1. ____ Set up you your ADVISORY TEAM and meeting schedule. List the names and contacts of all the members on an attached sheet.

2. ____ Contact small business advocacy groups and research your industry. Lay the groundwork for your business. List the new resources you've just learned about.

3. ____ What is your business focus? List the top two things your business will do or sell.

   _____   _____

4. ____ Start the outline for your business plan. What is your first business target?

   _____

5. ____ Start thinking about your business structure—to incorporate . . . or? Which business entity do you think is the best for you? _____ Why?_____

6. ____ Select a business name. _____

7. ____ Open a business bank account.

   a.   Bank name _____

   b.   Account # _____

8. ____ Select your accounting system(s). _____

9. ____ Research your business licenses. Make a list of all the licenses you need and have on an attached sheet of paper. Include the agency, license number, expiration date (if any), cost, and contact information.

10. ____ What insurance do you need? Make a list of all the policies you need and have on an attached sheet of paper. Include the name of the insurance company, broker, policy number, expiration date, cost, and contact information. For auto insurance, keep a copy of the policy data in your car and here.

11. ____ Where will you be working? From home or an outside office? Do a cost-benefit analysis to see which one works better for you.

12. ____ What business equipment do you need? Make a list of the equipment you need, including vehicles. Split the list up between equipment you will buy and equipment you will lease. On each list include the name of the equipment, license or serial number, purchase date, cost, warranty contact and expiration, loan or lease amount, and monthly payment. Include a copy of the purchase document in this file.

13. ____ What legal issues affect you? Make a list of the contracts and forms you need in your business, for customers or clients, vendors, subcontractors or freelancers, etc. Keep a master copy in this file.

14. ____ Research your vendors, especially insurance providers. Make a list of the main vendors or suppliers your business will use. List each vendor's name, the vendor's phone number and Web site (if applicable), the key contact (the top executive you can reach), the types of products or services the vendor will provide, the discount it will give you, and the payment terms.

15. ____ Make a list of all the service providers you need and have. Include on the list each vendor's name, the vendor's phone number and Web site (if applicable), the key contact (the top executive you can reach), the types of products or services the vendor will provide, the discount it will give you, and the payment terms.

16. ____ Find ways to consolidate your communications vendors and the related bills.

17. ____ When it comes to image and marketing, lay out your marketing plan. What are the first two things you will do to promote your business, besides the Web site?

_____   _____

18. ____ Address the money issues. Will you accept credit cards? PayPal? Will you factor your receivables? What key strategies do you plan to use to get paid soonest?

_____   _____

Remember to put a copy of each document into this expanding file.

SMALL BUSINESS CHECKLIST

Checklists are a helpful tool. Don't turn them into a crutch or limitation. When something is missing from your life or business checklist—add it!

—TaxMama

Starting a business is really easy. Many small business owners are in business before they even realize it. Someone likes something you make or do and offers to pay for it. Then another person asks. Pretty soon, something that started out as a hobby or family meal is bringing in a stream of income, even though you never intended to be in business. This is particularly true for the millions of people starting their own personal Web sites. Sure, the sites might start out as personal interest pages. But as they are filled with so much good information, they are suddenly discovered by hordes of people, and income starts rolling in. Oops, you're in business and didn't even know it. It is a wonderful feeling, though, isn't it?

Other times businesses are started with a clear purpose. Some people, for example, get frustrated because a type of product isn't available or because a service that should be there isn't obtainable. These smart people see the void and fill it. Sometimes, they simply start doing it for friends, like a carpool service, and a business grows from there.

Other people come up with a great idea to hit it rich and start building the business around the idea. Usually, they get so excited, their friends and family get caught up in the excitement and give them money. Or if they're really aggressive, they'll raise the money from strangers or through banks, loans, or venture capital.

And then there are those people who really want to start a business but don't know what business to start. If you don't have a clue but want one, read Paul and

Sarah Edwards's book *The Best Home Businesses for the 21st Century: The Inside Information You Need to Know to Select a Home-Based Business That's Right for You*, published by Jeremy P. Tarcher. It will not only give you ideas, but it will tell you what skills and tools you need to make that business work for you.

Which of these businesses will succeed? Which will fail? Can you tell just by reading about the personalities involved and the nature of the start-up? Not really.

Three Indicators Will Predict the Success of the Business

There are three key factors that will predict the success of any business. Look at the descriptions below and see how they fit your business.

1. **How big should your business be?** If a business stays small—such as a mom-and-pop operation—it may never make a fortune, but it can generate a nice, modest cash flow without a fuss. If handled properly, some of these businesses will support forever—without much stress—a household in modest, happy style.

2. **Has the business developed a plan—something to map out how it is organized and, when it grows, how to deal with success?** The people who have the foresight to treat their businesses as real enterprises generally grow them properly, make excellent profits, and have something solid to pass on to their children. Or they sell out to larger companies, for millions, when they are ready to retire or exit.

3. **Did the business owners take all the right compliance steps to learn of their tax and licensing obligations and stay on top of them?** Too many small business owners, even those who aren't home-based, just never take the time to look into the laws and rules that regulate their businesses. They just trip along blithely, doing what they do, and not dealing with licenses, payroll issues, or, sometimes, even filing issues, until these issues come and bite them in the derrière. Don't think I'm kidding. I've seen too many nice people come to me because they were in such trouble with the IRS (or city licensing people or sales tax departments) that they were about to lose their businesses—even though they were successful. Or maybe these people were in trouble precisely because their businesses were successful and had finally come to the attention of the authorities.

Remember, *ignorance of the law is no excuse*. It's your responsibility to learn what your business must do—it's not the government's responsibility to tell you.

On the other hand, most cities and states offer excellent free information on their Web sites and through local training sessions at colleges or other outreach programs. Or there are nonprofit organizations, like SCORE, ready to provide advice. This wealth of information and help is often free or costs very little. Using those resources, you'll also build a good contact network of the officials and bureaucrats who administer many of the programs. The small effort is well worth the trouble.

Let's ensure that your business is one of those that succeed. This book will help make sure you're one of the winners. Even if you're already in business, and have been for decades, the information you'll find here will help you.

Dennis Gaskill of BoogieJack.com said, "If you're already in business for yourself don't be fooled into thinking you can't learn plenty from this book. I've been in business for myself since 1997, and my eyes were opened wide in several places. In addition to gaining a greater understanding of tax issues, I found oodles of great business advice and a vast array of valuable resources that multiply the end value of the book.

"If I'd had this book when I started my business I'd have been able to spend more time growing it because I'd have spent less time working it. When you're working your business you're keeping it going, but when you grow your business you're increasing your income. With this book at hand, I'm giving myself a raise!"

It's not too late to get it right—to protect the time and dollar investment you've already made.

So What Do You Need to Do?

Before you get started, use the checklist in this chapter to get on track and make sure you are doing everything right. Try to follow the steps in the order they are presented. As you go along, you may think of some other things that need to be done at that particular point for your specific business or industry. Keep a stack of self-stick notes handy so you can record your thoughts when you think of them. (Did you know that Post-it pads came about as an error? 3M found a brilliant use for a glue that didn't stick.)

Many of the resources mentioned in this book will take you to the Internet. When I was starting my business, I had to drive 50 miles to the nearest Department of Commerce office in Los Angeles, or spend days in the little glassed-in room in the back of the Santa Ana law library to do my tax research. Today, you can get the same answers in a few minutes using the Internet. Most of the resources are free—at least, the ones I've found for you and included in this book. If you don't have Internet access, go to your public library. Most public libraries offer free Internet access, and the librarians can be very helpful. Perhaps it's time you were reacquainted with those libraries you loved as a kid.

You don't need a computer to start a business (e.g., house-sitting or dog-walking). You don't even need Internet access. But it helps. As Chapter 6 points out, the costs of a computer and Internet access are deductible as business expenses.

You'll be coming back to the checklist often. You would be wise to photocopy the pages and put them on a clipboard so you can work with them as you go along. In fact, make a few extra copies so you can use them in the first exercise. Each chapter will have a to-do list for you to use. Be sure to do everything that applies to you.

STEP 1. The first time you read the checklist, keep your mind open. Free-associate with the ideas and treat the time as a brainstorming session. Don't do anything yet—just add your notes.

STEP 2. Read the list through again. Treat the second read-through the same way. Only this time, make your notes more specific. Write the names of vendors or suppliers you already know, the ones you'll be contacting to implement the steps on the checklist.

STEP 3. Finally, start taking the actions and check them off when they are completed. Cross off anything that doesn't apply to you so that you're not distracted.

Ready? Let's go.

The Checklist in To-Do Order

Set Up an Advisory Team

Even if you're not incorporating your business, you need something similar to a board of directors. No one can run a business in a vacuum. Call upon professionals and people in your social or family circle or people in your community who've achieved success in the industries or fields you'll be servicing. You can't be expected to know everything, so don't try. Find an expert in each field to help your business succeed.

Plan to meet at least every month until the business is established. Then meet at least every quarter during the first year or two as the business develops. Meet at least once each year after that. Be sure these are people who are available for you to call upon throughout the year. Expect to pay them for their time. You might even want to keep them on retainer. Questions will come up that they can answer quickly and easily, saving you hours of research time, and perhaps quite a bit of money, in the process.

Who should be on your team? Your insurance broker, business attorney, tax professional, bookkeeper (if you have one), office manager, banker, largest vendor or supplier, largest customer, Web site manager, at least two people who have successful businesses in your community, perhaps your favorite marketing guru, and your spouse. Include at least one person who has been successful in your industry, too. Once you start hiring employees outside the family, add a human resources expert to your team.

Where can you find these professionals? Ask people you know for recommendations. Or visit the Web sites of your professional organization(s). These are the best places to find key tax and financial professionals:

- **Enrolled agents (EAs).** For tax specialists licensed to represent taxpayers before the IRS, people whose license allows them to work anywhere in the nation, contact the National Association of Enrolled Agents (NAEA), http://www.naea.org, (202) 822-NAEA (6232).
- **Certified public accountants (CPAs).** CPAs are authorized to perform certified audits and issue financial statements. For a referral, contact the American Institute of Certified Public Accountants (AICPA), http://www.aicpa.org/feedback/shortfb.htm, (888) 777-7077.
- **Attorneys with the American Bar Association (ABA).** For tax attorneys, business attorneys, and intangibles experts (patents and copyrights), contact the ABA, http://abanet.org, (800) 285-2221 or (312) 988-5522.
- **National Association of Tax Professionals (NATP).** You'll find a cross section of all kinds of tax professionals here—EAs, CPAs, attorneys, and licensed tax professionals. You can use NATP's online search function to find a local tax professional at http://www.natptax.com, or you can call the association's toll-free number, (800) 558-3402.
- **Insurance agents and brokers.** To locate insurance professionals, try the Independent Insurance Agents and Brokers of America (IIAA), http://www.iiaa.org, (800) 221-7917.

- **Certified financial planners.** To locate trained financial managers, contact the Certified Financial Planner Board of Standards, http://www.cfp.net, (800) 487-1497.

Incidentally, if a really big part of your business involves shipping, see if you can get your shipping company's representative on your team. People rarely think about including representatives from the shipping companies, but they often have worldwide contacts. They may be able to help you find the best vendors, as well as customers, for your business. And they can even design custom packaging for you at little or no cost if you're doing volume. For example, UPS created really beautiful packaging for Randazzo's Good Children Bakery Shoppe.

Get started now assembling your team; you'll need all these people to help you with the rest of this checklist.

Contact Small Business Advocacy Groups

Two of the most helpful advocacy groups for small businesses have Web sites with invaluable information. They are the Small Business Administration (SBA) at http://www.sba.gov and the Service Corps of Retired Executives (SCORE) at http://www.score.org.

On these Web sites, you'll receive lots of useful information about the business climate, your industry, and general business start-up help. SCORE even provides free advisors, or coaches, to help your business follow the right paths. Bear in mind that most of the people working for SCORE come from the corporate world and have little experience with small businesses. But they have good contacts, and if you let them guide you, they can help groom your business to grow in ways you couldn't do alone. What's the key thing to do with SCORE volunteers? Listen.

Decide Your Business Focus

Focus on one or two things you do well or products or product lines you want to sell or produce. If you think of many, list them so you don't forget about them. Then select only the top one or two things you can implement most easily. Once the business is running smoothly, you can always add products or services. Starting with too many services or product lines dilutes your focus and your market.

Think about McDonald's. It started with a core product line—hamburgers, fries, shakes, and filet-o-fish. That was it for decades until the company had built a solid reputation and market saturation. McDonald's does field-test new products in certain of its company restaurants. But it generally drops them before they are distributed nationally.

Prepare a Business Plan

We'll explain why you need a business plan and show you how to create one in Chapter 2.

Decide on Your Business Structure

Will you be a sole proprietor, corporation, or what? We'll help you decide in Chapter 3.

Decide on the Name or Names You Will Use

How do you decide on a name? Perform some searches first. Try looking online to make sure there isn't another company with the same name already in operation. Here are some other steps to take when selecting a name:

- **Trademark your name.** If you are planning for the long term or ever want to take your business public, this is an excellent precaution. You can do it yourself with the U.S. Patent and Trademark Office, http://www.uspto.gov/index.html. Before you file, even before you settle on your name, however, it may be worthwhile to run a trademark search to see if anyone is using it. A great Web resource for this is http://www.uspto.gov/trademarks/process/search. Once you've decided on a name, you may submit your application online at http://www.uspto.gov/teas/index.html. If you don't do it right up front, you may have to spend a fortune fighting to protect it. Because I didn't file right up front, it took me about three years to get TaxMama registered (see Figure 1.1). You can see the history of the battle here—http://vurl.bz/taxmama/TM-TaxMama.
- **Get an Internet domain name to match your business name.** Even if you're not planning to have a Web site right away, buy the name now and hold on to it until you need it. Otherwise, it will be gone when you're ready. Domains are cheap. GoDaddy.com (http://godaddy.com) sells

FIGURE 1.1 TaxMama Trademark

	Reg. No. 3,426,814
United States Patent and Trademark Office	Registered May 13, 2008

TRADEMARK
SERVICE MARK
PRINCIPAL REGISTER

TaxMama

ROSENBERG, EVA (UNITED STATES INDIVI-
DUAL)
P.O. BOX 280549
NORTHRIDGE, CA 91328

FOR: DOWNLOADABLE ELECTRONIC PUBLI-
CATIONS IN THE NATURE OF A SYNDICATED
COLUMN DEALING WITH TAXATION, PERSO-
NAL FINANCE AND SMALL BUSINESS, IN CLASS
9 (U.S. CLS. 21, 23, 26, 36 AND 38).

FIRST USE 7-10-1998; IN COMMERCE 12-11-1999.

FOR: PRINTED SYNDICATED COLUMNS DEAL-
ING WITH TAXATION, PERSONAL FINANCE AND
SMALL BUSINESS, IN CLASS 16 (U.S. CLS. 2, 5, 22, 23,
29, 37, 38 AND 50).

FIRST USE 7-10-1998; IN COMMERCE 12-11-1999.

FOR: PROVIDING A NON-DOWNLOADABLE
ONLINE COLUMN DEALING WITH TAXATION,
PERSONAL FINANCE AND SMALL BUSINESS;
EDUCATION SERVICES, NAMELY, PROVIDING
INTERNET-BASED AND E-MAIL COURSES IN
THE FIELD OF TAXATION, PERSONAL FINANCE
AND SMALL BUSINESS, IN CLASS 41 (U.S. CLS. 100,
101 AND 107).

FIRST USE 7-10-1998; IN COMMERCE 12-11-1999.

THE MARK CONSISTS OF STANDARD CHAR-
ACTERS WITHOUT CLAIM TO ANY PARTICULAR
FONT, STYLE, SIZE, OR COLOR.

SER. NO. 78-727,175, FILED 10-5-2005.

SUZANNE BLANE, EXAMINING ATTORNEY

domain names for about $10 per year. When operating online is important
to your business, your business name might depend on what's available as
a domain name. The very memorable TaxMama.com was chosen after just
such a search. The boring tax-related domains I wanted were no longer
available. So, to our everlasting delight, we came up with something clever
and original.

TaxMama Tip

The most important type of domain is the ".com" because it's the one most people automatically type
in. So if you use a domain with any other ending—without also owning the .com—people will be taken
to someone else's Web site.

- **File fictitious name announcements in your local newspaper, if necessary.** This step will protect your name at the local level. Generally, if you incorporate, you can skip the fictitious name filings because the corporate name is protected at the state level.

Set Up a Corporation, Partnership, or LLC—If You Plan to Be One

There are several documents that you have to fill out to become a corporation, partnership, or limited liability corporation (LLC). You'll need certain of those documents in order to take several of the next steps. So save yourself some time by filling these documents out now. You could use an attorney to handle the setup for you. I've found that attorneys tend to charge about $1,500 to $3,000 to set up your entity. They provide about an hour of advice and order the kit from an outside service that creates all the documents. The law firm turns it all over to you; then you have to get your own federal identification number, or your tax professional has to get it for you. Attorneys rarely remember to file the S-corporation election. That problem keeps cropping up consistently when clients come to me with their new corporations. What can you do instead? Do this. Pay your attorney for the hour of consultation about your business structure. Better yet, include your tax professional in that meeting, too. Then use one of these services to set up your entity. They are the same ones your attorney would use.

- **Incorp Services Inc. in Nevada**. http://vurl.bz/taxmama/Incorp, (800) 2 INCORP: You'll get 20 percent off on formation services and registered agent services when you use the coupon code TAXMAMA.
- **The Company Corporation.** http://www.accountstreet.com, (800) 315-9420: Register your corporation, LLC, or other formal structure at this site, which is one of the oldest incorporators in the country. Mention that TaxMama sent you to get a $25 discount.
- **Hubco.** http://www.inc-it-now.com, (800) 443-8177: Hubco has the cheapest prices for entity setup. Attorneys who prepare some of their own bylaws and articles use these folks. They service the public, too, but you'll need to take care of several aspects of the setup yourself. (They are also a good source for supplies, such as corporate seals, stock certificates, etc.)

It's essential to get the guidance of your team's attorney and tax pro on this issue before you take action. Read Chapter 3 to better understand why you need guidance.

Before you start working with a partner or an investor who plans to participate actively in your business, consider reading Doug Thorburn's *Drugs, Drunks and Debits: How to Recognize Addicts and Avoid Financial Abuse* (visit his Web site at http://www.preventragedy.com). Deciding to work with a recovering addict or obvious addict is easy. Once you know the person's condition, you can make your decision with your eyes open. It's the hidden addict who will destroy your business and your own emotional stability. Read the book and you'll know the signs going in; then you'll be able to decide if you want to go forward.

Open a Separate Bank Account for Your Business

Open a unique bank account for your business even if you plan to operate as a sole proprietor. Remarkably, many people overlook this fundamental business step. But it is crucial so that your personal money doesn't get confused with funds from your business. If you are ever audited, having a separate account can help you gather your paperwork quickly.

When you are picking a bank, shop around. Find a local bank with nationwide ATMs, willing to waive first-year fees on business accounts. Arrange to get copies of your canceled checks. Many banks are discouraging this service or charging for it. Pay the fee. Having those canceled checks at hand will save you a lot of time and money in audits and tough situations. Arrange for online access and downloads. Often with online banking, you'll get free accounting software. If you are given a choice, opt for Peachtree or QuickBooks, not Quicken (we'll cover this topic in detail in Chapter 4). You're welcome to establish a business savings account or an investment account to store your profits or start-up loans until you need the money.

Select an Accounting System or Software

Chapter 4 will guide you through the record-keeping process.

Research the Licenses You Need and Agencies to Which You'll Be Reporting

Gather all the forms and determine what your costs will be—both initially and annually. You'll need all this for your business plan and budget (we'll discuss this more in Chapter 2). In brief, though, here are several forms you'll probably need to fill out:

- **City or county license.** Even a home-based business may need one. Call your city, county, or parish clerk's office for more information. Bankrate.com has a resource linking to small business information in each state; see the State Resources list at the end of this chapter. Read your local government's business Web site carefully. Most localities have inexpensive licenses, around $25 to $75 per year. Be aware, however, that the Los Angeles license, based on a percentage of sales, could cost hundreds of dollars each year. And Los Angeles aggressively collects those funds.
- **IRS registration for an employer identification number (EIN).** File Form SS-4 online yourself. You'll find a link at TaxMama.com's Resource Center. *Note:* If you are a sole proprietor who doesn't plan to have employees, say you will have them, just to get the identification number issued. Having that EIN will make the difference between looking like a real business and looking like a hobby. (More about this in Chapter 2.)
- **IRS online payment system.** Sign up with the IRS's online payment system at http://www.eftps.gov. You can deposit your estimated tax payments, pay payroll taxes, and conduct other business tax transactions online.

Research State Taxes and Licenses

A variety of agencies may be regulating your industry, and you should learn the details about taxes, licensing, zoning, unions, etc., before you start. The fastest way to get the information you need is on the Internet. Start with your state's official Web site. When you get to the state's home page, look for a business link. If you need information about other states, use this link to all state tax agencies: http://www.taxadmin.org/fta/link/forms.html. This is the Web site for the Federation of Tax Administrators. The link goes to the federation's tax forms pages, but if you do a little backtracking, you'll find the tax home page of the state you are interested in.

If you don't have access to the Internet, pull out your residential telephone book. In the front, you'll find pages listing all your local and state agencies. Spend some time reading that whole section. You'd be surprised at the agencies you'll find. Some of them may even become a source of funding or contracts. Who knows? At least you'll find the key agencies that affect your industry. Be sure to call your city clerk (or local equivalent) about local licensing. For state issues, call your secretary of state's office. If that office is not the one you need to speak with, someone there will tell you whom you should call.

- **State income tax registration.** This is generally necessary only if you have formed an entity other than a sole proprietorship.
- **Sales tax.** You'll need to know about sales taxes even if all your sales are online sales. Chapter 12 explains why. You must collect sales taxes if you are selling products to the end user. Some states might charge sales taxes on services. Check with your state's department of revenue or its equivalent.
- **Payroll taxes.** Register with your state's payroll tax department if you plan to have employees. Your children might be employees—if they actually do the work they're supposed to do. (Chapter 9 will explain who is and isn't an employee.)
- **State licenses.** State licenses are usually required for child-care providers, cosmeticians, most professionals, contractors, those selling alcohol, anyone dealing with hazardous substances, truckers, and who knows what other industries. It's best to check before you find you're operating without a license.
- **Other.** Check to see what else your industry needs or requires. If you can't find answers online, interview people who are successful in your industry. Or just call your state and ask the folks there to point you to a list of your obligations. Better yet, have them mail the list to you. Save the list and use it as a checklist. Of course, hiring a good tax professional with expertise in your industry will save you hours or even weeks of research. A good tax professional already knows what you must do. Another way to save time researching all the licenses you need is to use BusinessLicenses.com (http://snurl.com/license-tax). It will do the research for you. For an extra fee, it will even fill in the forms for you.

Research Your Costs

Find the best vendors, providing good service at fair prices. Be willing to sacrifice a bit of price to get personal service. For instance, our toll-free line is through National Comtel, a small local company at (800) 987-0100. We can call the office and speak to the same two or three people every time, even the company president. No long waits on hold. No random customer service people who keep getting it wrong. I pay five cents per minute for incoming calls on my toll-free line. Small companies are willing to negotiate, which is great. But don't make them cut their prices low enough to put them out of business. With a little bit of work, you'll be able to find good suppliers in your own neck of the woods.

One of the first things you'll need to get quotes on is insurance costs. Consider working with good business insurance brokers. They'll know where the deals are and your coverage requirements.

- **Business liability, fire, theft.** Get a combined policy. For malpractice insurance, check with your professional association for the best prices.
- **Auto.** A good local broker can find you the best rates. You may be able to cut your rates by having one company carry several of your policies. Check several sources for better rates but be sure that the coverage you're pricing is equivalent across all carriers. Visit the American Automobile Association at http://www.aaa.com to find your local automobile club or call information to get the number of a local office. AAA offers some of the most complete insurance coverage and great service in case of accidents. GEICO, (800) 861-8380 or http://www.geico.com, offers different discounts for members of organizations, like government workers, AARP, etc. I started with a "Good Sam" discount. When I obtained a letter from my alma mater, the "university discount" cut my policy by another $116 for six months. Seniors taking driving classes can get another discount from most insurers. Mercury Insurance runs great commercials. It has good prices, but its policies do not cover other people driving your car or accessories on your car, even if the accessories were from the dealer. Read the proposed coverage before buying!
- **Health.** You'll probably need health coverage for yourself and your employees. Start out small. If you can't afford to pay your employees' insurance, consider setting up a Health Savings Arrangement (HSA) plan. Find an insurance carrier in your state at http://www.ehealthinsurance. com. HSAs were signed into law in 2003 and have become very popular. Read Chapter 10 for information on insurance benefits and tax credits.
- **Workers' compensation (WC).** Find a local carrier. Some WC carriers, especially the quasi-state agencies, will pay you dividends if the fund makes money. Those dividends can reduce your net premiums by 10 percent or more per year. If you belong to an association or a professional or trade organization, contact it. Some organizations have negotiated deals for their members. I got a substantial rate reduction through one of my accounting associations. For a comprehensive list of state agencies and carriers across the country, visit http://www.workerscompensationinsurance.com/links/index. htm or call your state insurance commissioner for carriers in your area.
- **Disability insurance.** If you can qualify, get covered. You'll need a source of income if you get sick or hurt and can't work for several weeks. Check

with your state if you can't get covered commercially. Many states offer state disability insurance coverage for small business owners that are similar to employees' coverage. The cost may be higher if you're on Schedule C rather than on payroll. Another way to get coverage if you don't meet the minimum health requirements is to buy a group policy for yourself and your employees. It usually requires a minimum of three people, but there are no medical exams. If you can find a really good policy, you'll be able to live on it if—heaven forbid—you become permanently disabled. If you don't have employees, look to your union or professional or trade association for group coverage. If that organization has not arranged for coverage, bug it until it does.

• **Life insurance.** Work with your advisory team on life insurance. Don't go overboard, but get the coverage you need. For instance, seriously consider getting key-man insurance, which allows you to buy out partners or their heirs in case of catastrophic injury or death.

• **Other.** There may be other insurance you will need, depending on your area, your business, and your industry. Your advisory team can alert you to the right coverage.

Select Facilities

Will you work from home, or will you buy or rent space? Whenever possible, look at the long-term picture. If you can afford to buy a place, do it. If you outgrow it, you can always rent it or sell it. Be unconventional, if you can. Will your business work if you put it into a house or an apartment? If it will, buy one. Many law firms and professionals take over old houses and fix them up as stately offices. If buying isn't an option, be creative. Can you share space with a vendor in exchange for some service? If the service doesn't interfere too much with your time, that may be a way to fund your first office space. (Read Chapter 5 about barter income.) If you must rent, negotiate. Offer to accept a higher monthly rent than you'd like in exchange for free months each year. That helps the landlord show a high monthly rental rate in case he or she wants to sell the building. Meanwhile, you end up paying a lower overall average rate.

The other option is to set up an office in your home, which has some excellent tax benefits—but could be too distracting to allow you to work. We'll discuss this in depth in Chapter 7.

One of my EA Exam students graduated and passed all three of the IRS's Special Enrollment Examinations. He met a man in church who ran a chain of check cashing outlets. They worked out a deal. Joe set up a tax office in one of the check cashing stores and did tax returns for the patrons. In exchange, Joe agreed to double his tithe to their church–paying the church 20 percent of his income instead of 10 percent. The arrangement worked out so well that the following year Joe had to hire staff and expand the arrangement to all the check cashing stores in the chain. Perhaps you can work out a mutually beneficial rental arrangement, too.

Make Lease-versus-Buy Decision on Equipment and Vehicles

When it comes to the equipment and vehicles you'll use, your first step is deciding whether or not you want to lease or buy. For equipment that either becomes obsolete quickly or is older and more subject to breaking down, a lease may be preferable. You can deduct the lease costs. Leases will often include service contracts, which will save you some money on that score. There are also benefits to buying automobiles you need for your job. We'll cover this in more depth in Chapter 8.

Arrange for Inventory

When manufacturing a product, inventory is the heart of your operation. Though you'll find suppliers around the world on the Internet, don't rely on people you've never seen at facilities you've never visited to make your main products. Legwork is critical. Inspect the facilities and talk to their customers. Once you have prices, plug them into your business plan. Let your advisory team help you find the right sources. Always be on site when the factory manufactures your products—or have a representative there to inspect the finished products—before shipping.

Several years ago, when computer ports were precious and not to be wasted, Chris invented the EasyStick, a mechanical joystick that could be strapped over the number pad on the keyboard instead of having to be plugged into the computer. He knew this device would only have a brief life before it became outmoded–perhaps two to three years at the most. It garnered rave reviews from the *Computer Shopper* and other major computer and gaming magazines. Chris found a major wholesaler who contracted with him to buy all the units he could produce. He raised money from a handful of investors, knowing he'd be able to give them a generous profit. Chris found a company in China to manufacture it, using Lexan. Lexan is a hard plastic that would withstand the heavy-duty use. Well . . . Chris wasn't there to oversee the process on the day the Chinese factory did its production run. It didn't use Lexan, but instead used a cheaper material. When people used them, the EasySticks broke almost immediately. The wholesaler canceled the contract. The company went bankrupt. Investors got nothing back.

Establish Supplies Accounts

Establish accounts with office supply houses, both locally and online. My company has worked with Quill (http://www.quillcorp.com) and Office Depot (http://www. officedepot.com) for decades. They both offer free overnight shipping for orders of $50 or more. Quill always includes something extra—cookies, briefcases, radios, and so on. Whenever a product is wrong or damaged, both companies take the materials back, no questions asked.

Develop a reasonable budget for the things you need and be careful not to spend money on things you don't need. Don't get things because they're cute.

Research Legal Issues

A variety of legal issues will affect your business. For instance, you'll need to know about your area's labor laws—so call your state's employment department.

- **Contract law.** Everything you sell is under contract, even if it is implied. Understand how to limit your responsibilities to your customers. The attorney on your advisory team can help.
- **Bad debts.** Customers don't always pay on time . . . or ever. Set up protections in your invoices and contracts before the problems arise. Search online for contracts similar to those you expect to use. Modify them for your business.
- **Liability laws.** When you have an online presence, your business is exposed to liability in a number of ways—sometimes through actions of others. As you're beginning your business planning, please read Jonathan I. Ezor's *Clicking Through: A Survival Guide for Bringing Your Company Online.* It will give you a handle on the legal areas you'll need to address so that you can develop your legal budget. There's lots of practical information in his book—if only he'd written it before I went online. Also, read Chapter 12 of this book to learn more about the nexus issues you face due to your Internet presence.

Consider Your Services Needs

Even if you decide not to hire employees initially, you'll still need help. There are many people who can assist you with their services. Get an answering service so that you're not constantly interrupted by calls. You may even need a virtual assistant. Certainly, you'll need an attorney and a tax professional, and you might need a consultant. For instance, you may not want to ship all your own products. Will you need a fulfillment house? Price out all the services you're going to need. Chapter 9 will give you a hiring setup checklist for freelancers and will provide you with more information on paying taxes for the people who work for you.

Select Communications

If there's a way to integrate your telephone, cell phone, Internet, and fax into one billing plan, do it. It's easier to get one bill from one service provider. On the other hand, it doesn't hurt to duplicate some of these services in case of trouble. For instance, my company has AT&T U-verse for the Internet. In case it goes down, we have Earthlink's dial-up service as a backup and Verizon's wireless thumb drive for our laptops. Since services like U-verse use your office's electrical supply, keep at least one old-fashioned phone line that is powered by the phone company's electrical supply at the socket. It doesn't hurt to also have a cell phone. That way, you have triple power redundancy.

Start to Work on Image and Visibility

Establishing brand awareness among your clientele and in the marketplace will help you keep your customer base in tough times. When they're devoted to your brand, you become their only choice.

- **Build your brand.** Rob Frankel's *The Revenge of Brand X* provides invaluable guidelines that you can use to cement your identity from day one.
- **Develop a presence in the marketplace.** Public relations is less costly than advertising—and more effective. Good PR will get you established as an expert in your industry. If you can't afford a public relations firm but you're able to speak clearly and eloquently about your business, sign up for Dan Janal's PR Leads service available at http://www.prleads.com and Peter Shankman's HelpAReporter.com at http://www.helpareporter.com. Having both services will give you access to the broadest base of journalists and publicists. Be prepared to invest a lot of time, at least initially. But if you

write good responses to journalists' requests for experts, you'll be flooded with calls. Press releases also generate attention when written well. For that, you will need an expert. Your advisory team can help you find the best person locally—or consult Dan Janal at http://www.prleads.com or Shel Horowitz at http://www.FrugalMarketing.com.

- **Consider advertising.** It's the lifeblood of a growing business. But don't shotgun your ads all over the place. Target your audience carefully and find the most effective, least expensive publications. If you're on a tight budget, Shel Horowitz's *Grassroots Marketing: Getting Noticed in a Noisy World* offers twenty-first-century tips for getting the most attention for your product or service—also found at http://www.FrugalMarketing.com.

Take Care of Money Issues

Some businesses or industries have a really long accounts receivable lag. Some businesses require you to advance money on merchandise or services. Then you must wait 30, 60, 90, or even 120 days to get paid. That's industry standard. Unless you have a charming and clever way to speed up the payments, you will need financing. Look into all the options available to you. In some industries, like the schmatte industry (the textile trade), "factoring" is common. Factoring is the practice of selling your accounts receivable to another company at a slight discount. Essentially, you're paying interest on your money in advance. The factor becomes responsible for collecting the money from your customers. Consider factoring or accounts receivable financing if you're planning to sell to any government agencies. They are notoriously slow pays—often 90 days or more.

This checklist (shown in shorter form in Table 1.1) is probably more comprehensive than you expected from a tax book, but you'll soon find that good tax planning goes hand in hand with good business planning. Without a solid business, who needs to worry about taxes? You'll have nothing but losses, and that requires a whole different set of plans—for failure. Well, this book isn't about failing. It's designed to make you a stunning success, without expending too much money or stress on your part.

TABLE 1.1 The Carry-with-You Checklist in To-Do Order

☐ Set up an advisory team.

    Tax advisors.

    Attorneys.

    Insurance agents and brokers.

☐ Contact small business advocacy groups.

    Small Business Administration: www.sba.gov.

    Service Corps of Retired Executives (SCORE): www.score.org.

☐ Decide your business focus.

☐ Prepare a business plan.

☐ Decide on your business structure.

☐ Decide on the name or names you will use.

    Trademark the name with the U.S. Patent Office: www.uspto.gov/index.html.

    Get an Internet domain name to match your business name.

    File fictitious name announcements in your local newspaper, if necessary.

☐ Set up a corporation, partnership, or LLC—if you plan to be one.

☐ Open a separate bank account for your business.

☐ Select an accounting system or software.

☐ Research the licenses you need and the agencies to which you'll be reporting.

    City or county license.

    IRS registration for an employer identification number (EIN).

    Sign up with the IRS's online payment system: www.eftps.gov.

☐ Research state taxes and licenses.

    State income tax registration if you are not a sole proprietorship.

    Sales tax.

    Register with your state's payroll tax department.

    State licenses.

    Other: Check to see what else your industry needs.

☐ Research your costs, especially insurance.

    Business liability, fire, theft.

    Auto: www.aaa.com to find your local automobile club; GEICO, (800) 861-8380, www.geico.com.

    Health—for yourself and your employees: www.ehealthinsurance.com.

    Workers' compensation (WC): www.comp.state.nc.us/ncic/pages/all50.htm.

    Life.

    Other—depending on your area, your business, and your industry.

☐ Select facilities: will you work from home, rent space, or buy it?

☐ Make a lease-versus-buy decision on equipment and vehicles.

continued

TABLE 1.1 *continued*

☐ Arrange for inventory.
☐ Establish supplies accounts.
☐ Research legal issues.
☐ Consider your services needs.
☐ Select communications: telephone, cell phone, Internet, fax.
☐ Start to work on image and visibility.
    Brand recognition.
    Public relations.
    Advertising.
☐ Take care of money issues.
    Loans.
    Other financing.

Checklist Resources

In this chapter, you saw a variety of resources. Here's a summary of them, so you can find them quickly and easily.

U.S. Government Resources

- **IRS.** http://www.irs.gov. For IRS forms and publications. Use the links on the navigation bar at the top of the page to find things quickly, or use the two search boxes to search the site or the forms and publications database.
- **Employer ID number.** http://vurl.bz/taxmama/IRS_EIN. This site explains how to fill out your SS-4 application and file for your EIN online.
- **U.S. Patent Office.** http://www.uspto.gov/index.html. This is the place to go for patents and trademarks.

State Resources

- **State-by-state business start-up information.** http://vurl.bz/taxmama/StateBusiness. Find out about local resources available in your state using BankRate's excellent online resource.
- **Small business information.** http://www.bankrate.com. This is a good resource for fundamental information on licensing and start-up tips.
- **State tax forms.** http://www.taxadmin.org/fta/link/forms.html. This site links to the tax agencies of all 50 states.
- **Business licenses.** http://snurl.com/license-tax. Save time researching all the licenses you need. BusinessLicenses.com will do the research for you. For an extra fee, it will even fill in the forms for you.

Business and Legal Resources

- **Incorp Services Inc. in Nevada.** http://vurl.bz/taxmama/Incorp, (800) 2 INCORP. You will get 20 percent off the price of formation services and registered agent services if you use coupon code TAXMAMA.

- **The Company Corporation.** http://www.accountstreet.com, (800) 315-9420: Register your corporation, LLC, or other formal structure at this site, which is one of the oldest incorporators in the country. Mention that TaxMama sent you to get a $25 discount.

- **Hubco.** http://www.inc-it-now.com, (800) 443-8177: Register your corporation, LLC, or other formal structure, and handle most of it yourself, a cheap option. It is also a great source of corporate supplies, such as corporate seals, binders, and so on.

- *Clicking Through: A Survival Guide for Bringing Your Company Online* by Jonathan I. Ezor (Bloomberg Press). The best book about how Internet issues affect your business. If you read nothing else I recommend, you must read this book. Ezor provides practical information in plain English about the issues you face the minute your business opens its Web site.

- *The Revenge of Brand X* by Rob Frankel (Frankel & Anderson Publishers). http://www.revengeofbrandx.com. Find out how to make your company the only choice.

- *Grassroots Marketing: Getting Noticed in a Noisy World* by Shel Horowitz (Chelsea Green Publishing Company). http://www.frugalmarketing.com. This book will help you focus your marketing efforts to get the most attention for the least amount of money.

- **Dan Janal's PR Leads.** http://www.prleads.com. Janal explains how to get interviewed by the top publications in the country.

- *Drugs, Drunks and Debits: How to Recognize Addicts and Avoid Financial Abuse* by Doug Thorburn (Galt Publishing). http://www. preventragedy.com. This book will help you avoid going into business with hidden addicts—or do it with your eyes open and precautions in place.

Internet Resources

- **GoDaddy.** http://godaddy.com. Domain names are only $8.95. Even though there are other designations you could choose to buy, like *.biz* or *.org*, if you can't get the *.com* version of the name, choose another name. Otherwise, whoever owns the .com site will get all your traffic.

- **Yahoo!** http://smallbusiness.yahoo.com. Yahoo.com has entered the domain name business. So if you're more comfortable with a brand name you recognize, Yahoo! is selling domains for $9.95. Naturally, it has added a host of Web site tools.
- **SiteBuildIt.** http://www.sitebuildit.com/taxmama.html. Ken Evoy has built an all-inclusive online business package. It includes the Web site, hosting, domain name, mailing lists, merchant accounts, shopping cart, all the tools you need to build a Web site and make it pay—even if you don't have a clue about programming or Internet mysteries. It even has a built-in affiliate program to let you track and pay for referrals. For little more than the price of hosting a Web site, you're going to get tools I've paid thousands of dollars to use. You really can put up your own site—even without the help of your 10-year-old.
- **National Comtel.** (800) 987-0100: Long-distance toll-free numbers.
- **Google.com.** This search engine will find what you need quickly. Google has the unique ability to perform subsearches. When searching for "office supplies," if you come up with 2,850,000 hits, Google can narrow that down. Scroll to the bottom of the page to the bottom search box and click on the text link to the right—"Search within results." Entering "filing cabinets" will bring the search down to only 17,900. Asking for "lateral" drops it down to 1,760. Search within again, this time for "discount," and the number drops to only 233 . . . and so on.

Office Supplies for Accounting and Taxes

- **Avery Labels.** http://avery.com, (800) GO-AVERY, (800) 462-8379.
- **Costco.** http://costco.com, (800)-774-2678: Shop online or visit a warehouse nearby.
- **Office Depot**. http://officedepot.com, (800) GO DEPOT: Shop online or visit a store nearby.
- **Quill Corporation**. http://www.quillcorp.com, (800) 982-3400: Great customer service.
- **Staples**. http://www.staples.com, (800) 3STAPLE: Shop online or visit a store nearby.
- **Viking Office Products.** http://www.viking.com, (800) 711-4242: For accounting forms and supplies.
- **Greatland**. http://www.greatland.com, (800) 968-5611: For accounting forms and supplies.

- **TaxMama's Quick Look-Ups.** http://www.taxmama.com/quick-look-ups. You will find all kinds of useful reference materials, Webinars you can replay, e-books, even the 100% Home-Based Business Tax Solution.
- **Your Business Bible.** http://www.yourbusinessbible.com. Look for worksheets and updates to this book.

✓ **CHAPTER 2   Business Plans You Know and Trust**
To-Do List and Questionnaire

Have you prepared your preliminary BUSINESS PLAN?_____

- Will it be for your own use only? If yes, *use a short version.*
- Will you use it with your ADVISORY TEAM? *Use a longer version with more details and explanations.*
- Will you be using it to raise money? *Use a software tool (see the Business Plan Books and Resources section) to develop a formal BUSINESS PLAN.*

1. Review it with your ADVISORY TEAM.   Date _____

- Separate out the short- and long-term recommendations.
- Revise your BUSINESS PLAN with the new information.

2. List the first FIVE things you must do THIS WEEK:

    (1) _____

    (2) _____

    (3) _____

    (4) _____

    (5) _____

3. What must you do TODAY? _____

    _____

4. Enter your target tasks on your calendar for the next 12 MONTHS.

5. Schedule the first two dates to reevaluate and rebalance your BUSINESS PLAN.

    Date #1 _____ Date #2 _____

Remember to put a copy of each document behind this page, folded in half.

2

BUSINESS PLANS YOU KNOW AND TRUST

I've been rich and I've been poor. Believe me, rich is better.

—Mae West

Chapter 2 Exercise—Create a Business Plan

We're just starting out and already you're ready to turn the page. You're thinking, I don't need a business plan. I know what I'm doing. It's just me, basically working from notes in my back pocket.

You might just do all right playing it by ear. But why not do great?

Frankly, you're going to need a business plan if you want to succeed. You will especially need a business plan if you fail (to protect your tax deductions—I'll explain in a moment). Without a plan, you're courting failure. There are so many details to remember in a business, it's hard to keep track of them without a scorecard, especially when you're working alone. Why sabotage your chances for success? Are you one of those people who are secretly afraid to succeed? Get over it! Take the time to sit down, make a few notes, and shoot for success.

Why You Need a Business Plan

The main reason you need a business plan is that the IRS will want to see it when your tax return shows losses for the first several years.

I know. You don't plan to have losses. But even the best-laid plans sometimes go wrong. When you run losses for more than two or three years, that business plan is going to make the difference between getting to keep those deductions and having the IRS disallow them all under the hobby-loss rules. We'll talk about those next.

You're almost asking for an audit if your business shows a loss for more than two years out of five (or five years out of seven if you're dealing with the breeding, training, showing, or racing of horses). With the country in financial crisis and with a tax gap of $350 million, the IRS is putting more energy into audits that it knows it can win. The IRS's audit software can be aimed to select returns that really do have something wrong with them. Businesses with constant losses are a prime target.

Why? What's the point of being in business if you cannot make a profit? You may as well go out and get a job! This makes perfect sense, doesn't it? After all, if this is your business, how are you going to live on losses?

Of course, if this is a hobby, that's another story. In that case, you are not entitled to be deducting those losses, without severe limits. That's where the IRS gets you—eliminating or limiting your deductions for what you thought were your business expenses.

A business plan can help overcome the "hobby-loss" argument during an audit!

What Is a Hobby Loss, and Why Do We Care?

Let's look at the information straight out of the tax code:

IRC §183(d) Presumption: If the gross income derived from an activity for 3 or more of the taxable years in the period of 5 consecutive taxable years which ends with the taxable year exceeds the deductions attributable to such activity (determined without regard to whether or not such activity is engaged in for profit), then, unless the Secretary establishes to the contrary, such activity shall be presumed for purposes of this chapter for such taxable year to be an activity engaged in for profit. In the case of an activity which consists in major part of the breeding, training, showing, or racing of horses, the preceding sentence shall be applied by substituting "2" for "3" and "7" for "5."

When the IRS considers your business to be a hobby, you have several strikes against you:

1. Your expenses are only deductible to the extent of your gross income. So if you have $10,000 worth of expenses, but your income is only $2,000, you waste $8,000. Those extra costs don't get carried forward, suspended, or anything. They're just gone. Poof!
2. You can't use Schedule C. You must report your expenses on Schedule A as miscellaneous itemized deductions.
3. Your "hobby" expenses are further reduced by 2 percent of your AGI, your adjusted gross income (the last number on page 1 of the Form 1040). That means if your AGI is $50,000, you lose another $1,000 worth of your expenses—aside from the expenses you lost because they were limited to your gross income.
4. You have to report the income on page 1 of Form 1040 on the "Other income" line, which increases your AGI. That could cause you to lose a variety of credits and deductions—and could throw your taxes into the alternative minimum tax (AMT) bracket.

Now that you understand a little about why you don't want hobby losses, here's how to avoid them. Look at these nine factors that the IRS considers important:

1. The manner in which the taxpayer carried on the activity
2. The expertise of the taxpayer or his or her advisors
3. The time and effort expended by the taxpayer in carrying on the activity
4. The expectation that the assets used in the activity may appreciate in value
5. The success of the taxpayer in carrying on other similar or dissimilar activities
6. The taxpayer's history of income or loss with respect to the activity
7. The amount of occasional profits, if any, which are earned
8. The financial status of the taxpayer
9. The elements of personal pleasure or recreation in this business

Real Business—Planned Losses

What if you know, at the outset, that it will take you 5 or 10 years of losses, as you build up your product or your market, before you make a profit? What if you know that if you can hang on for those 10 years, you're going to make millions?

The IRS doesn't know that. It has no way of knowing. But when the IRS comes along with its audit, the strongest defense you can have is your solid business plan in hand. Oh, you'll need a few more tools, as you'll see in Chapter 13, but the foundation of your audit defense will be your plan.

General Benefits

You're clear on the tax reason for the business plan, right? What other benefits can it give you? The five Cs!

- **Clarity and focus.** A plan can save you lots of time. You won't be floundering, wondering what to do next. You will understand your own business better.
- **Cost control.** A plan can help you keep your costs under control because you're not just shotgunning your spending. You only spend money on those things that are part of your plan.
- **Capital.** Except for small amounts of money, you won't get a bank loan or attract investors unless you have a business plan. Of course, you could use your credit cards . . . and with the no-interest or low-interest rate cards, that might even be a good option. But, at best, you're not going to get more than $5,000 to $50,000 that way. If you want real money—enough to fund your operation and let you fill large orders (for products or services)—you need a plan. No one will give you money if you don't understand your own business.
- **Confidence.** It's amazing the way your self-respect and confidence soar when you know what you're doing. You can look people in the eye and give them straight answers when they ask you how your business is doing.
- **Copiousness and growth.** Decide up front just how large you'd like your business to be. You may as well put the correct systems in place for the future—leaving room for expansion of software, phone systems, and so on. Decide if you plan to go public, build the business just so far and sell it, leave it to your children, or turn it into a franchise or a multilevel marketing operation. You can always decide to keep it small later. But to grow, when you haven't planned for it, will cost much more down the road.

The Fine Line between Success and Failure

Running a business was easy as long as I just had my tax practice. It was a cinch to plan out what needed to be done by what date, how many clients I had to see, by when, and so on. One of the things I've discovered since operating on the Internet is that the world is full of distractions, temptations, and opportunities. You're going to find yourself being torn in many directions. They all look like exciting opportunities. If you give in to those offers and invitations of quick money, you will slowly learn that if you had just stuck with your own business and your own plan, you'd be much further ahead.

The price of distraction is more than mere dollars. Time is also a finite commodity. My husband is too kind to point out that by simply focusing on my tax practice, I'd have more evenings and most weekends free. We'd be totally out of debt—even to the point of having our mortgage paid off. Instead, because I am guilty of succumbing to those alluring temptations, I work 12 to 15 hours each day, including most evenings and practically every weekend and holiday. (We're only nearly out of debt. The mortgage, which just dropped to a 4.375 percent fixed rate, will be paid off in a couple of years—but not yet.)

Sure, I love what I do—*all* the things I do. But sometimes it would be really nice to do a bit less—quite a bit less. That's my price of success, spreading myself too thin. However, I have a plan in place that will let me gradually reduce my workload and raise my income to the point where, in another year or two, my time and life will be in balance again. Oops! More interesting projects cropped up. I must redefine my time budget!

Is trying to do everything worth it? That's a personal decision. You'll have to decide. Let's see what happened to a few people and how they did or didn't focus.

Success

In 2004, we met Brad Waller and his partners, who started ePage, http://www.ep.com, in 1996. Brad and ePage just boringly focused on their business plan and deflected distractions. All their energies went into building an online classified system for Web sites to use as their own. They were pioneers in income-sharing programs, like affiliate commissions (Amazon.com's came later).

In 2004, they had 27,000 merchant sites, had run nearly half a million ads, and had attracted more than 5 million page views a month, with more than three-quarters of a million visitors. ePage never needed to get venture capital. The business has been supporting all the original founders, plus several employees, full-time for years. Better yet, Brad's marketing efforts require that he take an annual cruise to the Bahamas and trips to Hawaii and other exotic locations—as part of marketing conferences. Yes, life is tough.

What happened during the last six years? Growth is slow, but business is steady. ePage.com still serves half a million ads to over 850,000 visitors. It has more than 28,000 affiliates still telling the world about ePage.com.

Vision change—Brad recognized a powerful opportunity with telephone applications. He created a series of iPhone applications relating to online auctions and shopping. As a result of the success in this area, Brad's team has moved the company into a new market, with a do-it-yourself iPhone application site—http://uBuildApp.com.

Giving It Away Means More Profits

Philip Tirone's business ventures have done really well over the years, after a few bumps here and there. These days, he's feeling very fortunate. But Philip has seen others struggling through the credit disasters that befell them when they lost jobs and homes and destroyed their credit. Tirone set up a free credit resource, www.720.CreditScore.com, to provide information to help people fix their own credit. There's a credit gossary, links to the credit bureaus, the various laws that apply to credit ratings, and more.

That's a bit like the way TaxMama started waaay back when, teaching people to do their own tax returns. Most people, once they saw how much work was involved, hired TaxMama to do it for them. The same thing happened to Philip. Tirone's well-done site with free resources led to sales of his paid service. Giving away high-quality information builds confidence in the marketplace. People get to know who you are and the quality of your work. Incorporating the right set of free products or services, managed properly, can lead to financial independence. Today, Tirone works when he wants, where he wants (with an Internet connection, you can work from practically anywhere on the planet), and he relishes the time he spends with his wife and young children.

Too Much Success Equals Failure

Carolin Benjamin had the most charming idea for a site: http://www.dujour.com. When she started the site, it told you the holiday of the day. It was a place where you could play games, test your knowledge, compete against other people, and win prizes. Participants registered for free. Starting in November 1996, Carolin got the idea to invite merchants who wanted exposure to donate prizes, daily, weekly, or monthly, depending on the kind of visibility they wanted. The site was an instant hit, attracting more than 80,000 visitors a day, myself included. I loved to play there and won an elegant wooden pen and pencil set as well as other handcrafted items. Well, Carolin had the traffic and the prizes. But where was the revenue? She and her partner were too busy with their day jobs to plan how to make money.

Frankly, even with all the traffic, it was hard to find paying advertisers. Carolin maintained the site for several years, staying up most of the night to post winners, send out prize announcements, and respond to volumes of e-mail. She nearly collapsed from exhaustion. Carolin had to sell the site. Why was the workload too much? She made the same mistake many companies make—even large ones—she didn't plan for success. She had traffic but not the means or resources to respond to her members' needs—or the income to cover the costs of additional help.

Incidentally, as you can see, Carolin kept the URL. These days, it goes to the real estate business she runs with her husband in Arizona.

Failure, Well, Almost

In Australia, Ian Purdie started putting up articles about electronics, ham radios, audio devices, and all kinds of related technical and hobby information. His site, http://electronics-tutorials.com, became so popular that universities were using his free technical articles in their courses. Ian believed that if he put high-quality information out there, people would be sensible enough to contribute funds, or tip him, to support keeping the site alive. Even small sums would be welcome. Amazon offered a payment system, so Ian didn't need to incur the cost of merchant credit card accounts. His costs weren't high. Living on a pension, he could, essentially, get by.

Though users sent him many letters of high praise, few—if any—made donations. Few people used his links to buy their books or supplies, which would have let him generate commissions from their purchases. They'd buy those things—but not so he got the credit. Ian never diminished the quality of the articles he provided, despite years of frustration at the lack of financial support. Finally he just about gave up.

Why did he fail? He didn't have a business plan. Ian never arranged for a way to charge students and readers for his how-to articles. He never thought through the issue of where his income was going to come from. He just believed that people would be honorable and make contributions to support his useful site. To his credit, unlike Carolin, he didn't have to spend hours each night dealing with time-sensitive prizes and things. He could choose to add articles or not, as he saw fit. But he didn't have any money either.

He was just about to do something violent to his computer when he got really lucky. The Google folks came along with Adsense, which provides a stream of advertising revenues. But that's another story for another time. Today, Ian is in clover, and his business is a labor of love again.

Utter Failure

Mike was a very popular realtor in Southern California, earning a six-figure income as a sales manager for a real estate brokerage, when a friend of his invited him to open a business leasing private homes and condominiums. When Mike broached the idea to me, I did my best to persuade him to do two things: (1) work out a business plan, and (2) keep his day job. He could build up his new business slowly, from home, with a low overhead until it generated enough money to support him. In fact, if he'd told his boss about it, chances were, he'd have supported him, even to the point of helping him capitalize the business. No one else was making a concerted effort to tap into the San Fernando Valley market with a comprehensive service providing leasing and management for owners of single units. There was a demand for this service, not just among the homeowners, but by people looking for places to rent. Renters would keep running into those bait-and-switch ads, offering them attractive houses, condos, or guesthouses—then telling them they'd have to pay a fee to get the address. When they finally did get the addresses, those units were already taken (probably always were) or didn't exist.

So with this great potential market, off he went, returning to me several months later. Mike had skipped the business plan. He also had quit his job and opened an expensive office. His overhead, before he got to take home a single dime, was more than $17,000 a month, but his income was nowhere near that. He was lucky to generate $2,000 per month. To support his business, Mike was drawing money from savings.

Mike begged me to help, so I stepped in and cut his costs by $10,000 a month, even after my fees. It turns out that although he was an expert in real estate sales, he didn't understand how the leasing business worked. Mike was still paying out of his own pocket for expenses that the homeowners should be paying. The owners paid them willingly, once we rewrote the contracts.

We doubled his sales overnight by getting some high-end brokerages to refer their low-commission home leasing business to him. In fact, one brokerage owner told his staff that they must forward all leases to Mike. If he ever saw them wasting their time with a lease, they'd be fired. (You have to understand the economics. It takes about the same amount of time to find tenants as it does to find buyers, showing them lots and lots of houses. But where leasing a luxury home might garner a commission of $3,000, selling that same home will generate more than $30,000.)

Those referrals doubled revenues, but it was too late. Mike's business was still hemorrhaging money. Even though he'd been in business less than a year, Mike had dipped so deeply into his financial reserves that within a few more months, he had to file for bankruptcy. It's a real shame. He was one of the most popular members of the local Board of Realtors. The other members would have been very happy to refer their leasing business to someone reliable. Had Mike started out with a budget, low overhead, and better information, he'd literally be a millionaire today.

Exit Strategy—Taking It Public

A few years ago, Kevin Reeth and Ben Curren, both former Intuit employees, were immersed in their own Web development company. Seeing that the increasingly complex and function-packed software left the really small business owner totally confused, they took a gamble. They developed a versatile application to provide the individual business owner with simplified online bookkeeping services at http://www.Outright.com. A free application, it's funded by additional services they provide the owner to make life simple. Nearly from the outset, they structured the business for venture capital. The first round of investors came easily. By May 2010, they had processed over $2 billion in transactions. Their exit strategy is to take the company public, make millions of dollars, and stay involved because it's fun!

Letting Your Ego Rule

Can you name the one person who personifies great success, but turned it into a smashing failure? *Hint:* Living.

Yes, the answer is Martha Stewart. Her company, Martha Stewart Living, Omnimedia, Inc. (NYSE MSO), almost folded after her conviction. Large blocks of television stations dropped her show. Since the show was all Martha—and she was going to jail—even if they hadn't dropped her, who was in the wings to take her place? No one.

As a result, when she was indicted, then tried, and then convicted, the MSO stock went from more than $20 a share to below $10 in April 2004. In April 2010, the price was $7.30. But Martha's personal reputation has rebounded, and her popularity has soared.

What's the criticism here? Surely, Martha had a business plan. No one could be more focused than she was. The problem is the excessive focus—on her, on Martha. Unlike most media businesses that plan to survive for the long run, everything was about Martha. She made no provisions, even after the indictment, to introduce someone else into her television show or on her radio features. There should have been someone groomed to become her replacement if she were convicted—or if she died. The MSO business plan didn't have any continuity built in.

Be sure to treat your business as an entity of its own. Why build something up that no one can step into and take over if you get sick or die? If you tie it too closely to your irreplaceable personal services, your business won't have any value to anyone else. You won't be able to sell it.

Let's Not Fail Due to Success

Are you getting the idea? Even if you're on a success track, if you don't have a business plan in place to deal with that success, you're apt to fail. (Talk about a monotonous refrain!) These are the kinds of things to think about to prepare for success:

- Your ads are successful. Your phones are ringing off the hook. What do you do when the phone lines are jammed with customers wanting to give you money—but you haven't made any provisions for enough people to answer the phones?
- You get the largest order of your career. Where are you going to manufacture it? Or where will you get the trained staff to perform all those services on short notice?
- You get the largest order of the year. You can find the staff and facilities to fulfill it. But where are you going to get the money to pay for it all, until you collect your accounts receivable from this sale?
- You introduce a new electronic product that can be downloaded from the Web. It's all automated. No sweat, right? You get a great review in *PC Magazine* and David Letterman and Jay Leno are all over it with their jokes in their nightly routines. You get so much traffic that your Web site crashes. Can you bring new bandwidth online in time to save the sales? Or count on mirror sites?

Outline of a Plan

Many different books, software, and Web sites are available to help you create a good business plan. Whatever you use, even if it's only a simple list, there are 10 basic elements you'll need to consider (see Table 2.1). Answer these 10 questions. Use them to build your business plan using the books or tools that follow. With good planning, you are bound to succeed.

Important Things to Consider

When you sit down to develop your business plan, be sure to understand how you (and your partners) are going to be spending your time in this business. Face up to the tasks you hate to do. The simple fact is—if you hate to do something, you'll slough it off, do it poorly, or not do it at all. Don't economize by promising to do something you hate. The onerous tasks will be different for each person. Some people just dread having to sell. If you can't overcome that, delegate it. Or hire someone to do it. Others hate to do bookkeeping. If you have a mental block against it, don't torture yourself. Find someone on your team, or outside, who loves that task. Build the costs of delegation into your plan.

Sometimes, with the right team of people, it will work out perfectly. Be sure to have all the team members define their expectations—of themselves, of you, and of the company—so you're all going in the same direction.

TABLE 2.1 Ten Fundamental Questions for a Business Plan

1. What kind of business will you be? (sole proprietorship, partnership, corporation)
2. What will the business do? (products, services)
3. Where will you get the money to start and fund the business until it generates income? (you, investors, loans, credit cards)
4. How much money will you need to tide you over until income is generated? (to cover operations, wages, rents, supplies)
5. How will the business generate income? (sales, rents, grants, dues)
6. When will the stream of income start? (research time, construction time, sales cycle)
7. When will you break even?
8. What contingency plans do you have to back you up if suppliers or investors fail you?
9. What contingency plans do you have to be able to fulfill orders or sales when you succeed beyond your wildest dreams?
10. What is your exit plan? (sell, go public, invite partners, shut down, give to children)

Team Building in College

Working on my master's degree at California State University at Fullerton at night, I soon discovered that most of the courses required team projects. At first, I was incensed. My grade would depend on three other people, strangers, who were also working full-time during the day. Although most of them were men, somehow I always ended up being the group leader. That was fine with me. But assigning tasks would be touchy. Who's going to get the bad tasks or the grunt work? Well, drawing each person out, I learned that they each had a different idea of the chump job. There was usually someone who reveled in research. (Before the Internet, I hated that. Now, it's easy.) There was often someone who was a great typist (yes, before word processors and instant corrections) or had a secretary who was willing to type our papers. Most of them hated to write. For me, that was the easiest part of the job. They were relieved to be off the hook—I felt I was getting away with murder, sending them all out to dig up the information and present it to me. All I had to do was organize it and write it up. Someone else was going to make it look pretty. We each did our share of the work gladly, because we were each using our strengths. Those teams generally earned As.

Play to your strengths.

Of course, working to your strengths isn't just for college. Smart adults deeply engrossed in routine work will suddenly wake up to realize how much time they're expending on tasks that others should be doing. Robert MacPhee is the author of

Manifesting for Non-Gurus (http://www.manifestingfornongurus.com). He teaches a simple five-step approach to attracting more of the results that people want in their lives. With his help, people learn to be clear about who they are, clear about their intended results, and connected to the feelings and emotions they want to be experiencing. They learn to let go of attachments and consistently take inspired action, and by doing this they attract their desired results more quickly and easily. Robert says that the best part of teaching this work is getting the chance to practice what he preaches. That's how he ended up with his amazing assistant, Beth. I love this! Let's let Robert tell you his own story.

Manifesting My Assistant

I was sitting in my office one day, very busy as usual, feeling frustrated that I was unable to keep up with the demands of my workload. The thought occurred to me that I was spending way too much time working on things I did not need to be doing myself. I realized in that moment that I needed to get some help. But the thought of writing an ad, getting it printed, interviewing candidates, selecting someone, training that person, hoping he or she worked out . . . It all seemed like even more work, and I was not even feeling optimistic about the result!

But then I realized what I was doing. I was imagining the exact outcome I didn't want—doing exactly what I coach others not to do. So I decided to practice what I preach. I asked myself what result I *did* want. I realized I wanted someone I could trust, who wanted to work from home, who wanted to work part-time, who could work independently, and who would be fun to work with. I paused and tapped into the feeling and emotion of what finding that person would mean, and then I let go of any attachment to needing it to happen in any certain way or by any certain time (mostly because I was so busy I had to get back to work!).

The very next day, I received an e-mail from Beth, with whom I had worked before. She told me that she had recently had a baby and was looking for part-time work. Would I be interested in having her come back to work with me? She was able to work from home, only wanted part-time, and was fully capable of working independently. I knew I could absolutely trust her, and she was fun. Sound familiar?

She is still working with me to this day!

There's a big advantage to having a reliable assistant, even part-time. The right person can make your company look bigger and more professional. That person can take over tasks that don't require your personal spark of creativity. And he or she can free you up to take on projects you wouldn't otherwise have time to tackle. In Robert's case, when the opportunity arose to become director of training for Jack Canfield's Training Group, he had Beth to help keep his own business running.

Rebalancing Your Business Plan for Tax Consequences

You're always hearing stockbrokers and investment advisors talking about rebalancing your investment portfolio. That means once you've agreed on an investment approach, with a specific percentage of your money in various risk levels of investment, you need to review it each year. As the values of the investments change due to price fluctuations, dividends, and capital gains, one group may become worth more or less in proportion to the other groups. To keep the proportions in balance, you may have to sell some units of one group or buy units of another.

Use the same concept with your business plan. Review it annually to make sure you're on track with your overall goals.

Then review it again to see how any tax law changes, phaseouts, or phase-ins affect your business. Particularly, look at depreciation rules—politicians like to change this area often, increasing or complicating the deductions or credits. Look at business credits. Are there new incentives in place for hiring, locations, or special industries? Expect changes in the areas of travel, meals, and gifts. Those need updating for this millennium.

What are the top three best things about having a good business plan in place?

1. You'll spend much less time and money running your business. By not floundering and wasting time and money going in too many directions, all your investment will go toward producing profits.
2. You'll be able to take the best advantage of tax benefits available to your business, income level, or industry.
3. You'll be in good shape if you're ever audited. The IRS so rarely sees business plans for small businesses. When it does see that level of organization and discipline in that area, it will believe you've carried that thoroughness through into your accounting and tax areas, too.

Business Plan Books and Resources

If you're going to get tools and resources, don't go cheap. Saving yourself $50 to buy a cheaper resource may cost you much more in the time you'll spend to find the information that's probably already in the more expensive tool. Whenever possible, get the material on disk or CD so you can copy and paste or fill in forms. It will save you more time than you can imagine. Besides, electronic media lets you click on links to resources, which will take you directly to additional information as you need it.

Books and CDs

- *Small Business Management: An Entrepreneur's Guidebook with CD Business Plan Templates* (with CD) by Leon Megginson, Mary Jane Byrd, and William L. Megginson. Not only does this cover setting up a business plan, it guides you through marketing, budgeting, growing, and the continuity of the family business. It is a most comprehensive book.
- *Nolo's Tax Savvy for Small Business* by Frederick W. Daily. Looks at setting up a business and selecting a business entity from an attorney's point of view. It's an excellent companion piece to this book. You can get it from nolo.com or Amazon.com.
- *Nolo's Business Plan Pro* on CD. This includes sample business plans, financial statements for thousands of industries, SBA loan documents, and links to loan sources and venture capital.
- *Nolo's How to Write a Business Plan* by Mike McKeever. This book helps you evaluate your idea's profitability, estimate your expenses, and prepare your cash flow forecasts. It offers tips about sources of funds—and where *not* to get them. The Nolo books are available from nolo.com.

Online Resources

- **IRS audios on disaster planning and continuity planning.** http://www.tax.gov/Professional/DisasterInformation.
- **The Small Business Administration.** http://www.sba.org.
- **Links to business plans.** http://vurl.bz/taxmama/SBA_Plan.
- **Center for Business Planning.** http://www.businessplans.org. The center conducts a Moot Corp competition and posts the best sample business plans online at http://www.businessplans.org/businessplans.html.
- *Inc.* **magazine.** http://www.inc.com. *Inc.*'s Business Plan Guide walks you through your business plan, step-by-step, at http://www.inc.com/writing-a-business-plan.
- *Entrepreneur* **magazine.** http://www.entrepreneur.com. A series of articles and guides, including tips from Wharton's Business Plan competition, is available at http://www.entrepreneur.com/businessplan/index.html.
- **The Small Business Advocate.** http://www.smallbusinessadvocate.com. Jim Blasingame's radio show offers a flood of helpful information, and there's a wealth of articles, links, and interviews archived on his site. The "Gentleman of the Airwaves" (my title for him) is accessible for guidance if you need help.

- **CyberSchmooze at the IdeaCafe,** http://www.businessownersideacafe. com/cyberschmooz. Brainstorm with other business owners, and have those who've "been there, done that" examine your problems through fresh eyes.
- **Printable Checklist.** http://www.printablechecklists.com. For business or personal, you'll find a variety of fun and practical tools to help you get organized.
- **The Myth of Being Solo in Business,** by Mark Silver, founder of Heart of Business.com. http://vur.me/taxmama/Heart_Of_Business. Articles and information you will find interesting, along with a spiritual perspective on business.
- **TaxMama's Quick Look-Ups.** http://www.taxmama.com/quick-look-ups. You will find all kinds of useful reference materials, Webinars you can replay, e-books, even the 100% Home-Based Business Tax Solution.
- **Your Business Bible.** http://www.yourbusinessbible.com. Look for work-sheets and updates to this book.

✓ CHAPTER 3   ENTITIES
To-Do List and Questionnaire

1. What ENTITY is your business now?

2. What ENTITY have you decided to be? _____

3. In which state(s) must you register? _____

4. What service are you using? Name/URL_____

   Contact person _____ Phone(s) _____

   Cost _____ CK#/CC _____ Filing date _____

5. File IRS Form SS-4 online. TIN _____ Date _____

   Remember to print the page BEFORE saving it.

   a. Must IRS Form 2553 be filed? If yes, date filed. _____

   b. Must IRS Form 8832 be filed? If yes, date filed. _____

Remember to put a copy of each document behind this page, folded in half.

3

ENTITIES

A house divided against itself cannot stand.

—ABRAHAM LINCOLN (*from Matthew 12:25*)

To complete your business start-up and operations checklist as well as your business plan, you need to know what kind of body your business will wear. Why body? That's what *corporation* means.

> *Incorporate—1398, "to put [something] into the body or substance of [something else]," from L.L. incorporatus, pp. of incorporare "unite into one body," from L. in- "into" 1 corpus (gen. corporis) "body." The legal sense first recorded in Rolls of Parliament, 1461.*
>
> —From the *Online Etymology Dictionary,* http://www.etymonline.com

Decisions, Decisions, Decisions

Once you get past all the setup and planning, your business will be a joy to run. You'll love what you're doing. Everything will fall right into place, and you soon won't have to stop and make decisions each time you must make a move. So far, you've been doing drudge work, getting set up, but that will change. You have one more big decision to make. Then you'll be ready to go forth and conquer the world. (Of course, that one big decision comes only after lots more little decisions.)

What Do You Want to Be When You Grow Up?

The official term for the form—or body—of your business is *business entity*. There are two ways to decide what kind of business entity you are: decide for today or decide for the long run. Those not making plans, by default, decide only for today. But you—you have great plans. You want a dynasty! You want a piece of that IPO (initial public offering) pie.

There's no reason not to get it. *Wired* magazine claims venture capitalists (VCs) are flush with money, chasing too few good ideas. VCs are experiencing a funding hangover—"There's 50 times too much cash: The money has to go somewhere."[1] Why not tap into that?

To get it, you've got to start out with a corporation or limited liability corporation (LLC), and you must have the right accounting team. Your advisory team can help you find the right firm to lay the foundation.

Not everyone wants the stress of venture capital oversight. You might want the freedom to succeed or fail on your own strengths. That doesn't mean you can't have investors. You may—but you can keep them at a distance with smaller LLCs or limited partnerships composed of people you know. Before you decide, let's see what your choices are.

First, understand that what is presented here is just an overview of your options. To fully list all your options would take volumes. Use this information as a starting point for a discussion with your advisory team. There's just enough information here to help you frame intelligent questions.

Misplaced Generosity

Jerry, a new client, came to me one day to help him set up his brand-new business. After telling me a little bit about his new guitar lesson business, he proudly showed me the California LLC documents that Andrew, a friend of his, had paid for on his behalf. I cringed in horror.

His dear friend Andrew, though meaning well, had just obligated Jerry to a life of needless separate tax returns, an extra $800 annual fee to the California Franchise Tax Board, and a potential gross receipts tax. Plus Andrew had only loaned Jerry the money for the new LLC. Jerry also had to pay that back. All this, before Jerry even opened his doors. What a great friend!

Jerry and I sat down and outlined his business plan, determining his anticipated client base and potential income for the first three years, and then we outlined the expenses it would take to generate that income. In the end it was clear that with Jerry having a full-time job, this business would grow slowly

---

1. Gary Rivlin, "The Roots of Bust 2.0," *Wired*, April 2004: pp. 120–125.

but steadily. It would not earn enough income to make it worthwhile to incorporate, or set up any other entities, for at least the first three years. Perhaps, with some diligent marketing and referrals, Jerry would be in a position to quit his job and run the guitar business full-time in about five years. Not sooner.

Since a guitar business is not likely to cause expensive lawsuits, there was no reason not to operate as an uncomplicated sole proprietor.

We thanked Andrew for the LLC—and told him to either keep it or have his incorporator instantly revoke it before it started generating a mountain of paperwork for Jerry. Fortunately, the incorporator was able to revoke it quickly. But it did not return Andrew's money. After all, it did its job!

A Quick Overview of Entities

Presently, in the United States, there are only two basic types of entities—those that pay taxes and those that pass the taxes over to your personal tax return. Some entities swing either way. Once a small business decides what type of entity it is, it must stay with that decision. For some entities, like S-corporations, there are exceptions, but they may only change once every five years. Here are three of the key issues you'll need to understand before going deeper into the body of your business.

Taxation. Table 3.1 displays your tax-paying options. As you can see, corporations are the only businesses that must pay their own taxes. Table 3.2 supplies the tax rates. Income or losses from all other business forms are, or may be, passed on to you. You report them on your tax return and pay taxes at your highest tax bracket. These businesses are called "pass-through" entities.

Unless you're currently in the highest personal tax bracket, you're better off not forming a corporation. Corporations are notorious for double taxation. Corporations pay tax. Then you pay tax on the dividends or wages they pay you.

TABLE 3.1 How Income Taxes Are Handled by the Entity

You Pay	It Pays	Either Way
Sole proprietorship	Corporation	Limited liability corporation
General partnership		Trusts
Limited partnership		
Limited liability partnership		
S-corporation		

TABLE 3.2 Tax Rates

Corporations

Taxable Income Over	Not Over	Tax Rate
$0	$50,000	15%
50,000	75,000	25%
75,000	100,000	34%
100,000	335,000	39%
335,000	10,000,000	34%
10,000,000	15,000,000	35%
15,000,000	18,333,333	38%
18,333,333		35%

Qualified personal service corporation. A qualified personal service corporation is taxed at a flat rate of 35 percent on taxable income.

Personal Holding Company

Personal holding companies are subject to an additional tax on any undistributed personal holding company income. (IRS Code Sec. 541)

Year	Rate
2003–2010	15.0%
2002	38.6%

Accumulated Earnings Tax

In addition to the regular tax, a corporation may be liable for an additional tax on accumulated taxable income in excess of $250,000 ($150,000 for personal service corporations). (IRS Code Sec. 531)

Year	Rate
2003–present	15.0%
2002	38.6%
2001	39.1%
2000 and prior years	39.6%

None of the other entities pay tax at the federal level.

NOTE: Filing partnership returns late will result in penalties of $195 per partner per month, for up to 12 months. If you have a good enough reason for being late, do take the time to write to the IRS requesting abatement of penalties. The IRS will generally comply.

Self-Employment Taxes. Chapter 11 goes into self-employment taxes in depth. For now, all you need to know is that they cost you 15.3 percent of your business profits, even if your overall taxable income is zero. Income from all the "You Pay" entities is subject to self-employment tax, except one—the S-corporation.

Payroll. Working officers of corporations, S-corporations, and LLCs filing as corporations are required to take a reasonable salary. With a $290 billion "tax gap"[2] looming over the country, the IRS has hired an army of auditors. The newly trained auditors are visiting corporate books, looking for unreasonably low wages. They are looking for hobbies reported as businesses, incorrectly reported retirement deductions, unreported tips, and unreported eBay-type transactions, among other things. For all the other types of entities, wages are not permitted for the owners. Owners' families may be paid, if appropriate, as Chapter 9 explains. Owners may be required to receive "guaranteed payments."[3] But those are not subject to payroll taxes at the business level.

It's a real shame. Most working partners, even sole proprietors, would prefer to have a clear, definite payroll to deal with, rather than having to remember to make quarterly estimated payments.

Entities, in All Their Glory

So how do you decide? This section discusses all the major business formats with a brief explanation of how they work. Read the pros and cons carefully. There is no one perfect entity. Each one may have some advantages that are important to you. But there may be some other feature that makes it impossible for you to use. This will help you narrow down your decision.

Sole Proprietorships

This is just you, in business alone. You file your business tax return as a part of your personal tax return. (Some people call this a "DBA business.") Use the long version of Form 1040 and either Schedule C or Schedule C-EZ. If you're in business with

---

2. For an overview of the tax gap, see http://vurl.bz/taxmama/Tax_Gap.

3. Guaranteed payments are required when most income comes from services. The IRS requires that if one partner performs most of the services, then he or she gets a reasonable amount of income before the profits are split. This reduces the income that can be moved to children or other nonparticipating partners, who are apt to be in lower tax brackets.

your spouse, you're really a partnership, aren't you? The IRS thinks so and prefers that you report your income that way.

Pros
- It costs nothing to set up—unless you register a fictitious name, and then it's about $50–$100 every few years.
- You have complete autonomy in business operations and decisions.
- You aren't required to keep a balanced set of books. But do it anyway.
- You aren't required to have a separate bank account—but you should.

Cons
- Your profits are subject to self-employment taxes.
- Your business gets no tax benefit for medical expenses and insurance, without the complication and expense of a special plan, as described in Chapter 10.
- Without any structure, owners often get mentally lazy and don't think of their operation as a real business—so they rarely grow as they should.
- You are personally liable for everything that happens. All your assets, including your home and your savings, are at risk if you're sued.
- There is no continuity of life for the business. If you die, the business does, too.

General Partnerships

Two or more people in business together are considered a general partnership (GP). Income is reported on Form 1065, with Schedule K-1s issued to partners.

Pros
- They are inexpensive to set up. You may even write your own agreement. That's not a great idea, but it is a good starting point from which your attorney may prepare your partnership agreement. Even if there is no agreement, if two or more people are working together, you're automatically a partnership.
- General partnerships pay no taxes.
- Profits and losses may be split by formula, time devoted to the company, or other criteria, instead of only by ownership percentage.
- Losses are fully deductible on personal returns, unless they are real estate losses; those face passive loss limits, which are described in Chapter 6.
- Certain partnerships can get out of filing a tax return altogether. The partnership may file an election (which is a formal announcement to the

IRS) that the partners chose to report the transactions on their personal tax returns. You may do this with investment clubs, certain real estate rentals, or groups of people simply sharing expenses but not in business together.

Cons
- All the partners must be consulted for decision making.
- If loans are required, all partners must provide their tax returns and financial statements. Many refuse because they don't really want their partners to know how rich—or poor—they are.
- Profits are generally subject to self-employment taxes.
- All partners are personally liable for everything that happens. All their assets, including homes and savings, are at risk if sued.
- All partners are liable for the acts of other partners and employees, too.
- There can be continuity-of-life issues. This means if your partner dies, either the partnership is over or you're saddled with an heir (spouse or child) who's in a position to make business decisions. This usually results in conflict. Avoid this by using key-man insurance policies. These are insurance policies you take out on the life of each owner. When one of the owners dies, the policy pays the family of the deceased in order to buy out their interest in the business. This allows the survivor to own and operate the business without suddenly becoming partners with the deceased's spouse or children.

Limited Partnerships

Limited partnerships (LPs) are coming back into vogue. In a limited partnership, the limited partners put their money in and get complete protection from any liability or lawsuit of the business. However, limited partners don't get to participate in the decision making. There must always be at least one general partner who takes on the liability for the whole company.

Pros
- LPs are less complicated than corporations, LLCs, or LLPs.
- LPs don't pay federal taxes.
- They provide complete liability protection for all limited partners.
- Raising money from partners is easy. You don't have lots of general partners to answer to or get approval from.
- Getting loans is easier with LPs than with GPs. Only the entity's and the general partner's financial reports need to be produced for the lenders.

- Profits and losses may be split by formula, instead of only by ownership percentage. Some partners may want losses—others may not be able to use them at all.
- A benefit for the general partner in the LP is that partnership agreements may have buyout clauses or prohibitions against selling the partnership interest without the general partner's approval.
- Limited partners' earnings are not subject to self-employment taxes.

Cons

- LPs are more expensive to set up than GPs. You must get an attorney involved—whether it's yours or one recommended by the people investing with you.
- Limited partners have no control over decisions. They could lose their investment if the general partner is inept or crooked. They won't know in enough time to do anything about it, since the general partner often doesn't keep them informed.
- Some states, such as California, charge minimum taxes.
- For the limited partners, partnership agreements may have buyout clauses or prohibitions against selling the partnership interest without the general partner's approval.
- Limited partners' income or losses are considered passive. Loss deductions are limited to passive income from other sources.
- General partners are fully liable if the company is sued.

Limited Liability Partnerships

Limited liability partnerships (LLPs) are usually reserved for professional groups, such as attorneys, accountants, architects, and others with special licenses—or really good political lobbyists.

Pros

- LLPs don't pay federal taxes.
- They provide complete liability protection for all limited partners.
- They provide liability protection from the acts of other partners.
- No general partner is needed.
- Profits may be split by formula, time devoted to the company, or other criteria, instead of only by ownership percentage.
- There is continuity protection so that even if a member dies, the company continues. Do set up buy-sell agreements and key-man insurance policies in case of death or disagreement.

Cons

- They are expensive to set up. All partners have a say in the issues. And being professionals, they are all experts—so they do tend to put in their two cents' worth. All this "cooperation" pushes up attorney fees.
- Some states, such as California, charge minimum taxes.
- Rules are different in each state.
- Profits are subject to self-employment taxes.

Limited Liability Companies

Limited liability companies (LLCs) are an interesting creation. You'll see why when you read all the features in the "Pros" section that follows. LLC s are one of the most popular business forms with attorneys, since the attorneys can set them up easily using boilerplate forms. LLCs solve the problem of general partner liability. All partners, including managing partners, have liability protection.

Pros

- LLCs get to choose whether to report their business as a partnership, a corporation, or an S-corporation.
- One-person LLCs may report either as a corporation or on a personal Schedule C.
- LLCs may have multiple classes of ownership—this allows companies to give nonvoting shares to consultants and employees. Those members can share in profits but not decisions.
- LLCs are permitted to issue shares that may not be sold. Again, this is perfect for consultants and employees. If they leave, you may buy them out at a prearranged price or formula whether they like it or not.
- LLCs filing as a partnership don't pay federal taxes.
- They provide complete liability protection for all members.
- No general partner, with liability exposure, is needed.
- There is no requirement for keeping minutes, thus reducing paperwork.
- Profits may be split by formula, time devoted to the company, or other criteria, instead of only by ownership percentage.
- Even if a member dies, the company continues. Remember to set up buy-sell agreements and key-man insurance policies in case of death or disagreement.
- The manager running the LLC does not need to be an owner.

Cons
- They are expensive to set up properly.
- Some states charge minimum taxes. California also charges a gross revenue tax.[4]
- Rules are different in each state.[5]
- Profits are subject to self-employment taxes if the LLC files a Schedule C or a partnership return.

Corporations

Corporations (corps) are still the most common large business format used in the United States. Most publicly traded companies are corporations. Some, on the smaller stock exchanges, may be LLCs.

Pros
- All shareholders, including officers, have liability protection.
- Corps may have multiple classes of stockholders. Generally, preferred shareholders get a guaranteed rate of return, but they have no voting power. This allows companies to give preferred shares to consultants and employees. Those members get an assured stream of income but stay out of management decisions.
- Corporate dividends to shareholders have a preferred tax rate of 15 percent if the stock is held long enough.
- Corporations receiving dividends from other corporations they own may be able to exclude 70 to 100 percent of those dividends.
- No general partner, with liability exposure, is needed.
- Shares are easy to sell, though in small corporations the stock may have restrictions—or no market.
- Even if a member dies, the company continues. Remember to set up buy-sell agreements and key-man insurance policies in case of death or disagreement.
- Shareholders owning qualified small business stock (QSBS) for more than five years may exclude 75 percent of the capital gains on the sale (IRC Sec. 1202).[6]

---

4. If you're operating a small business in California, stay away from LLCs. They are usually your most expensive choice due to all the state taxes and gross revenue fees.

5. See "State Guide: Forms and Fees for Business Formation," with links to fees and filing requirements, at http://vurl.bz/taxmama/State_LLC.

6. In the December 2009 *Journal of Accountancy*, Tom Prieto offers a useful overview of the tax benefits of qualified small business stock. This takes into account the increase of the capital gains exclusion to 75 percent as a result of the American Recovery and Reinvestment Act of 2009 (ARRA). See http://vurl.bz/taxmama/QSBS.

- Shareholders of QSBS may deduct up to $50,000 ($100,000 for couples) per year on losses.
- You may have unlimited shareholders.
- Anyone anywhere on the planet may own your corporate stock, subject to any Homeland Security restrictions.

Cons

- Corporations are expensive to set up properly.
- Some states, such as California, charge minimum taxes, even when you have a loss.
- Profits are subject to double taxation. The corporation pays tax, and the shareholders pay tax on dividends issued from those already-taxed profits.
- The IRS may impose taxes for constructive dividends if you draw too much money.
- The corporation may be subject to an accumulated earnings tax if you draw too little money.
- The IRS may decide your wages are too high or too low and penalize you accordingly.
- If the corporation's income comes primarily from the services of shareholders, you may be subject to a flat tax of 35 percent as a personal service corporation.
- Undistributed income of personal holding companies may get hit with personal holding taxes.

S-Corporations

S-corporations (S-corps) have all the protections of corporations, but most of the advantages of partnerships.

Pros

- All shareholders, including officers, have liability protection.
- S-corporations don't need to keep detailed minute books, like a C-corporation.
- Corporations receiving dividends from other corporations they own may be able to exclude 70 to 100 percent of those dividends, using the dividends received deduction.
- No general partner, with liability exposure, is needed.
- Even if a member dies, the company continues. Remember to set up buy-sell agreements and key-man insurance policies in case of death or disagreement.

- You may choose to switch to a C-corporation format or back, once every five years, as long as you file Form 2553 by the fifteenth day of the third month of your fiscal year.

Cons

- Corporations are expensive to set up properly.
- Attorneys and corporate setup paralegals rarely file the S-corporation election. You must remember to file it yourself or have your tax pro do it for you. If you don't do it on time, you might lose the privilege of the S-corporation status.
- When shareholders are added, all shareholders must sign the S-corporation election, Form 2553, all over again. Companies often overlook this.
- Shares are not easy to sell because there is no public market. Generally, it's wise to place restrictions on the stock to keep outsiders from owning your business.
- There are restrictions on the employee benefits of shareholders who own more than 2 percent of the business.
- When it comes to health insurance for the 2 percent or more shareholders, there are special rules—a total pain. See Internal Revenue Bulletin 2008-27.[7]
- Some states, such as California, charge minimum taxes, even when you have losses.
- The IRS may decide your wages are too low and penalize you accordingly.
- S-corps may only have one class of stockholders. Profits and losses are allocated by ownership percentage.
- S-corp stock is not eligible for the qualified small business stock benefits.
- Nonresidents of the United States may not own S-corp stock.
- You may have no more than 100 shareholders.

Whew! That's a lot of data. How can you decide what your company will be? Photocopy these last pages. Draw a line through all the things that are unacceptable to you. Highlight the items you like. This will give you a visual feel for which entities will and won't work for you. To help you out, look at Tables 3.3 and 3.4, which give you a visual view of all the entities. Table 3.3 provides a side-by-side comparison of the primary tax considerations of all the entities. Table 3.4 provides a side-by-side comparison of the primary nontax considerations of all the entities.

---

7. IRB 2008-2 http://www.irs.gov/irb/2008-02_IRB/ar10.html.

TABLE 3.3 Summary of Tax Considerations for C- and S-Corporations, Partnerships, and Family Trusts

Tax Considerations	C-Corporation	S-Corporation	General Partnership	Limited Partnership	LLC	LLP	Family Trusts
Taxation	Corporation is taxed on profits. Shareholders are taxed on dividends.	Corporation is generally not taxed. Shareholders are taxed on profits passed on as dividends.	Partners pay taxes on their pro-rata share of income/losses.	Partnership is not taxed. Partners pay taxes on their pro-rata share of profits. Partners have passive loss restrictions.	Taxation method is dependent on whether a corporation or a partnership is elected.	Partnership is not taxed. Partners pay taxes on their share of profits.	Generally, income is allocated to beneficiaries at year-end.
Pass-Through of Income/Loss	No.	Yes.	Yes.	Yes.	It depends.	Yes.	Yes.
Property Exchanged for Ownership Interest	Nonrecognition treatment if control requirements are satisfied under IRC §351. Liabilities transferred in excess of basis may result in gain.		More flexibility than corporations. Generally no gain or loss is recognized at either entity or partner level. Guidance under IRC §721.		More flexibility than corporations. Generally no gain or loss is recognized at either entity or partner level. Guidance under IRC §721.		Property or money is transferred into or sold to trust.
Initial Basis	Basis in stock = stock purchase price + cash + adjusted basis of property transferred to the corporation. Liabilities do not increase basis.		Same as corporations except that a partner's share of liabilities increases basis.	Determined in same manner as general partnerships.	Determined in same manner as general partnerships.	Determined in same manner as general partnerships.	Fair market value of assets at time of transfer to the trust.
Income Allocation to Family Members	Not applicable.	Family members providing services must first be compensated prior to allocating income and loss to other family members.	Same as S-corps. Capital must be an income-producing asset in order for income to be allocated to a partner who is a family member and has received interest by direct or indirect gift.		Same as partnerships.		Specified in terms of trust agreement.

continued

TABLE 3.3 *continued*

Tax Considerations	C-Corporation	S-Corporation	General Partnership	Limited Partnership	LLC	LLP	Family Trusts
Alternative Minimum Tax	Subject to AMT.	Not subject to AMT at entity level.	Not subject to AMT at entity level.	Not subject to AMT at entity level.	Not subject to AMT at entity level.	Not subject to AMT at entity level.	Yes, either to the trust or beneficiary(ies).
Passive Loss Rules	Can generally offset passive losses against nonpassive income. C-corps are not subject to PAL rules except personal service corporations and closely held C-corps.	Shareholders may be subject to passive loss rules.	General partners are considered to participate materially if they meet any of seven tests in Reg. 1.469-5T, but LPs are more restrictive. Limited partners have only three tests by which they can be considered to "materially participate."		LLC members are treated as a general partner who has to satisfy one of the seven tests.	LLP members are treated as a general partner who has to satisfy one of the seven tests.	Subject to passive activity loss rules.
Fringe Benefits	Few restrictions.	Restrictions on 2% or more S-corp shareholders (may pay tax on fringe benefits).	Insurance, health, and welfare programs paid by partnership on behalf of partners are taxable to individual partners, deductible by entity, and reported as guaranteed payments to partners subject to SE tax.		Same rules as a partnership.	Same rules as a partnership.	Generally same rules as corporations.
Double Taxation	Yes.	No.	No.	No.	No.	No.	No.
Highest Marginal Tax Rate	Top rate: 38%.	Flow-through depends on individual's tax rate bracket. Top rate: 35%.	Flow-through depends on individual's tax rate bracket. Top rate: 35%.	Flow-through depends on individual's tax rate bracket. Top rate: 35%.	Flow-through depends on individual's tax rate bracket. Top rate: 35%.	Flow-through depends on individual's tax rate bracket. Top rate: 35%.	May flow through to individual or may be taxed as an entity. Top rate: 35%.
Filing Costs at Creation	Filing fee with the state.	Filing fee with the state.	None.	Filing fee with the state.	Filing fee with the state.	Filing fee with the state.	None.
Tax Forms and Applicable Publications	Form 1120/IRS Pub. 542.	Form 1120-S/IRS Pub. 589.	Form 1065/IRS Pub. 541.	Form 1065/IRS Pub. 541.	Form 1065/IRS Pub. 541.	Form 1065/IRS Pub. 541.	Form 1041/IRS Pub. 559.
Tax Return Due Date	15th day of 3rd month following entity's year-end.	15th day of 4th month following entity's year-end.	15th day of 4th month following entity's year-end.	15th day of 4th month following entity's year-end.	15th day of 4th month following entity's year-end.	15th day of 4th month following entity's year-end.	April 15; generally trusts must use a calendar year.

TABLE 3.4 Summary of Nontax Considerations for C- and S-Corporations, Partnerships, and Family Trusts

Nontax Considerations	C-Corporation	S-Corporation	General Partnership	Limited Partnership	LLC	LLP	Family Trusts
Ease of Formation	File and incorporate in any state for permission to conduct business.	File and incorporate in any state for permission to conduct business.	General partners must agree to form partnership. No state permission is required.	Certificate of limited partnership must be filed with the state.	File with state for permission to conduct business. Must follow specific procedures for formation and operations.	Register election of LLP with the secretary of state.	Set up trust, appoint trustee, and identify beneficiaries.
Legal Status	Corporate legal identity independent of shareholders.	Corporate legal identity independent of shareholders.	Legal business entity independent from partners.	Legal business entity independent from partners.	Legal business entity independent from members.	Legal business entity independent from partners.	Independent taxable entity.
Eligible Entity	No restrictions.	Citizens, resident aliens, estates, certain trusts.	No restrictions. Any person or entity qualifies as an eligible partner.	No restrictions. Any person or entity qualifies as an eligible partner.	No restrictions. Any person or entity qualifies as an eligible partner.	No restrictions. Any person or entity qualifies as an eligible partner.	No restrictions.
Management	Board of directors and officers are elected or selected by shareholders.	Board of directors and officers are selected by shareholders.	Partners generally have equal voice in decision making.	General partners manage according to partnership agreement.	Operating agreement outlines management.	Partners generally have equal voice in decision making.	Trustee decides on most issues.

continued

TABLE 3.4 *continued*

Nontax Considerations	C-Corporation	S-Corporation	General Partnership	Limited Partnership	LLC	LLP	Family Trusts
Choice of Tax Year	No restrictions.	There are certain restrictions in choosing a fiscal tax year (Section 444 election).	Must adopt same year-end as partner(s) with 50 percent interest. When no partner with 50 percent interest has same year-end, must adopt same year-end of principal partners with 5 percent interest in profits and capital. Otherwise, calendar year is adopted or show a business purpose.	Must adopt same year-end as partner(s) with 50 percent interest. When no partner with 50 percent interest has same year-end, must adopt same year-end of principal partners with 5 percent interest in profits and capital. Otherwise, calendar year is adopted or show a business purpose.	Must adopt same year-end as partner(s) with 50 percent interest. When no partner with 50 percent interest has same year-end, must adopt same year-end of principal partners with 5 percent interest in profits and capital. Otherwise, calendar year is adopted or show a business purpose.	Must adopt same year-end as partner(s) with 50 percent interest. When no partner with 50 percent interest has same year-end, must adopt same year-end of principal partners with 5 percent interest in profits and capital. Otherwise, calendar year is adopted or show a business purpose.	IRC §645 provides tax year as the calendar year. Exempted are tax-exempt trusts under 501(a) and charitable trusts under 4947(a)(1).
Dissolution or Liquidation	Perpetual life. Shareholder approval normally is required. State law dictates approval procedure and necessary percentage of shareholders that can effect a liquidation.	Perpetual life. Shareholder approval normally is required. State law dictates approval procedure and necessary percentage of shareholders that can effect a liquidation.	Death or exit of partner may cause dissolution.	Generally limited to a fixed amount of time.	Generally limited to a fixed amount of time.	Generally limited to a fixed amount of time.	Generally limited to a fixed amount of time.
Owners' Liability	Shareholders are typically not personally liable for the debts of the corporation.	Shareholders are typically not personally liable for the debts of the corporation.	Partners may have unlimited liability.	General partners have unlimited liability, and limited partners have limited liability.	Members are not typically liable for the debts of the LLC.	Partners are not typically liable for the debts of the LLP.	Owner is not generally liable for debts of trust.
Ability to Raise Capital	Sell shares of stock or bonds to raise capital.	Sell shares of stock or bonds to raise capital.	Obtain additional partners or investments from existing partners.	Obtain additional partners or investments from existing partners; bank loans.	Possible to sell interests, subject to operating agreement restrictions.	Obtain additional partners or investments from existing partners.	Owner can sell assets in trust. Income from assets is held in trust.
Transferability of Interest	Shares of stock in a corporation are easily transferable.	Yes, subject to shareholder consent.	Depends on partnership agreement.	Depends on partnership agreement.	Possibly but usually restrictive.	Limited partners may transfer their interests subject to partnership agreement.	No.

A Brief Word about Nevada, Delaware, and Wyoming Corporations

You've probably heard many radio ads tempting you with the virtues of the Nevada or Delaware or Wyoming corporations. The ads encourage you to set up your corporation in Nevada or Delaware or Wyoming. They promise to fix your credit, get you loans without your guarantee, and help you do other things you could never do as a small business. Sure, there are good things about them—privacy, for one. The corporate registrars of Nevada, Delaware, and Wyoming won't reveal your identity, only the identity of your agent for service. If you're hiding out from creditors or former spouses, this may be a way to tuck away your assets.

None of these states have corporate, LLC, or partnership income taxes. They don't even require state tax returns. All you have to do is fill in an annual report about the current officers and agent for service—and pay them a franchise fee.

What's bad about using them? If you're not living in one of those states, you'll have to register your corporation to do business in your own state, too. Often, that will require you to reveal who you are. It will mean filing and paying your state's taxes. It will mean extra forms and registrations.

What if you follow the advice of those aggressively pushing the Nevada and Delaware corporations and you don't register in your home state? If someone doesn't want to honor any of your contracts, he or she doesn't have to and you have no standing in your state. Someone who figures out your company is not registered to do business in your state can walk away from your bills, and you can't sue. Your own state, when it catches you, will charge you taxes, penalties, and interest for all the years you didn't file tax returns locally. Try getting the courts to hear your case.[8] You won't have any luck.

If you feel you must set one up, because you think "Someday I'm going to leave my state. Besides, nothing really happens in my state. It all happens on the Internet," it will cost you. To legitimately have all your transactions take place in Nevada, Delaware, or Wyoming, you'll need a local address. All your mail must be delivered to that state and then forwarded to you. Not only does this cost you money, but it adds about a week of time to each of your orders or banking notices. You must have either a phone number in that state or a toll-free number. Even local customers in your hometown must use that out-of-state phone number. Your bank account must be in that state. You must pay an agent for service. How much extra

---

8. In order to file a lawsuit to collect bad debts, or anything, you must have legal standing in the state where you are filing the lawsuit.

can you expect to pay so that you can avoid taxes in your own state? Here are some annual numbers:

Post office box ($25 per month)	$300
Postage—mail and package forwarding	$360
Agent for service	$150
Extra bank costs due to late notices[9]	$240
Toll-free phone number or call forwarding	$300
Annual franchise fee (approximate)	$125
Total cost of tax-free corporation	$1,475

If you set up an out-of-state corporation or LLC to save the annual $800 minimum fee in California (one of the more expensive states), you've just outsmarted yourself. You've spent $675 more than the taxes would have been. If you're in a less expensive state, as far as corporations go, seeing how high the costs can run may make you think twice—the inconveniences generally outweigh the benefits.

The Real Benefit of Incorporating in Places Like Nevada, Etc.

Sometimes you team up with partners, friends, or business associates who will work with you actively in a business. Your associates are all in different states. Set up the main entity in Wyoming, Nevada, or Delaware. Then register as a foreign corporation in each state where your business associates live and operate. Remember to register in the state where your fulfillment takes place (storage and shipping of inventory), if that takes place in yet another state.

Another good reason? You are at a point where you want to establish a solid business. You know that you will be moving to a different state within the next two to five years. You're not sure where you will be moving. You can protect your company's name, trademark, identity, and presence by establishing the master incorporation (LLC, etc.) in a neutral state. By setting up your business in neutral territory, you can move anywhere in the country without having to close your business and reincorporate elsewhere.

---

9. The extra fees result from the delays in learning when some of your Internet sales have been questioned or deemed fraudulent. Due to the mail delay, you might not get the notice in time to respond and save your sale—or your standing with the bank.

What about Nonprofits?

If you want to get attention and raise money quickly, a nonprofit organization is a great structure. The right cause will open lots of corporate doors and treasuries. Radio and television stations are required to run public service spots, so advertising is free. The big drawback to being a nonprofit is that you can get voted out if you don't structure your organization properly. You don't actually "own" the company. So don't set your business up as a nonprofit entity unless you're prepared to do it right. Otherwise, the IRS will come down on you like a ton of bricks.

You can start out with a nonprofit entity to establish yourself, your image, and your credibility. Use that as a jumping-off point to create a parallel business, funneling part of your profits to your nonprofit. You'll be helping yourself and doing good at the same time. Simply take a decent compensation as director of your nonprofit and make a remarkable improvement in the world around you. That's what Fred Jordan did. His Fred Jordan Mission started by feeding and sheltering Los Angeles's skid-row homeless. Today it helps people as far away as Africa and Hong Kong. Or take actress Carmen Zapata of the Bilingual Foundation of the Arts, which promotes cross-cultural understanding by bringing the Latino experience and culture, through the medium of bilingual theater, to English-speaking and Spanish-speaking audiences. And there's Rose Martin, whose Peace Neighborhood Center in Ann Arbor, Michigan, raises millions each year to help local people in need—and shares the wealth with other organizations in need.

The organization doesn't have to be a charity. It doesn't have to be depressing. You can start something that's fun or that's for people in specific professions or that gathers people with similar interests—like bowling, surfing, scrapbooking, video games, movies, eating, anything your imagination can dream up. Imagine devising a way to get paid for doing something you love!

Don't you admire people who can bring their passion to their work and create a win-win situation for all concerned? That could be you—and your family.

Entities We're Not Discussing

This book doesn't cover the use of trusts or cooperatives as a business format. There are advantages to all those forms, too, along with pitfalls. If you're feeling really aggressive, consider chatting with your advisory team about those alternatives.

All the Highlights in One Place

Let's summarize what you need to know about entities. First of all, avoid Nevada, Delaware, and Wyoming corporations, unless you're located in Nevada, Delaware, or Wyoming—or you run a business across several states. Don't start a business thinking you can hide income offshore.[10] Cut taxes, but don't make that your only consideration. Factor in long-term issues, such as health, retirement, and your family's and staff's needs.

The following overview lays out reporting requirements for each type of entity discussed in this chapter.

Sole Proprietorships

Report income and expenses on the following forms:

- Use Schedule C for most businesses.
- Use Schedule F for farms, florists, and ranches.
- Use Form 4835 if your farmland was leased to a tenant farmer. Income from this form is not subject to self-employment tax.
- Use Schedule E, page 1, for rentals of real estate or equipment.
- Use Schedule E, page 1, to report your royalties from books, films, and other intangibles.
- Use Form 8829 to deduct your home office.
- Use Form 4562 to deduct depreciation.

All Partnerships and LLCs Reported as Partnerships

Report income and expenses on the following forms:

- Form 1065 is the overall tax return. Use page 1 to report your general business income and expenses.
- Use Form 1040, Schedule F, to report farm and ranching income. Include it with Form 1065.

---

10. To the IRS, "offshore" means "outside the United States." That includes Canada, Mexico, and all those tempting tax-free islands and havens, like the Caymans and the Bahamas. See Chapter 5 for a discussion of offshore income and abusive schemes.

- Use Form 8825 to report your real estate rental activities. Include the form with your Form 1065 package.
- Schedule K-1 is issued to each partner or member, reporting the person's share of income, expenses, and credits.
- Use Form 4562 to deduct depreciation.

S-Corporations

Report income and expenses on the following forms:

- Form 1120-S is the overall return form.
- Use Form 8825 to report your real estate rental activities. Include the form with your Form 1120-S package.
- Schedule K-1 is issued to each partner or member, reporting the person's share of income, expenses, and credits.
- Use Form 4562 to deduct depreciation.

Corporations

Report income and expenses on the following forms:

- Form 1120 is the overall return form.
- Use Form 8825 to report your real estate rental activities. Include the form with your Form 1120 package.
- You will generally need Form 4562 to report your depreciation, amortization, and business miles driven.
- Use Form 4562 to deduct depreciation.

Your Big Decision

You have the tools to decide. Before you go to the next chapter, reflect. How will you set up your business, your legacy? What will the body of your vision be? Will it be you alone or one of those alluring corporate or partnership entities? You'll need to know how your business will operate before you can set up the structure of your accounting system. Don't agonize over the decision. Please, don't let it paralyze you. Pick an entity. If you're wrong, it's all right. You can always change it later. Sure, it will cost a bit of money to convert to another entity. Don't worry about it. By then, you'll have the money. So before turning to Chapter 4, decide!

Entity Resources

- **Online etymology dictionary.** http://www.etymonline.com.
- **Form 1040, U.S. Individual Income Tax Return.** http://www.irs.gov/pub/irs-fill/f1040.pdf.
- **IRS Publication 334, *Tax Guide for Small Businesses.*** http://www.irs.gov/publications/p334/index.html.
- **Form 1040, Schedule C, Profit or Loss from Business.** http://www.irs.gov/pub/irs-pdf/f1040sc.pdf.
- **IRS Publication 541, *Partnerships.*** http://www.irs.gov/publications/p541/index.html.
- **Form 1065, U.S. Return of Partnership Income.** http://www.irs.gov/pub/irs-pdf/f1065.pdf.
- **IRS Publication 542, *Corporations.*** http://www.irs.gov/publications/p542/index.html.
- **Form 1120, U.S. Corporation Income Tax Return.** http://www.irs.gov/pub/irs-pdf/f1120.pdf.
- **Form 1120S, U.S. Income Tax Return for an S Corporation.** http://www.irs.gov/pub/irs-pdf/f1120s.pdf.
- **Form 4835, Farm Income and Expenses, Not Subject to Self-Employment Tax.** http://www.irs.gov/pub/irs-pdf/f4835.pdf.
- **Form 8825, Rental Real Estate Income of a Partnership or S Corporation.** http://www.irs.gov/pub/irs-pdf/f8825.pdf.
- **States' business start-up information.** http://vurl.bz/taxmama/BR-Sts. Bankrate.com provides fundamental information on licensing and start-up tips and links to various state agencies.
- **State tax forms.** http://www.taxadmin.org/fta/link/forms.html.
- **Wyoming—50 States Resource.** http://vurl.bz/taxmama/Wyo_States. One-stop access to business sites of all 50 states.
- **State Guide: Forms and Fees for Business Formation.** http://vurl.bz/taxmama/State_LLC. Has links to fees and filing requirements.
- **Incorp Services Inc. in Nevada.** http://vurl.bz/taxmama/Incorp, (800) 2 INCORP: To get 20 percent off on formation services and registered agent services, use the coupon code TAXMAMA.
- **The Company Corporation.** http://www.accountstreet.com, (800) 315-9420: Register your corporation, LLC, or other formal structure at this site, which is one of the oldest incorporators in the country. Mention that Tax-Mama sent you to get a $25 discount.

- **Hubco.** http://www.inc-it-now.com, (800) 443-8177: Register your corporation, LLC, or other formal structure, and handle most of it yourself—the cheapest option. Also, a great source of new or replacement corporate supplies, such as the corporate seal, binders, and so on.
- **TaxSites.com.** http://www.taxsites.com. A great starting point for any tax or accounting search.
- **Legalbitstream.** http://www.legalbitstream.com. This site is a free tax law research Web site offering comprehensive and timely updated searchable databases of federal tax law, consisting of tax cases from the federal courts and IRS materials that were issued from the present back to 1990 in most cases (contains 50,000 documents).
- **IRS—Starting, Operating, or Closing a Business.** http://vurl.bz/taxmama/IRS_Business. The IRS has built a small business resource that features articles, tips, and information to help you start a business, operate your business, and close your business. You may even find some brief videos.
- **IRS—Life Cycle of an Exempt Organization (a nonprofit entity).** http://vurl.bz/taxmama/IRS_NonProfit. Step-by-step information on setting up, operating, and dissolving your charitable institution, trade association, social welfare organization, labor organization, or agricultural or horticultural organization.
- **TechSoup.org.** http://home.techsoup.org. Get free software, technology, and other resources if you are a nonprofit organization. Often, you can get several copies of software products for all the key members of your organization for free or at significant discounts.
- **GuideStar.org.** http://www2.guidestar.org. Look up most legitimate charities and nonprofits. You can find their financial reports and all public information in this master database. Some of it is available for free simply by registering. Other data may require a fee.
- *Bottom Line/Personal.* http://www.bottomlinepersonal.com. This site has a searchable database with at least the last three to five years of issues online. This is an excellent place to start a search. Subscribe to *Bottom Line/ Personal* for $39 per year for short, to-the-point financial articles, information about tax issues, and money-saving tips. They're written in plain English, so you'll have no trouble understanding them.
- **TaxMama's Quick Look-Ups.** http://www.taxmama.com/quick-look-ups. You will find all kinds of useful reference materials, Webinars you can replay, e-books, even the 100% Home-Based Business Tax Solution.
- **Your Business Bible.** http://www.yourbusinessbible.com. Look for worksheets and updates to this book.

✔ CHAPTER 4   RECORD KEEPING
To-Do List and Questionnaire

1. Will you be doing your own record keeping? ____ YES ____ NO. If no, enter contact information and dates you collected documents, as needed:

    a. ____ Will you hire an outside or virtual bookkeeper?

    b. ____ Hire an in-office assistant?

    c. ____ Hire an accounting or tax firm?

    • Name _____ Phone(s) _____

    Address _____

    E-mail _____

    W-2 _____ I-9 _____ W-9 _____

2. What accounting system will you use? List the name of the tool(s):

    a. Paper-based _____

    b. Software _____

    c. Both _____

3. What online accounts will be integrated?

    (a) Bank accounts _____

    (b) Credit cards _____

    (c) PayPal or shopping cart _____

    (d) Other _____

4. Are you using a ____fiscal year or _____calendar year? End date _____

5. _____ Accrual or _____Cash basis?

Remember to put a copy of each document behind this page, folded in half.

RECORD KEEPING

Delegate your record keeping. But more importantly, make sure the person you are delegating to has impeccable ethics and independent oversight by a quarterly accounting audit.

—Adryenn Ashley of WowIsMe.com

You've probably never thought about it this way, but record keeping is a language. In fact, it's a series of different languages, depending on who will be using or reading your records. In Chapter 3, you made the big decision. You picked out the body your business will be wearing—even if it's just for the short term. Now, it's time for you to learn to communicate properly for the body you've chosen.

While the languages are different, they have the same roots. Just as French, Spanish, Portuguese, and Italian all come from Latin, English also has a strong Latin influence. If you listen closely to those other languages, you'll find you can understand them a little, because you speak English.

It's the same thing with your records. The basics are the same across the board. The words used to describe concepts and transactions are the same, but the nuances and details are different the higher up the food chain your business gets. Refer to the glossary later in this chapter to demystify the terminology that tax professionals and accountants use.

Keeping Records Is a Pain!

Many small business owners are so busy trying to run their businesses, hold it all together, keep the bills paid—that there just isn't time for bookkeeping, too.

Besides, who knows how to do it correctly. If you can't do it correctly, it can be daunting, can't it?

But you have to do it. Really, really, you do. If you don't keep decent records, how can you possibly know how your business is doing?

Some people operate on the principle that if there is money in the bank account, everything is fine. One set of business owners I knew used to call up the bank in the morning to find out their balance. (Today, of course, you can look it up online.) If there was money in the account, they wrote checks. They didn't take into account the fact that the checks they wrote yesterday had not cleared yet. As you can imagine, they were bouncing checks all over town without understanding why. Their employees understood. The minute they got paid, they ran to the bank to cash their paychecks before any of the owners' wild checks hit the bank.

Making It Painless

Adryenn Ashley has some tips for you. Adryenn is an award-winning author, filmmaker, and speaker, and the founder of Wow! Is Me (http://wowisme.net).

When you're just starting out, you do your own "expense reports" to give to the bookkeeper. OK, when you're really starting out, you hand over a shoebox full of receipts with a slightly apologetic look on your face and say, "Can you make sense of this?" Once you have a system in place, then it's up to you to mark your receipts. Well let me tell you, when you get to a certain earning level, it is actually more practical to have a savvy bookkeeper do it all, import the data from the bank (so that means limiting cash spending and using debit cards for easy tracking), match the data up to appointments in the calendar, and only spend 10 minutes asking me to identify the dozen or so transactions from the month she can't figure out. Time spent on bookkeeping per month? Ten minutes. It all boils down to having a bookkeeper who is a self-starter and understands your habits.

But don't forget quarterly audits, not done by the bookkeeper, but by a third party. I once discovered my bookkeeper had been writing herself checks (using my signature stamp) for her pay. Rather than putting herself on payroll, she had been deducting herself as office supplies so she wouldn't get a 1099 at the end of the year! Tsk-tsk! I would never have found that without the audit. So, yes, delegate, but more importantly, make sure the person you are delegating to has impeccable ethics and independent oversight by a quarterly accounting audit.

I use QuickBooks Accountants edition because I have multiple entities in different segments! I have the bookkeeper come in, and the auditor comes in quarterly on the sly. I don't want people to behave because they know they're being watched; I want them to do an honest job because they're honest people! I love, love, love my bookkeeper now! She's amazing. She used to work for a bank doing very complex stuff, and so I'm a walk in the park for her!

I hired a more expensive bookkeeper who is a QuickBooks guru to make sure that it was properly done. You can also have your CPA's office do it. It's just more expensive. For me, having things in the right category was the most important. I did a full 10-year audit of a company (I was a forensic accountant for the movies for a while), and it was amazing what I found . . . designer sunglasses written off as utilities . . . once you get a feel for how the company runs and what's normal, the abnormal stands out.

Types of Accounting Systems

It's very important for you to track your incoming funds and your expenditures if you want to have success as a small business. The simplest of accounting systems is just a summary of your various sources of income and a list of your expenses. Since that's essentially a list of numbers, there's no real way to tell if anything's missing. That's called a single-entry system. Whether you maintain these records manually or on a computer—using something like Quicken or Nitro Tax Helper—you have no cross-reference to ensure your books are in balance.

Here's an example of a single-entry system's transactions. In August, John fixed his car for $250. He paid his printer $150. John picked up office supplies for $75. His rent was $550. He bought a copy machine for $775 using his credit card. John's expense records might look like this:

Description	Amount
Auto Expenses	$250
Printing	$150
Office Supplies	$75
Rent	$550
Copy Machine	$775
Total for August	$1,800

As you can see, there's nothing to show you how much money came from his bank account or from increasing the balance due on his credit card.

There's no balancing factor in single-entry systems. Being in balance is an obsession for accountants and bookkeepers. It tells us that all the pieces of the puzzle are there. That's why businesses generally use a double-entry accounting system. Both sides of each transaction are recorded, and when the numbers don't balance—we know something's missing or something's entered incorrectly. In a double-entry system, John's transactions for August would look like this:

Description	Amount
Asset—Bank Account	($1,025)
Asset—Copy Machine	$775
Liability—Credit Card	($775)
Auto Expenses	$250
Printing	$150
Office Supplies	$75
Rent	$550
Total for August	-0-

Using a double-entry system, you always come out to zero, because assets = liabilities + capital.

Not everyone will need a double-entry bookkeeping system. Corporations will. Very small businesses can get by with the most casual of records. Although if you start out with a balanced bookkeeping system, even for a tiny business, you'll already have your system in place when growth is better than you expect. You can save the cost of converting or entering a year's worth of data.

While paper-based bookkeeping systems are perfectly adequate, I recommend that you don't use them. If you're starting a business in this millennium, do your accounting on a computer. It's much easier and faster to correct posting errors. Reports are at your fingertips whenever a banker, your tax professional, or anyone else asks. The software will give you enough information to prepare budgets or to catch fluctuations in costs or income.

One of the things I love about today's computerized accounting systems is that you no longer have to sort checks into numerical order or invoices into date order before you enter them. You just enter everything in any order you find it—and the computer puts each transaction into the right order. When working with people who haven't done bookkeeping for years, this is especially helpful. As I come across checks or invoices from other years, I can enter them into QuickBooks as I go along. I just need to remember to set the paper aside and file it in the box or drawer for the right year. You'll find that feature very helpful if you have receipts in your car or your kitchen or with your children, your boss, or your staff. As you get things in piecemeal, you don't need to stress about redoing the entries to get them into the right month.

Another advantage to the computerized system is that it will give you reports for any time period. If you need to get a profit and loss statement for January through May in order to compute your estimated tax payment, it takes seconds with a good software program.

One feature that some of the accounting software companies are offering these days is online accounting. You pay a monthly fee, and they keep the software updated. You can access your accounts from practically anywhere on this planet. You and your tax professionals don't need to exchange files. You can go online together and discuss the accounting and make revisions or corrections any time you like. The only drawback is that when you use an online accounting system, you can only use it for one company. If you buy bookkeeping software, on the other hand, you can generally use it for as many companies as you like.

Do yourself a favor and get the computer and the accounting software or use an online system—whatever works for you. Just be sure to automate your accounting.

Doing It by Hand

If, on the other hand, you really prefer to do your bookkeeping by hand, take a look at Tables 4.1 and 4.2, which show how to set up a multicolumn spreadsheet. (If you want to do this on paper, you can buy 13-column spreadsheets.) As you can see in both tables, all the numbers to the right of the totals must be added together to equal the total in Column D, the "Total Check" column.

If you're going to do your bookkeeping by hand, be sure to total each page separately. Then have a total page for the month for both cash receipts and cash disbursements reports. Once the month is balanced, total all 12 months to get the whole year.

Use the "Other" column (see Table 4.2) for expenses that are not necessarily recurring. At the end of the month, subtotal each item in the "Other." Add those sums together for the year.

Hand all these pages over to your tax professionals, who can review them and use the information to complete your business taxes.

The IRS Says It All

If you prefer not to take a full-blown bookkeeping course, start out by reading (or skimming) two IRS publications. The first one is IRS Publication 583, *Starting a Business and Keeping Records* (available at http://www.irs.gov/publications/p583), and the second is IRS Publication 334, *Tax Guide for Small Business* (available at http://www.irs.gov/publications/p334). Keep a highlighter pen and a pad of small Post-its handy to mark the passages that apply to you.

TABLE 4.1 Company Do-Re-Mi Cash Receipts Journal, November 2010

A	B	C	D	E	F	G	H	I	J
Date	Item #	Received From	Total Check	Net Sales	Sales Tax	Shipping Income	Reimb. Exp.	Late Fee	Rental Income
11/1/2010	2245	Newman Sound Systems	650.00	577.37	47.63	25.00			
11/5/2010	813	Ansty Tenant	825.00						825.00
11/17/2010	11612	Speakers City	923.18				923.18		
11/25/2010	945	Later Tenant	803.85				-62.40	41.25	825.00
		Total November	3,202.03	577.37	47.63	25.00	860.78	41.25	1,650.00

Totals in Columns E through I must equal the total in Column D.

TABLE 4.2 Company Do-Re-Mi Cash Disbursements Journal, November 2010

A	B	C	D	E	F	G	H	I	J	K	L	M
Date	Check #	Paid To	Total Check	Product Purchases	Office Supplies	Travel	Meals and Ent.	Rent and Utilities	Phone, Fax Internet	Auto	Other (Describe)	Amount
11/1/2010	811	Janice Janeway	321.83			200.00	75.83			46.00		
11/5/2010	812	Landlord	1,165.00					1,165.00				
11/17/2010	813	Electric Company	224.16					2,24.16				
11/21/2010	814	Sally Staff	115.94		32.00		61.99		21.95			
11/26/2010	815	City of LA	109.00								Bus. license	109.00
		Total November	1,935.93	0.00	32.00	200.00	137.82	1,389.16	21.95	46.00		109.00

Totals in Columns E through K must equal the total in Column D.

Fiscal Year

In general, you will set up your bookkeeping system using a calendar year for most entities. Sole proprietors may only use calendar-year bookkeeping systems. Partnerships and pass-through entities may use the year of the majority owner. If that owner is a person, it will be a calendar year. When corporations or other partnerships own the majority interest, the partnership may use the fiscal year of the owners.

Corporations may select any year that suits them. Once the year is established, however, you may only change it with written approval from the IRS.

Accounting Styles

You have a choice of using either cash or accrual accounting—right? Nope, there's also the hybrid method and percentage of completion.

The cash method of accounting is the simplest and the most confusing. As with all things tax, there's always a dichotomy. It's the easiest method for people to use because you only report income from money you've actually received. You only report expenses for bills you've paid.

If it's that simple, why is it confusing? Perhaps it has something to do with the definitions of what is considered "received" and what is considered "paid," and the exceptions to the rule. Chapter 5 will explain "constructive receipt"—or define when money is considered received. Chapter 6 will explain when the money is considered spent—and the few exceptions that crop up.

A key area of confusion for people who have not studied accounting (in other words, most of the business population) is why they can't write off bad debts—bills clients or customers never pay.

That's because you must be on an accrual basis to use bad debt write-offs. Even then, it's not as useful as you might think. You see, when using an accrual basis, you're reporting income when you send out the invoice to the client. So you're paying tax on income you haven't received—or may never receive. That's why you may write off bad debts when you can't collect the money. You've already included that debt in income.

Why would anyone want to use accrual accounting (aside from the times it's required by law)? Because you also get to deduct your bills before you pay them. Some companies have customers who pay them quickly, so their accounts receivable (money from clients) is low. But they have 60-day or 90-day terms on their accounts payable (bills they pay), so they have large unpaid balances—that they get to deduct at the end of the year.

Typically, businesses such as medical practices, which have large unpaid accounts receivable balances, should always be on a cash basis. There are always more and more invoices that patients are refusing to pay. By using the cash basis of accounting, a practice never has to report all the income it never received.

Larger corporations tend to use the accrual method. This lets them enter all their purchase orders, purchases, and shipping manifests or bills of lading into accounts payable in their accounting system. Doing this makes it easier to match up purchase orders with what was actually delivered. The company then has the invoice in its cash management system and can do a better job of tracking when to pay the bill. Companies on the accrual system also enter all the invoices for their sales into the system. That way, if a customer pays off only part of an invoice, the computer can keep track of the amount of money the customer still owes.

If you use the accrual method and know how much cash you have, how much you expect to come in, and how much you have to spend, it becomes much easier to take advantage of vendors' discounts.

The hybrid method allows a business to use the accrual method for its stock and inventory, but the cash method for everything else.

Percentage of completion is generally used for large projects, like construction and engineering. You report your income and expenses based on the percentage of the project that has been completed. So if 15 percent of the bridge has been built, you'll report only 15 percent of the contractual income—even if you've received 30 percent of the payment. And since you often must buy half the materials in advance, you'll still only deduct 15 percent. The rest will be inventory.

Records You Must Keep

In our office, we keep everything. Our office and our storage area are overflowing with paper. Why? I don't trust magnetic media to be readable when I need it. It's happened in the past, when something we meticulously backed up was corrupted by time or heat or . . . never got backed up properly to begin with. Besides, how many times have you changed your backup devices? You've used discs, then ZIP drives, then tapes, then CDs, DVDs, and now—thumb drives. Do you still have a 5¼-inch "floppy" drive to read those old discs?

These days, the technology is better, easier, and faster when it comes to scanning. If you're smart, you'll get a scanner with a feeder so that you don't have to scan each page by hand. When you store the images electronically, make sure you get the front and the back, as appropriate. The best format to use is Adobe's PDF file format. Adobe seems to be smart enough to keep its technology backward-compatible. In other words, you can still read a PDF file from 2005 even though the PDF technology has advanced dramatically since then.

What Kind of Documents Should You Keep?

- **Most important, make copies of all checks.** When customers pay you, copy their checks. Then copy their checks again, this time with your deposit slip. Put the copies of the checks in your customer files, with their invoices. Put the deposit slip into your banking file. Later, when you reconcile your bank account, if you've overlooked an entry, you can find the details quickly.

  Consider making two copies of the invoices you send to clients, one to go in the client's file and the other to go into a master invoice file. All the invoices in the master file should be in numerical or date order. If you use numbers on your invoices, make sure you have each one, even if it's voided. The IRS looks for gaps in numbering sequence. To them, that means you invoiced someone and pocketed the cash off the books. To you, it probably meant your printer ate it or you messed up and prepared a new one. Just reprint it, mark it "void," and add it to the stack.

  Making copies will also help you during an audit if the check you're depositing happens to be a loan from you or a cash advance. It will be easy to prove to an auditor that this was not income.

- **Next, save the canceled checks as a record of your spending.** You don't need to copy them; just be sure to keep them safe and dry. You need them to prove you paid a bill when a vendor says it never received your check. You'll also need canceled checks for tax agencies. And you'll need the information for audits.

- **It's very important to save paid bills.** Some people chill my soul: when they pay a bill, they throw it out. *Nooooooo!* The IRS wants to see what you're paying, not just how much. Do you like doing this with credit card bills? Please stop. Save all your paid invoices and your credit card statements.

- **Save bank statements.** Keep them all—from all accounts.

- **Save receipts.** Save receipts when you've been out of the office doing shopping. Bring back all the receipts for the money you took from petty cash and for the things you charged on your credit cards. You'll be able to match the invoices up with the statements. If there are errors, you'll catch them and get your refunds. Sometimes, the computer system produces posting errors, or it gets hacked. With the receipt in hand, you have proof of the correct charge.

- **Keep copies of purchase contracts on all assets.** When you buy a car, a copy machine, a computer, or whatever, keep copies of all purchase contracts in a master file. You'll need copies of those invoices to support your depreciation expenses. Even though the IRS can, technically, only go back and audit you for three years, if there is something on a tax return that was bought six years ago, the IRS has a right to request the original documentation. For instance, you bought an editing machine for $30,000 in 2010. You didn't need the deduction the first year, so you depreciated it over seven years. Your last year will be in 2017. An auditor comes along to audit in 2015. He or she may audit 2012, but the year 2011 is not permitted. However, you bought this editing machine in 2010, and it's still generating a deduction. The auditor may ask to see the purchase document, even though you bought it five years before the audit. Save time—just have it handy.

- **Keep information about loans.** Keep a copy of the full loan contract, with all the details on the payoff terms. To verify the interest deduction, the IRS will want to see the contract so it can do its own calculations. Having a copy will also be a big help to you in case the interest charges are in error. I have seen banks and finance companies make errors all too often. You can prove the correct interest using your paperwork and your own loan amortization schedule. Use Bankrate.com's loan calculators and print out the report. (It's available online at http://www.bankrate.com/brm/popcalc2.asp.)

- **Retailers, keep cash register receipts.** Always make sure that you match the information on your cash register receipts with the entries in your accounting system. If your cash register software is properly programmed, it should give you separate totals for cash and for credit card payments by customers. Match that up with your accounting entries. If the cash is short because you kept some of it to use for purchases and errands, record the total income received. Then deduct the amount you kept as a charge to petty cash on hand. Be sure to bring back the receipts. For some reason, I find that with retail establishments, somehow the income on the books rarely seems to match the tape. We spend a great deal of time tracking down inconsistencies. Please make sure your tax professional helps you reconcile any differences.

- **Save tax returns of all kinds.** You file paperwork with your city, county, state, and federal governments. Keep copies of each item in its own file in date order with the most recent on top. Add up all your sales tax returns to make sure you've reported the same income on your income tax return as you did on your sales tax return. The IRS is on a payroll audit kick. Be sure to keep all your payroll records, time cards, and paychecks or proof of electronic payments. Also, keep copies of all the expense reports and reimbursements—to prove those payments were not payroll.

How Long Should You Keep Records?

Keep all tax returns forever. Ignore what anyone else tells you. There have been too many times that the IRS or the state has made demands on tax returns filed 8 or 10 years ago, saying they were never filed. If you have a copy, you can insist it was filed.

If you send money in with those tax returns, keep a copy of the canceled check in the file with the returns. If you got a refund, make a copy of that, too. If the IRS grabbed your refund, you won't have any check copies, but you'll have a letter saying it grabbed the refund from a given year. One of these three items will prove that your return was filed.

Keep copies of all asset purchases for the life of the asset plus 10 years or for the life of the loan on the asset plus 10 years. If it's real estate, keep the paperwork until you sell it, plus 10 years.

Basically, keep everything for at least 10 years after its useful life or tax return filing date is past.

You realize, of course, there is this rule in the universe: As long as you keep it, you won't need it. The minute you throw it out, everyone will need it.

Until two years ago, I kept all my client records, from way back in the 1970s. Finally, I got bold and decided to give the records to the clients whose addresses I still had—and to shred the files of people I couldn't reach. I only shredded files that were at least five years old, plus my own personal records.

One hour after I finished shredding, a client who'd filed bankruptcy a couple of years earlier, owing me money, called. He wanted the paperwork on the money he owed me so he could pay it off. (He had never listed my debt in the bankruptcy.) Well, I didn't have the papers, so I couldn't prove what he owed me. If it had been anyone else, I could have waved good-bye to that money. Luckily with Adam, he just shrugged and sent me what he thought he owed me.

Glossary of Bookkeeping Terms

Above the line. Accounting industry jargon for expenses that are deducted on the first page of Form 1040. These expenses are generally deductible as adjustments to income. They reduce your adjusted gross income, which allows you to increase medical expenses and miscellaneous itemized deductions. (*Also see* Below the line.)

Accounts payable (or A/P). Invoices you've received, or are expecting, for things you have purchased or things you have had delivered to your place of business or to your clients. For record-keeping purposes, only accrual basis companies report A/P on their financial statements.

Accounts receivable (or A/R). Money owed to you by your customers or clients after you have sent them an invoice. A/R does not include loans that are being repaid to your business or anything else. It is just income due to you, in whatever form, as a result of a business transaction.

Accrual. An accounting method that includes all your company's sales and purchases, even if you haven't collected the money from clients or paid your vendors. Most people in business alone are wise to avoid this method. It involves an assortment of complexities and rules. (*See* Cash basis.) Accrual accounting is good when your outstanding business debt is high, but your accounts receivable are low.

Adjusted basis. The tax cost of your asset, with improvements added in and things such as depreciation and casualty losses deducted. This is the tax cost after all adjustments mandated by the tax code have been applied to the cost. (*See* Basis.)

Adjusted gross income (AGI). The last number on the first page of your Form 1040. The lower this number is, the more apt you are to be able to deduct IRAs, take advantage of various credits and losses, and use medical expenses and miscellaneous itemized deductions. Several other numbers use this as a starting point. Please get familiar with AGI.

Advances. Loans, often to employees or owners, that will be repaid from their next payroll check or from their draws. They could also be funds given to workers before they go on a trip or to a business event. In that case, the workers must submit an expense report with receipts or mileage data adding up to the amount of money advanced. If they have money left over, they must either return it or have it deducted from their compensation. They may opt to have it added to their compensation and taxed, instead.

AGI. *See* Adjusted gross income.

Amortization. Derived from the Latin word for "death," the value of certain designated assets prorated over a period of time. You deduct a portion of it each year, much like depreciation.

Assets. Things the business owns that aren't part of the product being sold. Assets include bank accounts, investment accounts, inventory, vehicles, loans to people, equipment. They also include intangibles such as patents, copyrights, client lists, and goodwill. Businesses on accrual will also report their accounts receivable under assets. Assets are the first section of the balance sheet.

Audit trail. The details of all the transactions behind a number on the financial statements, including all adjustments. Most consumer accounting or bookkeeping software has good audit-trail features. It lets you run reports and then click on the number to get the details within that account. However, it also lets you correct the entry directly. Once you do that, there is no evidence of the error. Professional accounting software requires you to make a journal entry to correct each error, leaving a history of entries.

Balance sheet (BS). A report that shows the following relationship of your finances: assets = liabilities + capital (or equity). The balance sheet does not include your expenses or income—just the profit resulting from them. The "income" line on the balance sheet must equal the net income line on the profit and loss statement. All prior year's profits are rolled over into retained earnings.

Basis. Tax cost of an asset. It generally consists of the purchase price. For some assets, the basis is the fair market value (FMV). To keep things interesting, when it comes to depreciating business assets, the basis is the *lower* of cost or FMV. But for estates, it's often the *higher* of cost or FMV. (*See* Adjusted basis, Fair market value.)

Below the line. Accounting industry jargon for *itemized deductions*. These are expenses deducted on Schedule A. They don't reduce your adjusted gross income.

Capital (*also called* owner's equity). Capital represents investments in the company. Depending on the type of company, it might include stocks (corporations), shares (LLCs, LLPs, partnerships), or simply owner's equity. The capital section of the balance sheet includes the money invested in the business, the draws taken from the business, and the profits or losses of the business. It also includes any money spent to buy back company shares or stock from owners or partners.

Cash basis. The most common method of accounting. As income, you only include the money for which you have constructive receipt. (*See* Constructive receipt.) Under expenses, you include only the bills you've paid. Certain things that look like accruals also get picked up—payroll and sales taxes to be paid in January (or at the end of your quarter). Credit card purchases are included in cash basis reporting, even though you have not paid for the purchases. They are treated like loans you've taken out at the time you made the purchase.

Check register. That little booklet the bank sent you with your checks. You're supposed to list all the checks you write and the deposits you make. Add your deposits and deduct your checks and bank fees. *Et voilà!* You know how much money is in your bank account, at a glance.

Closing the books. When a company finishes the accounting for a month, quarter, or year, and reconciles all the accounts, it closes the books for that period of time. No more entries are made into those ledger or journal pages. If errors are found later, they must be corrected using a journal entry. You can't just go back and erase the wrong entry. You must either debit or credit the error to get it right. That's in formal accounting systems. Today's software doesn't require that you close the books. It lets you make corrections later, if that's when you reconcile your bank statements or decide to enter your transactions.

Constructive receipt. Money you've received at a specific time, with the right to use it. (*See* Cash basis.) Usually this is important at year-end. A check was mailed to you by your customer in December, but you received it on January 2. Did you have constructive receipt of that check in December or January? Here are some common examples.

- If someone gives you a postdated check, you don't have the right to deposit that check until the date.
- On the other hand, let's say you own a controlling interest in another business. That business owes your company $5,000, but you tell the business to hold on to your money until next year. The IRS considers this as if you have constructive receipt of that money. You're the one who is in control of when that check is issued.
- A third case is where someone owes you money. You tell the person to pay that money to a third party to whom you owe money. Even though that check never hit your books, the IRS treats that as if you had constructive receipt of the money. You controlled how that money was spent.

Credit. In accounting, a credit is the negative half of an accounting entry (debits and credits). It reduces the balance of the account it's posted to. On the asset section of a balance sheet, it reduces the asset. A credit to the bottom of the balance sheet increases liabilities or equity. On the profit and loss statement (P&L), a credit increases income and decreases expenses. A credit balance on the P&L means you have a profit. (*See* Debit.)

Debit. The reverse of a credit. (*See* Credit.) A debit balance on the P&L means you have a loss—you're in the red. When you debit your bank account on your books, it means you've made a deposit. When the bank debits your bank account on *its* books, it means you have drawn money from it. Debits and credits are a confusing concept if you can't visualize both sides of the transaction.

Depreciation. The act of writing off the cost of an asset over a specific period of time, as designated by the tax code. Chapter 6 expands on this issue.

Double-entry bookkeeping. A balanced system in which each transaction has two sides; e.g., when you write a check for office supplies, you reduce the balance in your checking account and increase the balance in an account called office expenses.

Draws. In partnerships or pass-through entities, funds paid to partners or members. They are considered advances against income. This is not income. Draws are reported on the books as a negative amount under capital. At the end of the business year, they are netted against retained earnings—or the owner's capital account. (*See* Capital.)

Expense report. A worksheet submitted by employees wanting reimbursements for out-of-pocket expenses. It may also be an accounting for monies advanced before a business trip or shopping trip was made. Generally, receipts are attached to substantiate the expenses.

Fair market value (FMV). The price a stranger would pay for your asset in an arm's-length transaction. If you put it up for sale, what would someone pay for it? Try to avoid using sample prices you find on eBay as your source for FMV because you'll end up with a lower value.

General journal. Within the bookkeeping system, this is where adjustments are entered.

Journal entry. An accounting entry posted to the general journal. Most entries come into the books via money transactions—deposits or purchases. They are entered in the cash receipts journal or cash disbursements journal. However, corrections, depreciation, amortization, the splitting of payments between loans, and interest—all those noncash or correcting transactions—are entered in the general journal. Year-end adjustments are entered on the books using journal entries.

Liabilities. These represent money the business owes, including unpaid payroll and sales taxes accrued at the end of the year, credit card debt, loans, and monies owed to employees or officers. Accrual basis companies will include their accounts payable here.

Nexus. This is a business presence in a state or tax area. See Chapter 12 for a detailed explanation.

Offshore income. Income held in accounts outside the United States. *Offshore* doesn't necessarily mean "on an island." It could just as easily be in an account right across the border in Mexico or Canada.

Owner's capital account. An account in the equity or capital section of the balance sheet that tracks the partner's, shareholder's, or member's ownership interest in the business. When the investor contributed very little money but has received a lot of draws or losses, his or her capital account may be negative. When capital is negative, an investor is usually not permitted to deduct any more losses.

Owner's equity. *See* Capital.

Pass-through entities. Business entities that do not pay federal taxes. They pass their profits and losses through to owners, who report the amounts on their personal tax returns. Chapter 3 explains this concept.

Payroll. Wages and salaries. Payroll is not just any money you hand to the workers. Payroll has a specific meaning. If you use *payroll* to refer to the compensation you're paying your freelancers within earshot of an auditor, you've just turned them into employees. Chapters 9 and 10 cover this topic.

Percentage of completion. Another accounting method. It is a way of reporting income when you're on a long-term project and receive progress payments. This is used in construction and engineering projects, among others.

Profit and loss statement (P&L). A financial report summarizing a business's income and expenses, resulting in either a profit or loss on the bottom line. (*See* Balance sheet.)

Purchase order (PO). A written document letting a company know that someone in authority approved a particular order. It also defines what was ordered and usually includes a promise to pay for a specific number of units at a specific price.

Quarter. When used in financial reporting, generally a three-month period. There are four each year. You'll often see quarters noted as Q1, Q2, and so on. They usually run as follows—Q1 5 January–March; Q2 5 April–June; Q3 5 July–September; Q4 5 October–December. The IRS, of course, has a whole different schedule for quarters (see Chapter 11). Quarters are particularly important for payroll, sales taxes, and estimated taxes. In the financial world, publicly traded corporations release their profit and loss statements each quarter—to the acclaim or jeers of analysts.

Retained earnings. Profits the business has earned that have not been distributed to owners or shareholders. (*See* Balance sheet, Draws)

Tax year (*also* fiscal year). The accounting year established by your business. In general, it should start on January 1 and end on December 31. However, corporations have the option of selecting their own year-end, to simplify accounting. If taxes will be deferred (delayed) more than three months, the IRS may require the company to pay the difference earlier as estimated tax payments.

Terms. The period of time by which an invoice must be paid; may also include a discount code. For instance 2/10 means if you pay the invoice within 10 days, you're welcome to deduct 2 percent of the invoice.

Trades. An advertising industry term that describes formalized barter transactions.

Transposition of numbers (*also called* "transpo"). A mistake that occurs when writing numbers or keying them into your accounting program—when your fingers get dyslexic and two numbers switch places. Instead of typing "976," you type "796." The difference is 180. You can always recognize a "transpo" because your out-of-balance number will add up to a multiple of three.

Trial balance. A list of all the accounts your company uses in its accounting system, with a balance in each account. When you total up the balances in all the accounts, you should get zero.

Wages. *See* Payroll.

Record-Keeping Resources

Online Glossaries
- **The AICPA (American Institute of Certified Public Accountants).** http://www.aicpa.org/members/glossary/a.htm. Has a glossary of terms, acronyms, and abbreviations.
- **VentureLine.** http://www.ventureline.com/glossary.asp. Offers an extensive tax and accounting glossary.

IRS Publication
- **Publication 583, *Starting a Business and Keeping Records.*** http://www.irs.gov/publications/p583/index.html.

Free Bookkeeping and Record-Keeping Resources
- **FreshBooks.** https://taxmama.freshbooks.com/signup. Free basic bookkeeping. Simple, online way to track your time and your income, do your billing, and get paid quickly. If all your income comes from three clients, you can use **FreshBooks**'s full range of services for free. The site has a community forum where you can learn—and even meet new clients, perhaps.
- **Outright.** http://www.outright.com. Free bookkeeping for sole proprietors. Kevin Keeth and Ben Curren used to work for the QuickBooks folks. They realized how excessively complex the software had become for the really small business owner who simply wants to keep track of records. Not only is this free, but it lets you import information from your online bank accounts, credit cards, and other applications, such as Shoeboxed, PayPal, eBay, and FreshBooks.

Bookkeeping Resources
- **One-Write.** http://www.one-write.com (double-entry cash journals). This is one of the older manual systems for small businesses. Basically, it's designed so when you write your checks, the information is duplicated directly into the cash disbursements journal. At the end of each day, week,

or month—depending on how many transactions you have—you simply total up each page. Just follow the formula at the bottom of the page to see if you're in balance. It's a little old-fashioned, but I remember having more free time when we used this system. You will still need to enter the data into a general ledger. Or have your tax pro do that for you. One-Write also offers a software system.

- **Dome.** It produces a variety of record books and bookkeeping systems that are inexpensive, including a 13-column pad in a 3-ring binder, with tabs for cash receipts pages, cash disbursements pages, payroll journal, and general journal. You can find the products at all office supply stores and at online bookstores, and your tax professional can show you how to set things up.

- **Tax MiniMiser.** http://snurl.com/homebiz-tax. This system allows you to log usage of vehicles or mixed-use assets. You can use it to track income and expenses as a complete accounting system—on paper. Or you may give the monthly envelopes to your accountant to record for you. The envelopes will contain all your receipts and backup for the deductions on your business tax return.

- **Nitro TaxHelper.** http://www.nitrotaxhelper.com. This is the simplest software system—a single-entry bookkeeping system with easy-to-customize accounts. It lets you track mileage right up front. Reports include P&L and expense or income detail. There's a version for multilevel marketers, too, which can be customized for your downline, available at http://www.mlmtaxhelper.com.

- **Quicken.** http://www.quicken.com. This is a single-entry system with lots of bells and whistles. With its banking and investment tools, it has terrific value for personal use. But don't use it for business. Buy its big sister, QuickBooks, instead.

- **Peachtree.** http://www.peachtree.com. This is very popular with larger businesses and accountants but is more complex than QuickBooks. It's easier to use if you have some accounting or bookkeeping background. Generally, users set it up to work with account numbers, which are harder to use when trying to make entries quickly. The software is slow. I have tried it with various systems, and it is always slow.

- **QuickBooks.** http://www.quickbooks.com. A full double-entry system for small businesses, QuickBooks is available in many versions, including customized versions for various industries and point-of-sale systems for retail shops. This program can work with online banking systems. Add-on payroll systems are available. When buying the box, instead of using the online version, you may track many companies. It's one of the most popular systems. Intuit is buying up smaller companies, so a few years from now, it may be the only one left standing. But as improvements are made, it gets more and more confusing to users. Newer versions are not backward-compatible. So to enable your tax pro to review your work, or for you to see your tax pro's changes, you both have to constantly buy updates, which can be very frustrating. *TaxMama Recommendation:* To avoid the compatibility problem, consider the online version. You, or your accountant, can access it from anywhere and make entries even when you're on the road. QuickBooks does the backups for you. Mac and PC versions are available. *Note:* The company offers a free starter version. It's perfect for small businesses.

- **Acclivity's AccountEdge.** http://www.accountedge.com. This system offers software for both Windows and Mac systems, with accounting software for several countries and currencies. It's a more sophisticated system, allowing you to add more modules as your business expands to include manufacturing, payroll, and other accounting functions. The company offers free conversions from QuickBooks (formerly MYOB).
- **Sage ACCPAC** (formerly ACCPAC)**.** http://www.sageaccpac.com. Another step up, this system works best for larger organizations needing a more formal accounting environment. The company offers free conversions from QuickBooks and Acclivity.
- **Shoeboxed.** http://www.shoeboxed.com. For those who don't have the time to record all their invoices, receipts, etc. this is a terrific service. It is especially good for folks who experience total resistance to bookkeeping. Shoeboxed integrates with Outright.com, FreshBooks, and more—and is adding features all the time. In fact, you can even scan receipts directly from your phone.

Tax Resources—Calculators and At-a-Glance Summaries

- **CFS Tax Software.** http://www.taxtools.com. This site has an excellent, inexpensive array of tax tools and special calculation tools, including payroll tools, you won't find anywhere else.
- *TMI Quickfinders Handbook.* http://www.quickfinder.com. Good for daily look-ups on how to handle issues, this book contains worksheets and basic explanations, with index versions for individuals and businesses. Great for at-a-glance information.
- *The TaxBook.* http://www.thetaxbook.com. TaxMama's favorite look-up resource. Similar to the *Quickfinders Handbook*—but better and cheaper. I use

The TaxBook Deluxe in the TaxMama's Enrolled Agent Exam Review Courses because the one volume covers individuals, partnerships, corporations, and more.

Tax Resources—Research and Academia

The following publishers provide tax updates and resources to accounting firms and colleges. You can get a copy of the tax code, regulations, or analyses on any tax issue. They have books for specific industries and entities. Teaching tools and study guides are available, too.

- **Bureau of National Affairs (BNA).** http://www.bna.com, (800) 372-1033: It provides folios and in-depth analyses of tax issues.
- **Commerce Clearing House.** http://cch.com, (800) 248-3248.
- **Lexis Nexis Matthew Bender.** http://bender.lexisnexis.com, (800) 227-4908. The original in-depth legal database teamed up with a major analytical publisher.
- **Thompson-RIA.** (800) 950-1216: Publishes in-depth analyses of tax and accounting issues.
- **TaxMama's Quick Look-Ups.** http://www.taxmama.com/quick-look-ups. You will find all kinds of useful reference materials, Webinars you can replay, e-books, even the 100% Home-Based Business Tax Solution.
- **Your Business Bible.** http://www.yourbusinessbible.com. Look for worksheets and updates to this book.

✓ **CHAPTER 5   INCOME**
To-Do List and Questionnaire

1. What are your business's sources of income? Which can you increase? By percent.

   - Sales of products   _____   _____
   - Sales of services   _____   _____
   - Consulting fees   _____   _____
   - Contracts   _____   _____
   - Commissions or referrals   _____   _____
   - Registrations   _____   _____
   - Rents   _____   _____
   - Royalties   _____   _____
   - Other   _____   _____

2. Is your industry changing? Are any of those income sources about to start declining? If yes, which ones, and by how much?

   _____   _____   _____

   _____   _____   _____

   _____   _____   _____

3. What can you do to replace those sources of income? With what cost?

   Increase advertising? _____

   Eliminate that revenue source? _____

   Concentrate more energy on other existing revenue streams? _____

   Close the business and seek employment? _____

Remember to put a copy of each document behind this page, folded in half.

INCOME

It's just as easy to love a rich man as a poor man.

—Your Mother

Money In, Money Out, Wave Your Hands All About

You'd think income would be the easiest concept for a business owner to grasp. It seems completely obvious to you, right? Income is the money that came into the business. Clearly, it's all the money that was deposited into your account.

But what if you don't have a business account? Or you use your personal account most of the time instead? Then, how much is income?

The following question is typical of a new business owner:

I am self-employed as a carpenter. When someone pays me for a job I've done, and he pays me by check, how can I keep "supply" costs separate from "labor" costs? For example, if I charge $500 to do a job and spend $800 in supplies, I'll get a check for $1,300 in payment. I don't want the IRS to think I've earned $1,300 when in fact I've only earned $500. Help!

Other troubling concepts involve understanding the difference between income and deposits to the business account. They're not necessarily the same thing. Let's take a little test. All the following are examples of items deposited in your business account. Can you tell which ones are income?

- Client reimbursement of your out-of-pocket expenses
- Customer's payment for completed work

- Your money, deposited to prevent an overdraft
- Cash advance from a credit card or your home equity
- Royalty for the oil under your home
- Money from investors or partners
- Money you borrow from Mom (Shhh. Don't tell Dad.)
- Insurance settlement for your pain and suffering arising from a work-related auto accident
- Money you took from your IRA to cover payroll
- Repayments of advances you took earlier

Which ones are income? Only the first two. All the rest are often deposited into business bank accounts, but they have nothing to do with income.

It's really important to get this right because most small business owners don't bring their bookkeeping with them to their tax appointments. Instead, many only bring their profit and loss statements, some neat printouts on a spreadsheet, or a couple of scribbled pages of data. Your tax professional generally never gets to see your income records. So when you overstate your income, he or she has no way of knowing. The good news is that if you've reported these deposits as income, your audits will result in refunds.

A Capital Idea

If eight of these sample transactions aren't income, then what are they? Most of them are capital transactions. The rest are strictly personal and never belong in a business account at all. Money you receive for personal reasons, such as the royalties related to your residence and personal injury settlements, should be deposited into your personal bank accounts. If your business really needs that money, fine—write a check and lend it to the business. Then you'll have an audit trail of a loan transaction.

Capital transactions are things that belong on the balance sheet side of your financial statements. They include loans, credit card debt, and investment assets bought or sold for business use.

Investor's Money

How do you report the money you receive from an investor? It depends on the nature of the investment. If an investor lent you money, which your business must repay, it's a loan. Sometimes the money an investor lends you is a hybrid of a loan and profit sharing: You're going to pay the money back to the investor, plus 6 percent interest, plus 10 percent of profits. It's still a loan. Report the funds as a debit to the bank account and a credit to a loan account. Be smart. Use the name of the person as the name on the account, e.g., Loan from Rich Guy Malone.

To make it an investment, as opposed to a loan, the investor must have bought a percentage of your business—not just a percentage of your profits. We discussed the nuances of this in Chapter 3. Record this as a debit to the bank account where the money was deposited. The credit will go to stock if it's a corporation. It will go to owner's equity—George Generous—if it's a partnership.

What if you're a sole proprietor? Well, if you sold part of your business, you're no longer alone. If you file no formal paperwork, you're automatically a partnership. Remember to get your federal identification number for the new entity.

Did I tell you the best thing about investor's money? If everything falls apart, you don't have to repay it. That's the big difference between a loan and an investment. Lenders avoid risks. Investors share the risk with you. You succeed—the investors get a windfall. You fail, and so do they.

So if these eight transactions weren't income, what is?

What *Is* Income?

Income is all the compensation you receive for your goods or services. Note the word *compensation*, as opposed to *money*. Sometimes you don't get money—you get stock or a share in a partnership or LLC. Perhaps you trade your expertise for services or two chickens, or you get a painting or your lawn mowed.

To determine whether an unfamiliar transaction is income, ask yourself this—"Would they have given this to me if I didn't provide them with a product or service?"[1] If the answer is no, you have income.

If the answer is yes, you probably have a gift. Of course, what if your family and friends are using your services just to help you out? Well, even if it's a pity sale, it's still a sale.

Look back to Chapter 3 to review which IRS forms to use to report your income.

---

1. Read the income chapter of IRS Publication 334, http://www.irs.gov/publications/p334/ch05. html#d0e3424.

Timing of Income

Chapter 4 explained the difference between accounting on a cash basis and accounting on an accrual basis. Most small businesses are on a cash basis. Essentially, you report your income when you get the money. But even for cash basis businesses, there are times when money received is not income, such as the following:

- **As a landlord, you receive a security deposit; that's not income.** It's not your money. You must return that money to the tenants if they leave the premises in good condition when they move out. But last month's rent is rent. So that *is* income.
- **You're an attorney and receive a settlement from an insurance company for your client.** That's not your money. It belongs in your trust account until you pay all the costs and all the parties. Once the case is settled, the fee is income. When you draw money from the trust account specifically as fees, it's income. *Note:* If you don't draw the money, but could have drawn it—it's income when the money was available to you.
- **You're a contractor and receive a third of the project cost from your client for the building you're erecting.** That money might be required to last several months as the construction progresses. You're only entitled to draw money for yourself at certain stages of completion. You'll be reporting that income on a "percentage of completion" basis.
- **You're a retailer, and someone buys something on layaway.** The money isn't yours until the person finishes paying for it and picks up the merchandise. If the person never does, how much of that money are you entitled to keep before you refund the difference? There may be a processing fee at the time the transaction is canceled. The fees will depend on your layaway contract. Until then, the money is a deposit.
- **You put on seminars or workshops for which people must pay in advance.** People pay an attendance fee weeks or months ahead of time. They are entitled to a refund, less a cancellation charge, at any time before the event. Before the event, the only part of the money you've received that is considered income is the cancellation charge. Once the event takes place, naturally, the rest of it is realized as income.[2]

You're getting the idea. Money isn't treated as income until you earn it.

---

2. *Realized* in tax lingo means the event has now taken place or the income is now earned.

Tip

The abbreviated explanation of income: when there are strings attached to money, it becomes income when the strings are gone.

A Brief Note about Accrual Basis

Small businesses that work on the accrual basis report the income as it is invoiced.[3] You only send invoices when you've earned the money. So when people pay you a retainer or advance for services to be rendered, you record the money received as a debit to cash and a credit to accounts receivable instead of as a credit to income. It gets treated as income when you work off your obligation. When you issue your invoices for this work, you'll be crediting income and debiting accounts receivable.

Sales Taxes Received—Are They Your Money?

Bookkeeping can frequently be a messed-up area, but it's actually much simpler than it looks. You want your books and your deposits to balance to the income reported on your tax return. To do that, you must include the sales tax you collect as part of your income. Simple. Yes, include it.

Then, see the line of your tax return that asks about tax expenses? Deduct the sales taxes you paid to your state on that line. In fact, this is one of those expenses you get to deduct even before you pay it. Since you received all the sales taxes with your sales by December 31 (or your fiscal year-end), you deduct it in the year the taxes were collected. You'll be paying it by January 31, or the alternate due date if January 31 falls on a weekend.

Income Rarely Reported

There are three kinds of transactions most people either forget to report or don't bother to—illegal income, offshore income, and barter. I'll cover each of these briefly, just so you know the issues associated with these types of income.

---

3. *Accrual basis* means that you report income when you send out the invoice. You report expenses when you receive the invoice or when the merchandise you bought is received into your office or warehouse. See the glossary in Chapter 4.

Illegal Income—Can't Report It?

If you're engaged in criminal activities, the last thing you want to do is report your income to the IRS and turn yourself in. You're not an idiot. Well . . . you are a criminal, so there's room for doubt.

Remember, the arm of the IRS is all-powerful. Before Homeland Security was created, the IRS was the only agency of the U.S. government that operated on the Napoleonic Code—guilty until proven innocent. The IRS has the distinction of catching Al Capone, where the relentless pursuit of the FBI brought no results.

So, yes, if you're a drug lord, a thief, an illegal prostitute (it's legal in some states), an embezzler, whatever—report the income. You're welcome to call it "other" income. But report it. Since being a criminal is a business, report it on Schedule C and pay the self-employment taxes on it. Enter 999999 as the activity code on Schedule C—it stands for unclassified establishments, or unable to classify. If you consider yourself a professional, use 541990—all other professional, scientific, and technical services.

Oh, go ahead, pay the tax. Just because you're a criminal doesn't mean you can't be a good citizen, too.

Offshore Income and Abusive Tax Schemes

Offshore income[4] means income generated outside the United States. Sometimes you have transactions with businesses outside the United States. As a U.S. citizen or resident, your business is taxed on its worldwide income, not just on its domestic revenues. With the Internet, it's easy to open a bank account in another country without ever setting foot there. You can deposit your offshore sales into that account and keep it as a secret nest egg until you're ready to retire. Or just have the bank issue you a debit card, and you can spend the money here at home. Most people think that the IRS will never see a record of that money, but those people aren't thinking straight.

The world is getting smaller and smaller. The IRS already has arrangements with Visa and MasterCard (your debit cards) to audit their offshore accounts. The unprecedented arrangement with the Swiss government shocked the world! Small countries often rely on U.S. financial assistance or tourism. When the U.S. government starts threatening to withhold those benefits, countries often elect to enter into treaties that effectively rat you out.

---

4. The IRS's Abusive Tax Schemes warning is available at http://vur.me/taxmama/IRS_Abusive_Schemes.

There are some very heavy fines, penalties, and even jail time if you're caught. The IRS is making a powerful effort to make the public aware of this—and paying rewards for information. So beware. Your friends who don't have money offshore might just get irked enough that you're flaunting your wealth. That reward is really nice.

Seriously, don't go there. It's not worth the price.

There are legitimate ways to legally set up businesses and partnerships with people or businesses in other countries. If your business is heading that way, go for it. Be sure to report all your earnings when you do. It's done all the time. You've seen Coca-Cola, Motorola, McDonald's, Federal Express, and many other very successful international businesses do it. When you reach this point in your business, add an expert in international taxation to your advisory team. Otherwise, you're bound to step on the toes of other countries' tax systems, too. If you don't know where to find an international tax expert, Team TaxMama may be able to help.

Bartering—You May Not Even Know You're Doing It

Barter happens more often than you realize. It's not just a function of formal barter clubs or exchanges.

You do it without even thinking. Barter is older than speech. It's the foundation of civilization. Barter made it possible for people to specialize since they no longer had to do everything themselves. I cook and feed you. You weave and clothe me. I farm—and give you food. You shoe my plow horse and make my tools.

How does this translate into today's world? You have skills and trade your services for someone else's products. When each side of the transaction has equal value, and both sides are providing something related to business, it's not nearly such a problem when you don't report it. There would be no tax effect.

The advertising industry commonly gets columns, space, or air time in "trade." Instead of paying for the ads, the client provides goods or services. When I was working for a radio station, in exchange for ads, FTD delivered flowers to each office every Monday. On Fridays, we'd all get Winchell's doughnuts. Licorice Pizza provided records (what, you were expecting pizza pie?). When the Shubert Theatre opened in Century City, we were all invited to a private, press-only performance of *Grease*. For the most part, both sides of the transactions were business oriented. Even though it may look personal, the station received certain merchandise and used it in the course of business. Staff benefited from all the goodies we were given, so we could spread word-of-mouth recommendations.

However, barter isn't usually done by contract. It's usually a casual exchange of a business product or service for a personal one. For instance, you're a plumber with a shop on Main Street. You provide $1,200 of plumbing services to your gardener at his home. In exchange, your gardener mows your lawn and maintains your landscaping for a year. You must record the value of your plumbing services as a sale. You have $1,200 in income.

Since the gardener is providing you with a personal service, you don't get to deduct the cost of the gardening. The gardener must report the $1,200 he would have been paid for his services as income. May the gardener deduct your plumbing bill? Perhaps a part of it. The gardener has an office using 33.3 percent of his home. He'll be able to deduct one-third of the expense. As a result, the gardener has net income of $800 from this transaction.

When you add them together, that's $2,000 worth of income never reported to the IRS. The IRS understands this. Wherever the IRS stumbles across barter during an audit, it's assessing taxes. Your innocent remarks may incriminate you, even when you didn't realize you'd done anything wrong.

So please be careful. When trading with people, be sure to think through the details of the tax implications of your transaction.

The IRS Has a New Audit Guide

Since there is such a healthy, abundant cash-based economy prospering in the United States, the IRS decided to develop an audit guide to train its examiners to "cherchez le cash." It targets specific industries and ways cash is transferred—digitally and in person. It addresses online businesses, as well as Laundromats, bail bonds, car washes, salons, etc. Is your business income mostly via cash, or do you cash your clients' checks at their bank or check-cashing establishments? It is in your best interests to read the IRS Cash Audit Guide. (http://vur.me/taxmama/IRS_Cash_Audit_Guide)

1099s Your Business Receives

1099 forms are sent only to sole proprietors and partnerships. In the past, corporations did not get them at all, except for medical and legal practices. Effective in 2012, all businesses must be issued 1099s when they are paid $600 or more. While a business might get an assortment of 1099s, here are the principal kinds to expect, in order of frequency:

- **1099-MISC.** Your company provides $600 or more worth of services to another company or person in a given year.

- **1099-INT.** Your company lent money to another company or person. You are receiving $10 or more in interest income.
- **1099-DIV.** Your company used some excess cash to invest in stocks. This might also come when you receive income from a corporation your company owns.
- **1099-B.** Your company sold stock or engaged in barter transactions.

The IRS's computer receives millions of 1099s from all over the country and matches up the amounts with everyone's tax returns. If a 1099 was issued to you, the IRS is going to be looking for that number on your tax return. You'd be wise to include the full amount shown on that 1099—even if it's wrong. Chapter 13 explains what happens when the numbers don't match. Here are some tips to ensure you don't get those nasty notices.

What If a Company Sent You a 1099 for More Money Than You Received?

Of course, a person would be daft to pay tax on money he or she has never received. How can you fix the problem without getting yourself into trouble? You have two choices—contact or correction.

Contact the company that issued the 1099 and ask it to issue a correction. Or, as I always like to do, ask the company to pay you the difference. Pity, it rarely does.

If it is smart enough to hold off filing the 1099s with the IRS until it has received feedback from recipients, the company will be most agreeable. Simply provide some proof or documentation explaining why the 1099 is too high. The company will be happy to help—or it will show you why you're wrong. See how easy that is?

I wish it were so. Unfortunately, this avenue usually results in an argument with some closed-minded bureaucrats who stubbornly refuse to help. They get defensive because they didn't have the foresight to wait for feedback from the recipients. They've already submitted the 1099s and don't want to file amended forms. Amending them attracts attention. The 1099s also are used in audits or court cases when examiners are looking for evidence of fraud. One of my longest, nastiest audits started when a corporation was audited and the examiner happened across an amended 1099 with my client's name on it. He jumped on that amended 1099, deciding he'd found fraud. In fact, the auditor was so aggressive, he was shooting for a RICO audit.[5] But . . . that's a story for another day . . . and another book.

---

5. *RICO* is the acronym for the Racketeer Influenced and Corrupt Organizations Act—we're talking about organized crime here!

What If the Money Is from Last Year?

Be aware that sometimes the 1099 will be right—as far as the sender is concerned. It's a timing difference. Take the example of my client, Eddie the Entertainer. Eddie is on the road most of the year. He does his darnedest to keep up with his book-keeping, but it's tough when you're rarely home. As a result, my office always calls Eddie's agent to verify his earnings for the year. In 2009, the agent reported $20,000 more than Eddie had on his books. That's a large sum. Eddie couldn't really account for the difference. Tracking down the payments, we learned the agency issued some checks at the end of 2009 that Eddie didn't receive until 2010. That accounted for the difference. As far as the agency was concerned, it paid the bill in 2009—it wanted the deduction. There was no error.

How can you fix this when it happens to you? When the money was sent out in one year, but you received it the next, report the full income, but adjust your expenses to account for the difference in income. The tax code, when it comes to cash basis taxpayers, operates on the doctrine of "constructive receipt." You don't report the income until you receive the money in such a way that you can actually use it. (For example, a postdated check received on December 20 that is dated January 15 is considered received in January.)

As far as I am concerned, this is the easiest and fastest course of action. If the amount in dispute is really large or if it's a substantial part of your overall income for the year, it would be wise to attach proof with your deduction.

To prove you received the money in the following year, here are some things you can use:

- **A copy of the postmarked envelope the check arrived in will help.** If the envelope was postmarked on December 31, no matter where you are, you didn't get it until the following year. If it was postmarked earlier, maybe the 28th or 29th, it will depend on how far you are from the sender. So be prepared to describe the normal travel time for letters between your locations. If the envelope has stamps or notations about being misdelivered, that will also help demonstrate you got it later.
- **A copy of the check and the deposit slip can also prove your case.** In Chapter 4 you were advised to make copies of all deposits, with the deposit slips. Here's a perfect example of an instance when you'll need it.
- **A signed statement from your bookkeeper or accountant that states you didn't receive the check until the following year can help.** If the person doesn't really have firsthand knowledge, don't put him or her on the spot. Be kind to your staff.

- **When all else fails, you can use your bank statement.** Circle or highlight the deposit in the following year. I don't like providing bank statements if I don't have to. It gives the IRS too much information about your bank account. And there might be some innocent deposit of a loan or something that the IRS will jump on as unreported income. So use this as a last resort.

There's one timing issue that may be a gray area with respect to constructive receipt. Suppose the check was sent so that it arrived at your business before December 31, but you were out of town or the office was closed. There was no one to receive or deposit the check until January. When do you report it?

Use your best judgment. The answer to this question will depend on how well you can support your position that you didn't have constructive receipt.

When the Issue Is Not a Timing Difference

Suppose you flat-out disagree with the amount on the 1099. You know you keep good records, and you know you never got that money. What do you do?

First, let's examine why the 1099 is wrong. Did the company you worked with report that it paid your whole invoice, but didn't really pay you? Check with the company's accounting department. It may have a check that never cleared, got lost in the mail, or is sitting in someone's drawer, forgotten. All these scenarios are common. Who knows, perhaps you just found some money. Collect the money—and include the adjustment to your tax return. Regardless, ask the accounting department to give you a printout of checks it paid to you. Sometimes, you'll catch a posting error. Perhaps the department posted someone else's payment to your name.

If the company you are working with refuses to cooperate and the difference is substantial, you may want to pursue the issue. After all, the company might owe you money. Most likely, you're no longer working with that company.

At the very least, you should look into why the company is so insistent on reporting a larger amount. Do they do this to others too? What other fraud is going on? Send a letter via certified mail, return receipt requested, asking for the detail on all the payments to you. Give the company 10 business days to respond. If it doesn't, be prepared to go to small claims court, or superior court depending on the amount, to collect the difference. Clearly, if the company says it paid you that much money, but you didn't get it—the company owes it to you. You'd be surprised how quickly a company will cooperate with you once it's been served with a lawsuit. You'll either get your information—or get your money.

If it's not a lost check and not unpaid bills but simply a completely wrong number, it will be up to you to convince the IRS you're telling the truth. In this case, be very sure that all your bookkeeping is up to date and that you've identified all your mystery deposits. (Yes, even I have those—when my filing hasn't been done for a while and I can't find my copies of the deposits where they should be.) Attach a statement to your tax return, containing a list of the checks you did receive from that company, with the dates and check numbers. Include some words about the steps you took to straighten the problem out and the company's lack of cooperation.

To What Do You Attach All These Statements?

The tax return you use will depend on the business format you've chosen. Chapter 3 gives the details and the forms. For our purpose, you need to know where on those forms to put your adjustments. Bear in mind, you will not be e-filing. You will file a paper tax return.

- **Sole proprietorships.** Look at page 2 of your Schedule C. There are empty lines in "Part V Other Expenses." On one of those lines, enter "1099 income in error. See Statement XXX attached." Replace the XXX with the heading you put on the statement. Incidentally, if you run out of lines on Part V, you're welcome to attach a list of expenses. Simply save one line for this purpose and on it write "See additional expenses on Schedule XXX attached." After you've listed the overflow of expenses, put the total on the line you saved for this schedule.
- **Partnerships or LLCs filing as partnerships.** There is a line on Form 1065 for "Other deductions (attach schedule)." Most business expenses end up on that attached schedule. On one line of that list of other deductions, simply enter "1099 income in error. See Statement XXX attached."

You can add the statements even when you file electronically. Simply be sure to check the box on your software that says the note or statement is to be printed or included with the tax return. All the major software providers give you this option.

If you're worried about this getting you audited, don't be. I'm going to give you some really great news. The IRS hardly ever reads these statements—especially not when you file electronically. Your electronically filed return is rarely touched by human hands.

What about that difference you just adjusted? The IRS's computers only match up to the income reported on line 1 of your Schedule C and line 1a of your Form 1065. So be sure to include the full amount of the 1099 on those lines. The computers doing the matching have no way of cross-referencing your miscellaneous expenses.

What Should You Do If the 1099 Never Showed Up?

The purpose of the 1099 system is for the IRS to catch cheaters. It's not designed for you to have someone else do your bookkeeping, though many small business owners rely on 1099s for just that purpose. If you're already doing everything right by keeping proper books, the way you were taught in Chapter 4, you already know your income. Don't wait for the 1099s to come in. If you haven't received one by March 15, use your own records.

Generally, when companies send out 1099s, they tend to be correct. If you get one later and it's wrong, be prepared to amend your tax return solely to report the additional income and deduct it back out at the bottom. Usually, that's not a problem. Then again, if you're working with a spouse, partner, or boss who doesn't remember to tell you everything, here's what might happen to you.

One of my clients, the Big Macher, is the embodiment of the entrepreneurial spirit. He's the golden boy that everyone trusts and loves. You probably know someone like him—or are like him yourself. Family and friends gave him lots of money to invest in real estate. In the 1980s, Mr. Macher was the limited partnership king. He was the general partner in dozens of partnerships, owning millions of dollars of property across the country. His management company wasn't incorporated—he filed on a Schedule C. He operated his business on a handshake. While emotionally satisfying for him, it was a nightmare to his accountant. Trying to get the details of agreements and contracts was harder than holding on to a snowflake. Not surprisingly, Macher received an audit notice. The IRS was concerned about him because he never reported $33,000 of interest income from a company in Long Beach, California. That made no sense. I logged in each 1099 meticulously. If it wasn't reported, we never received it. Besides, if we'd received $33,000, I'd know about it. It never happened.

The auditor faxed me a copy of the incriminating document. I asked Macher if he knew anything about this. He just shrugged it off, saying, "I don't think so." Furious, I called the company that issued it. Bob explained what it was. Macher was a partner in one of Bob's partnerships. The venture came up short, and it had to borrow money. Macher was responsible for his share of the interest payments. However, Bob happened to owe Macher a chunk of money. So Bob wrote a check to Macher for the $33,000 interest. Macher endorsed the check back to Bob to pay his own obligation. That's why I had never seen the income. Bob sent me a copy of the front and back of the check Macher had received and endorsed. He also sent me paperwork on the interest Macher was paying. (He never explained why he didn't send us a copy of the 1099 in the first place.)

Net tax effect? There was $33,000 interest income received and $33,000 interest expense paid. Taxable total: 0!

Cost to Macher? Plenty! Lots of fees. Despite the fact that there was clearly no taxable error, the auditor insisted on auditing three years' worth of tax returns. He felt this was a big enough omission that he wanted to see what else was missing. After months of work, he found—ta-daaaa! A couple of thousand dollars of expenses he disallowed. There was no tax due—just a minor reduction of the net operating loss carryforward.

The key points of this story are:

1. No matter how careful you are, there's always something outside your control.
2. For heaven's sake, if you're the Big Macher, have pity on your support staff and debrief them at the end of each day. If you're not a report-and-staff-meetings kind of person, set up a voice mailbox you can call, using your voice-activated, hands-free cell phone (no accidents or distractions, please). You can tell the story of your last meeting. Be sure to brag and include all the details and nuances you're so proud of. Your assistant will be able to check the messages throughout the day. One of those offhand remarks will alert your assistant to ask you about a contract, order, or whatever.

So What the Heck *Is* Income?

And you thought this was easy. Income is more complex than you think it is. Some funds you intuitively consider income aren't. Other things you'd never dream of as income really are. If you're not sure, call your tax advisor.

The best thing to do to keep yourself on track is to have your accountant or tax professional review your books each quarter. Errors will be caught before they cost you money.

Income Resources

- **IRS Publication 334, *Tax Guide for Small Business.***
  http://www.irs.gov/publications/p334, (800) 829-3676: Order this book; it is a must-have reference source, covering all the tax-related aspects of your business.
- **IRS on Barter.** http://www.irs.gov/taxtopics/tc420.html.
- **IRS on Barter Clubs and Exchanges.** http://vurl.bz/taxmama/IRS_Barter.
- **IRS Cash Audit Guide.** http://vur.me/taxmama/IRS_Cash_Audit_Guide.

- **TaxMama on Barter.** http://taxmama.com/barter-category/unreported-barter-income. An overview of how and why barter is taxable using a real case that the IRS took to court.
- **FreshBooks.com**. https://taxmama.freshbooks.com/signup. Collect your accounts receivable more quickly by e-mailing a more professional-looking invoice with a variety of payment options.
- **Chapter 2 of this book—"Business Plans You Know and Trust."** Devote some time to understanding your income and how to increase it.
- **TaxMama's Quick Look-Ups.** http://www.taxmama.com/quick-look-ups. You will find all kinds of useful reference materials, Webinars you can replay, e-books, even the 100% Home-Based Business Tax Solution.
- **Your Business Bible.** http://www.yourbusinessbible.com. Look for worksheets and updates to this book.

1. What "listed property" do you use? And how many of each?

        ___Vehicle   ___Camera   ___Video equipment

        ___Cell phone ___Other

What kind of a log have you decided to use for each "listed" asset? Enter the date you have created it (or bought it),

implemented it, and updated it through the current date, for this year, for each asset (use another sheet).

        ___ Excel spreadsheet   ___ Tax MiniMiser   ___Calendar

        ___ Appointment book   ___ PDA/cell phone ___Other

2. Are you logging both personal and business use? ___Yes ___No

3. Is each user logging his or her personal and business use? ___Yes ___No

4. Start tracking your mileage—business and personal, RIGHT NOW.

5. If you carry inventory, when do you take your year-end count? Date_____

6. Collect copies of the written contracts for your facilities and equipment into one file.

7. What expenses are specific to your industry? List them on another sheet.

8. What questions do you have to ask your ADVISORY TEAM or TAX PROFESSIONAL?

_____

Remember to put a copy of each document behind this page, folded in half.

COMMON DEDUCTIONS

Time is worth more than money. You can always earn more money. Can you replace lost time?

—TaxMama

The best part about being in business for yourself is all those luscious deductions. You can't go to a cocktail party, networking meeting, or any place people gather without hearing how someone deducted a cruise, a party, a luxurious car, a home—in fact, most kinds of living expenses. Owning your own business is great, they say, because most of your living expenses are deductible.

Listening to what other people say, you might as well get the best of everything—the most expensive briefcase, watch, PDA, computer, and cell phones for everyone! After all, it's practically free. It's all tax deductible.

Please curb your euphoria for just a moment.

Even if all those things are acceptable as deductible business expenses in your particular business, your tax savings is only a percentage of the amount you spend. It's not more than 50 percent of the price. You're still spending $100 for every $50 you save.

No, you can't make it up in volume.

How do you know what you can deduct and what you can't? This chapter explains it all for you.

Rule of Thumb

Actually, you're really rather right to rejoice in your expenses. Let's face it; if you must spend the money, you might as well enjoy what you've bought. In most cases, the IRS doesn't really have the right to dictate how much you spend on any given item. Would you like to have your business carry you around first class? If you can afford it, go for it!

Looking at the cost of something I want to use for business, this is my rule of thumb: How many hours will it take me to pay for this thing or this experience? Do I want to devote that many hours after I've consumed this trip or bought this device?

Think about it. Once you develop a business, money will come. On the other hand, time is not a renewable resource. Think about that when you pull out that credit card to pay for a needless extravagance or excessive expense.

Universally Deductible

As long as we're in a spending frame of mind, what shall we spend money on that we know the IRS is used to seeing on business tax returns? The following are some of the items you can deduct.

Mixed-Use Assets

Car, computers, cameras, cell phones, and even other things that don't start with a *c* are mixed-use assets—things you need both personally and for business. We'll talk more about them later in this chapter.

Office Expenses

Especially when working at home—out of your back pocket, so to speak—you overlook a substantial part of your office costs. You may pick up supplies while you're out running around, shopping for the family, but you often forget to split the receipts you've collected. Some of those family supplies were used in the business office. This category is often used as a catchall for all general business expenses. Don't dump everything in here—or in office supplies. Look at each purchase and put it in the category where it belongs. Stamps and postal supplies belong in postage or in postage and shipping. Software, if it's renewed annually, should be considered computer supplies. Software that has a long-term life is capitalized. It's an asset that gets depreciated. Auto expenses, including gasoline and parking, don't belong in office expenses. They belong in auto expenses and parking, respectively. The $1,000 down payment on the copy machine doesn't belong here either. That's an asset. Here's how you enter the copier purchase on your books.

When you take out a loan to buy an asset, such as a copier, you must put the full cost of the copier on the books, as well as the loan. Here are the entries you'll be making when you purchase the copier (journal entry #1) and when you make payments (journal entry #2):

Account Name (Description)	Debit	Credit
Copy Machine (cost of asset)	$5,000	
Bank Account (wrote check)		$1,000
Loan Payable (borrowed money)		$4,000
(Journal Entry #1) Record the purchase of the copier		
Interest Expense (make loan payment)	$25	
Loan Payable (principal part of payment)	$75	
Bank Account (wrote check for payment)		$100
(Journal Entry #2) Record monthly loan payment		

Cost of Goods Sold

This deduction is generally for merchandise or inventory. When you're selling a product, wholesale or retail, your merchandise is considered your cost of goods sold.[1] That cost gets reported on the second page of the Schedule C for proprietorships and on the second page of the 1065 or 1120 for other entities. Other costs of goods sold include the labor to make it, to get it ready for sale, or to install it. Freight to ship it to your facility is also a cost of goods sold. The freight to ship it to customers, however, is part of the sales costs.

For attorneys, your cost of goods sold would be the clients' costs on a specific case, e.g., the filing fees for the case, the doctor's bills, investigators' costs, and things like that. For someone putting on seminars, the cost of goods sold would include the fees to instructors or speakers, the cost of the facility and the refreshments, and the costs of the handouts or books.

When you're involved in manufacturing, there is a raft of direct and indirect costs that may end up in this part of the tax return. It's much more complicated. Be sure to have your tax professional set up your accounting system so you get it right.

---

1. Cost of goods sold is the hard costs involved with producing your product or delivering your service.

Advertising, Marketing, and Publicity

The IRS clearly has no trouble with these obvious expenses. For some reason, though, people don't deduct these correctly. When I see a business growing that doesn't show anything on the advertising line, I wonder where the business misposted those costs. On the "Advertising" line, you may include trade shows where you exhibit your company. Include print, radio, television, or Internet advertisements; open houses, if you're a real estate agent; and mailers, brochures, and flyers.

Commissions and Fees

Be sure to issue 1099-MISC forms to everyone you pay $600 or more in a year. Chapter 9 tells you how to make the experience painless. I have seen people lose these deductions because the 1099-MISC forms were not issued. Be careful in this category. If your professional code of ethics doesn't permit commissions to be paid to anyone who isn't licensed in your field, you may not want to report illegal commissions. (Those are also known as bribes.) On the other hand, even during an audit, I haven't seen examiners question the legality of commission paid by real estate agents to unlicensed individuals.

Interest Expense

Most businesses borrow money. In fact, it's a good idea to establish a business line of credit now, when you don't need it. Your bank will give you a better rate of interest now—when you're flush with cash—than when you're broke and begging.

Do you understand how lines of credit work? The money is available for your use whenever you need it. You pay no interest unless you use the money. And if you're really sweet, your banker will waive the annual fees. So what interest expenses are deductible?

- If it's a business loan, deduct the interest.
- If it's a personal loan, the interest deduction does not belong on your business books. Period.
- If it was a personal loan, but you used all the money for the business, put the proof into a file with each year's tax return. You may deduct the interest.
- Credit card interest is easy to deduct if you use a separate card for all your business purchases. *Personal interest expenses are not deductible.* So if your funds are limited and you have to choose between paying off the balance on a personal credit card and paying off the business one—pay off the

personal card first. *Let the business card earn the interest fees. Those are deductible.* When using the same card for both personal and business use, you'll have to do some computations to see what percentage of the interest on that card can be treated as a business deduction. For the future, set aside one card just for business use. It will make your life much easier, and your record keeping, too.

- For vehicle loans, if you use the car for personal purposes, be sure to deduct only the business percentage of the auto interest. For example, if you use the car personally 15 percent of the time, deduct only 85 percent of the vehicle loan interest. *Note:* When you use the car as an employee (even as an employee of your own corporation), you may not deduct the interest.
- Be careful with loans from owners. Write up a loan contract for each loan, with an interest rate. Even if you don't pay the interest, compute it for the year and accrue it. [Journal entry: Debit to interest expense. Credit to interest payable (or to loan from officer).] For corporations, be sure to put the decision to borrow this money from the officer or shareholder into your minutes. Have all the officers or members of the board of directors sign the minutes to approve them.

Rent and Utilities

The IRS expects going concerns to rent office or manufacturing or storage space. That won't attract any attention. But if you're trying to deduct your home office expenses, please read Chapter 7 for instructions.

Insurance

Business insurance premiums, including workers' compensation, business liability, malpractice, and facility and equipment coverage, are all deductible. When it comes to health insurance or life insurance, Chapters 9 and 10 explain what you may and may not deduct. Health insurance issues are complicated for planning purposes. Take the time to learn the tricks. Health credits and deductions are available to those who make the effort to invest the time.

Taxes and Licenses

One of the things I always find in this account is estimated payments on the owner's personal income tax. Sorry, my friend, those are not an expense of your business. Deductible taxes include the employer's share of the payroll taxes, personal property taxes, fees paid to your secretary of state, the fee for your city business license, the cost of your professional license, sales taxes you collect from your customers, and if you're a corporation, the state taxes your business pays. *Note:* The state income taxes or franchise taxes are generally not deductible on your state corporation tax returns. Some people advise you to pay them in December of the year before they are due so you can take the deduction early. That's great for one year. The next year, if you don't also do that, you won't have a state tax deduction at all. See how that works?

Education

It doesn't matter what industry you're in, whether you're a professional or a tradesperson or a truck driver, you must keep up with the latest news, information, and technology relating to your business. Classes, seminars, workshops, books, and magazines—all these are acceptable—and expected. You're entitled to deduct travel costs. So why not look for courses in places you'd like to visit? Combine your personal and business interests. Who knows; if you're having fun, you may even attract other people who are apt to become future clients or customers.

You may not deduct courses taken toward your degree if having that degree is a minimum requirement of the job. Nor may you deduct the cost of education to learn a new career. These sound like foolish rules, but that's the law. You would think our legislators would do everything in their power to encourage Americans to have the best education and skills in the world. We have all seen major shifts in the workforce several times over the years. You've seen times when entire professions or trades were put out of work. (Engineers in the 1970s, teachers in the 1980s, engineers in the 1990s, data entry folks in the 1990s . . . just to name a few.) It's important that people and businesses look toward the future and learn skills to fall back on if things go poorly in their present industry. That can cut social welfare costs way down. Even if no deduction is available, have the good sense to keep learning new ways to support yourself. It may also provide new, lucrative directions for your business. Besides, learning can be very satisfying!

Travel and Transportation

General business travel is deductible, and so is travel to attend trade shows and courses. However, if your spouse or family members come along just for fun, you don't get to deduct their expenses. You may only deduct their travel expenses if they are an integral part of the business.

You have a choice of keeping careful receipts and deducting the actual cost of your lodging or using rates set by the IRS. If you're frugal, the IRS's standards, called per diem rates, may be higher. Look up current, or prior, per diem rates at the General Services Administration Web site, available at http://vur.me/taxmama/PerDiem.

Meals and Entertainment

Except for places in the business of serving food (like restaurants and day-care centers), you only get to deduct 50 percent of this expense. That's why it's so important that you post your travel expenses properly. You don't want to find yourself in shock right before an audit, when you pull out those credit card receipts and see that a hefty part of your travel deduction was really meals. When you travel, you may use the per diem rates for meals instead of your actual expenses. They are often higher than what you normally spend. Look up current, or prior, per diem rates at the General Services Administration Web site, available at http://vur.me/taxmama/PerDiem.

Uniforms

Aside from the tax deduction, there are other advantages to having uniforms. You know exactly what you're going to wear each day, and your wardrobe costs drop. Uniforms create brand awareness, spreading your company name wherever you go. They also can give you and your staff a sense of pride. *And* they're deductible. You can turn anything into a uniform. Simply sew your logo onto your jackets, shirts, or other garments. Establish a particular look to enhance your image and to be remembered. (Don't look; there's a guy wearing a brown shirt and shorts, with heavy shoes. Who is he? We all know it's the UPS guy.) Create your own look so that people seeing you will instantly associate you with your business.

As far as the IRS is concerned, uniforms are something you only wear for work. If you can wear those clothes in places not related to work, I have seen the IRS disallow them as a uniform cost. In fact, one taxpayer went to his audit in his uniform to prove that he wore uniforms. The auditor took one look at him and said, clearly, this is street wear. No deduction! Nasty!

Special TaxMama Tip

How do you overcome this? Treat these costs as advertising, not uniforms. You are proudly wearing your logo to create brand awareness. In fact, those clothes are a conversation starter—and they do attract clients or customers.

Now that you know different specific items you can deduct, let's look at expenses specific to some industries.

It's All about You

Each industry has certain characteristic deductions to consider. These deductions won't apply to all members of the industry, but they apply to enough to make them worth knowing. To find out the deductions unique to your industry, the best place to start is with your industry association. Often, national trade and professional associations hear from their members when they face audits relating to the industry. The better associations track the information about what was handled incorrectly by members. Either they will educate members to avoid that accounting practice, or they will lobby to change the law so that it coincides with industry practices.

While there's no room to cover all industries, here are some tips on a few industries. Use a search engine on the Internet, such as http://www.google.com, and look for your own trade or profession to find tax issues relative to your business. That's how I find my best resources.

Beauty Salons, Barbershops, and Other Salons

For beauty salons, barbershops, massage salons, etc., your biggest issue is determining if the people working at your shop are employees or independent contractors. Chapter 9 describes the results of a barber's audit. To avoid paying employment taxes on your tenants (or people renting out chairs in your shop), get rental contracts signed with your operators. They must be responsible for rents, even on weeks they are not using their stations. When renting out space in your salon, don't deduct the money from customers' payments. Have the operators write you monthly or weekly checks.

If you are processing customers' credit card payments, the contracts should include a provision allowing you to do that, spelling out the fees or percentage you will charge the operators for this service.

Remember to include laundry costs for the towels and robes you clean at home each day. The following are some sites you will find useful:

- **The Cosmetology Fairness and Compliance Act of 2001.** http://www.govtrack. us/congress/bill.xpd?bill=s107-879. This is the salon industry's reply to provisions affecting it in the 2001 Tax Act.

- **Beauty Salon Defined.** http://vur.me/taxmama/IRS_BeautySalons. This beauty salon guide is composed of collective information from audits, interviews of salon owners, and contacts with the state departments. This guide is intended to provide an overview of the industry.
- **IRS's Salon Industry Audit Procedures, Including Allowable Expenses.** http://vur.me/taxmama/IRS_Salons. This is the IRS's guide for its auditors to use when they audit salons and shops.

Child-Care Providers

Many child-care businesses are operated in the owner's home. IRS Form 8829 has a special computation for your office in home. Rather than basing your business use on square footage, it is based on the percentage of hours your facility is in operation. It's imperative that you keep daily logs. Often, you have parents coming very late to pick up their children—that's still business time. The IRS has standard per diem–per student rates for the food you provide. The amounts appear to be low, to my eyes, so track your actual food costs. At the end of the year, see which is higher—your actual costs or the IRS's rates. When buying groceries and class supplies, get separate receipts for your school purchases and household purchases. If you don't, keep the receipt in your business and circle the business purchases.

The IRS regularly audits such businesses, since so much cash changes hands. You can read the audit guide that IRS auditors use—the IRS's Child-Care Providers Industry Audit Procedures and Allowable Expenses—available at http://vur.me/taxmama/IRS_ChildCare.

Construction Industry

Many states have rules requiring construction businesses to pay their workers as employees if they are not licensed contractors. While you may not have specific uniforms, for many trades, you can only wear your jeans or shirts once. After that, they are too caked with cement or other dirt to be washed. Since those items of clothing are disposable and definitely cannot be used on the street in that condition, pick up the costs. Keep receipts for all your tools, gloves, boots, safety equipment, and the toolbox on the back of your truck. Your office in home (see Chapter 7) probably includes the whole garage and additional storage units you've built. Taking that into consideration, your ratios of business use may change. On some projects, using percentage of completion costing will let you delay paying taxes on some of the money you've received. Sometimes, the completed contract method will work better for you. Check with your tax professional for some tricks of the trade.

An excellent resource for the construction industry is the McGraw-Hill Construction Web site at http://www.construction.com. During the years I spent working in this field, the *Dodge Reports* were an excellent source of bidding opportunities for larger projects we would never have know about on our own.

Here's an exciting resource I just found. Howrey's Construction WebLinks at http://www.constructionweblinks.com. Wow! You'll find a wealth of links to resources, legal information, licensing, and more for construction companies and construction workers provided by a law firm (Howrey, LLP) specializing in the construction industry.

Protect yourself from audits by understanding the IRS's Construction Industry Audit Procedures, Including Allowable Expenses. This guide, which the IRS auditors use, is available at http://vur.me/taxmama/IRS_Construction.

Multilevel Marketing Industry (MLM)

Surprisingly, the IRS does not list an audit guide for MLM companies, yet the IRS has instituted an aggressive push to shut down abusive MLM schemes, such as the Tax People prosecution in Kansas.[2] Think carefully before treating this as a business. If you're only buying the products or services for personal use, then all your expenses are personal. If you get a 1099 for your sales to yourself, report the income, and on page 2 of Schedule C, on the "Other expenses" line, enter "Not income—personal use discount only," and deduct the same amount. If you're getting a discount on merchandise you purchase for use in your business, your commissions are income. Add the commissions to your business income. However, if you are actively and aggressively building your downlines,[3] selling products, and generating revenues, then you should take all the deductions you're entitled to use. In case your income never builds up enough to show a profit, keep a log of all your marketing activities and marketing expenses. You'll need them to fight the IRS in the event of a hobby-loss or fraud audit.

---

2. Analysis by attorney Jeffrey A. Babener of the 2001 prosecution of Kansas-based company Renaissance, The Tax People, available at http://www.mlmlegal.com/taxpeople.html.

3. In multilevel marketing terminology, *downlines* are the members that you have recruited to the company. These are the people whose sales earn you a commission.

Truckers

If you're a trucker, you're subject to a variety of gasoline, road, and vehicle taxes; tolls; and weight charges. Keep all the receipts for those fees in a safe place for each year. Even as an owner-operator, you've contracted with one or two companies that give you the majority of your runs. Have you ever looked at the pay stubs they give you? They have deducted for at least two kinds of insurance and several fees they share with you. Usually, the 1099-MISC they issue to you is for the *gross* amount of your income or the contracted fee. Yet the check you actually get might be at least 10 percent less. Ask the accounting department if this is the case. Or hold on to every single check from that company and add them all up. Odds are, you haven't been taking a deduction for this 10 percent or so worth of fees. There's also an annual heavy vehicle use tax due, $100 minimum (Form 2290). It is due on the anniversary date of your vehicle purchase plus one month. The IRS includes a chart in the instructions to Form 2290, in case the due date confuses you—see http://www.irs.gov/pub/irs-pdf/i2290.pdf.

The IRS's per diem rates allow truckers to get a standard daily meal allowance, just like other business travelers. There's a special rate for transportation workers, like truckers, railroad personnel, etc.—see http://vur.me/taxmama/Trucker_Per_Diem. While the rate changes every year, expect it to be somewhere around $50 per day. Please note, if you are subject to "hours of service limits" by the Department of Transportation, you may only use 80 percent of the per diem amount. Keep an eye on this at http://vur.me/taxmama/Hours_of_Service. It may rise to 100 percent someday.

Since you're usually on the road, your administrative time is limited. Here are some resources to cut your time and costs of tax administration.

- **Flatbed Owner Operator Tutorial.** http://www.mitchell-bros.com/oo_flatbed.htm. A list of the kinds of deductions you can expect your carrier to take from your check when you drive for a truck line.
- **Drivers' Daily Log.** http://www.driversdailylog.com. A software tool to help you maintain daily logs and hours of service.
- **Trucking Success's Tax Organizer for the Road.** http://virl.ws/taxmama/Trucking_Organizer. This tool will help make it easy for you to keep your tax data and records in one place.
- **IRS's Trucking Industry Audit Procedures, Including Allowable Expenses.** http://vur.me/taxmama/IRS_Trucking. It would be wise to get familiar with the IRS's perspective on what is and isn't deductible by truckers. (Here is an old audit guide from 1995: http://www.unclefed.com/SurviveIRS/MSSP/truck.pdf.)

- **Form 2290, Heavy Highway Vehicle Use Tax Return.** http://www.irs.gov/
  pub/irs-pdf/f2290.pdf. You must file Form 2290 within the first month that
  you put any heavy highway vehicle, with a taxable gross weight of 55,000
  pounds or more, into use.

Cash-Intensive Businesses

One of the wonderful things about a business that collects cash from its customers
is that there is little or no accounts receivable. The big drawbacks are that you are
a frequent target for thieves—and for IRS audits. After all, since all the revenue is
cash, it's easy to skim some money off each day without paying taxes. The IRS has a
special audit guide (available at http://vur.me/taxmama/IRS_Cash_Audit_Guide)
to help close that insidious tax gap. Read it carefully if you own a restaurant or
a grocery or convenience store—in other words, an establishment that handles a
high volume of small-dollar transactions. The IRS also uses the audit guide for
industries that engage in services, such as construction or trucking, where independent contract workers are generally paid in cash.

Mixed-Use Assets

Mixed-use assets were introduced earlier. Now is the time to look at them in depth.
Cars, computers, cell phones, cameras, and other property used for entertainment,
recreation, or amusement are called "listed property"[4] and have the honor of occu-
pying their own special place, taking up most of the second page of Form 4562.

Computers, video equipment, cameras, monitors, and beepers—you can't
run a business today without them. They're no longer a luxury. In fact, they're so
reasonably priced that many children have their own electronics. Parents and their
businesses no longer share the home computer. Since the initial public offerings
(IPOs) of the 1990s, everyone is trying so hard to re-create the phenomenon, who
has time for a personal life anymore? Besides, with digital cameras and reality television, everyone's family and home is going online.

Let's talk about how you can make the most of your deductions with each of
these mixed-use assets.

Cars, aside from real estate or a complete manufacturing plant, are likely to be
the biggest one-shot expense to a small business. In the American economy, your

---

4. Internal Revenue Code §280F(b) applies to less than 50 percent business use of listed assets.

car is the key to your image. Chapter 8 tells you all of the most effective ways to squeeze deductions out of it—whether you lease or buy.

Would you like to get even more money out of your car dollars and be able to get something better than you thought you could afford? Go to the dealer selling the model of your dreams—and buy a used model. New luxury cars lose value instantly when taken off the lot. That's not just an old wives' tale. So let someone else pay for that quick devaluation. You buy the completely refurbished one- or two-year-old dream machine with most of the warranty left, and have the dealer detail it for you before you pick it up. If you don't squeal, people will think you bought the car new.

The listed-property rules with respect to just about everything except cars, televisions, and stereos are obsolete. They should be removed from the tax code. Even the IRS isn't paying attention. The IRS used to target the split usages of listed property. Aside from personal use of cars, I haven't seen an auditor ask about personal use of property (except for television or cable) since the early 1990s. In fact, just as we were going to print, Congress passed the Small Business Jobs Act of 2010 removing cell phones from "listed property" permanently, effective January 1, 2010.

What Do the Listed-Property Rules Mean to You?

For all listed property you want to deduct, you must track the business and personal usage so you know what percentage of that usage is for business. If you want to treat your camera, stereo, DVD player, and television as business property, you have to keep logs of all the usage with a separate column for business. That's right. Can you just see yourself sitting down to watch television and making a notation in your log with the date, starting time, and list of the programs you're watching? Be sure to include a few lines about how you're using the time or the programming for business purposes. If other family members use the TV, they have to make log entries, too. After all, your family's time counts toward total use of the asset. At the end of the year, you'll be able to deduct about 20 percent of the expenses, based on the few business hours you actually logged. Yes, it's a pain. That's the point. Congress wants to discourage you from deducting personal assets. Many entertainment industry folks set up their equipment in a separate screening room, even if it's just a separate bedroom, to use for business viewing.

The main thing you need to know is when business use of the asset falls to less than 50 percent, you can't take a depreciation deduction for the asset. If you've been depreciating over several years and business use falls below 50 percent, you may have to recapture, or pay back, some of the depreciation. This is what you have a tax professional for—to help you in times like that.

As for the special rules for cars—and there are many—we've devoted Chapter 8 to this subject. But we didn't explain what depreciation is all about—that comes next.

Depreciation

Back in the good old days, a depreciation deduction was provided so companies could write off a portion of the cost of their large capital expenses (buildings, equipment, fixtures, and so on) over the item's useful life. This was to provide them with the incentive to put that money aside so they could replace items as they wore out. Back then, depreciation life was related to how long a piece of equipment or building would last without substantial repairs or improvements.

Depreciation was also easy to figure out back then. Using a simple mathematical formula or two, you could determine depreciation without a scientific calculator or slide rule—just a pencil and paper . . . and perhaps an extra finger or toe. We used these nifty worksheets, which you can use too. (See Table 6.1.) Really, depreciation was logical: you could use straight line, declining balance (DB), or sum-of-the-years digits.

Straight line was the easiest type of depreciation. For this, you just had to divide the cost of the asset by the number of months in its useful life. Then all you had to do was multiply that result by the number of months the asset would be in use during the year:

Cost ÷ useful life in months × months used this year

Straight Line

Trixie bought a computer for $1,200 on September 5. It had a 5-year useful life: 5 years × 12 = 60 months. Dividing $1,200 by 60 = $20 per month. She used the computer for 4 months this year. The deduction is 4 × $20 = $80.

Next year, Trixie will depreciate it for a whole year: $20 × 12 = $240, or 20 percent per year.

In a double-declining balance (DDB) or a 1.5 declining balance (1.5 DB), you simply took the first formula and multiplied it by 2 or 1.5:

(Cost ÷ useful life × months used this year) × 2

or

(Cost ÷ useful life × months used this year) × 1.5

The only difference in the declining balance method is that you multiply your resulting percentage against the undepreciated balance of the asset. Let's go back to Trixie, shall we?

TABLE 6.1 Form 4562, Depreciation Worksheet

Depreciation Worksheet (Keep for your records.)

Description of Property	Date Placed in Service	Cost or Other Basis	Business/ Investment Use %	Section 179 Deduction and Special Allowance	Depreciation Prior Years	Basis for Depreciation	Method/ Convention	Recovery Period	Rate or Table %	Depreciation Deduction

Double-Declining Balance

Divide the number of months the asset was in business use this year by the total life. Trixie had 4 months of use, divided by 60 months' life. Her straight-line depreciation rate would be 6.67 percent. Using DDB, she would multiply that rate by 2 = 13.33 percent. Trixie's first-year depreciation would be $160 (13.33 percent × $1,200).

The following year, Trixie deducts the $160 already written off from the full purchase price of $1,200 to equal $1,040. She would multiply this reduced asset cost by the second year's depreciation. In Trixie's second year, she used it 12 months out of a total of 60. That's 20 percent. Remember, we multiply that number by 2 to equal 40 percent. So the second year, Trixie's depreciation is $416 ($1,040 × 40 percent). From then on, Trixie's rate would be 40 percent, but the balance will keep decreasing. In the third year, the asset cost is $624 ($1,040 − $416). Multiplying $624 by 40 percent gives Trixie a smaller deduction than last year, equal to $250. And so forth.

The formula is:

(Cost ÷ useful life × months used this year) × 2
   × (cost − previous depreciation)

or

(Cost ÷ useful life × months used this year) × 1.5
   × (cost − previous depreciation)

Halfway through the useful life, you'd switch back over to straight line.

Depreciation in Today's World

Aside from mere historical value, there's a reason for explaining the old way of determining depreciation to you. The present depreciation system still has a little resemblance to these two computation methods.

The IRS changed its depreciation rules in 1986. It introduced concepts such as the accelerated cost recovery system (ACRS) and modified accelerated cost recovery system (MACRS). For the present, you'll be using MACRS, which is based on the two systems described above. (See Table 6.2.)

Depreciable assets are categorized in groups called classes. You can look them up in IRS Publication 946, *How to Depreciate Property* (available at http://www.irs.gov/publications/p946/index.html) or read IRC §168. Most businesses only need to know about these four classes. The life is called a recovery period.

TABLE 6.2 MACRS Percentage Table Guide

MACRS Percentage Table Guide
General Depreciation System (GDS)
Alternative Depreciation System (ADS)

Chart 1. *Use this chart to find the correct percentage table to use for any property other than residential rental and nonresidential real property. Use Chart 2 for residential rental and nonresidential real property.*

MACRS System	Depreciation Method	Recovery Period	Convention	Class	Month or Quarter Placed in Service	Table
GDS	200%	GDS/3, 5, 7, 10 (Nonfarm)	Half-Year	3, 5, 7, 10	Any	A-1
GDS	200%	GDS/3, 5, 7, 10 (Nonfarm)	Mid-Quarter	3, 5, 7, 10	1st Qtr 2nd Qtr 3rd Qtr 4th Qtr	A-2 A-3 A-4 A-5
GDS	150%	GDS/3, 5, 7, 10	Half-Year	3, 5, 7, 10	Any	A-14
GDS	150%	GDS/3, 5, 7, 10	Mid-Quarter	3, 5, 7, 10	1st Qtr 2nd Qtr 3rd Qtr 4th Qtr	A-15 A-16 A-17 A-18
GDS	150%	GDS/15, 20	Half-Year	15 & 20	Any	A-1
GDS	150%	GDS/15, 20	Mid-Quarter	15 & 20	1st Qtr 2nd Qtr 3rd Qtr 4th Qtr	A-2 A-3 A-4 A-5
GDS ADS	SL	GDS ADS	Half-Year	Any	Any	A-8
GDS ADS	SL	GDS ADS	Mid-Quarter	Any	1st Qtr 2nd Qtr 3rd Qtr 4th Qtr	A-9 A-10 A-11 A-12
ADS	150%	ADS	Half-Year	Any	Any	A-14
ADS	150%	ADS	Mid-Quarter	Any	1st Qtr 2nd Qtr 3rd Qtr 4th Qtr	A-15 A-16 A-17 A-18

Chart 2. *Use this chart to find the correct percentage table to use for residential rental and nonresidential real property. Use Chart 1 for all other property.*

MACRS System	Depreciation Method	Recovery Period	Convention	Class	Month or Quarter Placed in Service	Table
GDS	SL	GDS/27.5	Mid-Month	Residential Rental	Any	A-6
GDS	SL SL	GDS/31.5 GDS/39	Mid-Month	Nonresidential Real	Any	A-7 A-7a
ADS	SL	ADS/40	Mid-Month	Residential Rental and Nonresidential Real	Any	A-13

Chart 3. **Income Inclusion Amount Rates**
for MACRS Leased Listed Property

	Table
Amount A Percentages	A-19
Amount B Percentages	A-20

- **Three-year property.** This property includes manufacturing equipment, certain racehorses, tractor units, and rent-to-own property.
- **Five-year property.** This category includes autos, taxis, small aircraft, trailers, computers and peripherals, office equipment, apparel manufacturing equipment, certain construction equipment, and fixtures and appliances used in rental properties.
- **Seven-year property.** Office furniture, manufacturing equipment (not already included in the first two classes), oil, gas and mining equipment, agricultural buildings or structures, and anything that isn't classified anywhere else fit here.
- **Real estate (buildings only, not land).** Commercial real estate is depreciated over 39 years using a straight-line method. Residential real estate is depreciated over 27.5 years, straight line.

Don't worry; you won't have to do the calculations. You'll be able to look up depreciation in the tables. Table 6.3 gives you the most commonly used depreciation table for small businesses. Table 6.4 covers residential real estate (apartments and homes rented out) and commercial and business property. This also includes your home office. Although you're living in the house, the office part makes it subject to the 39-year rules.

In addition to recovery periods, you have "conventions" that dictate adjustments in the MACRS tables. Did you notice that "half-year" designation in the title of Table 6.1? It refers to the date you bought your assets.

- The half-year convention treats all your property as if you bought it in the middle of the year.
- The mid-month convention applies to real estate. It treats all buildings as if they had been bought in the middle of the month.
- The mid-quarter convention comes into play if more than 40 percent of your assets (based on cost) were bought in the last three months of your tax year.

I'm sorry; despite the title of this book, there is no way to make depreciation easy. All this, and we haven't even talked about the part you're most excited about—bonus depreciation.

TABLE 6.3 MACRS Depreciation: 3-, 5-, 7-, 10-, 15-, and 20-Year Property; Half-Year Convention

Year	Depreciation Rate for Recovery Period					
	3-Year	5-Year	7-Year	10-Year	15-Year	20-Year
1	33.33%	20.00%	14.29%	10.00%	5.00%	3.750%
2	44.45	32.00	24.49	18.00	9.50	7.219
3	14.81	19.20	17.49	14.40	8.55	6.677
4	7.41	11.52	12.49	11.52	7.70	6.177
5		11.52	8.93	9.22	6.93	5.713
6		5.76	8.92	7.37	6.23	5.285
7			8.93	6.55	5.90	4.888
8			4.46	6.55	5.90	4.522
9				6.56	5.91	4.462
10				6.55	5.90	4.461
11				3.28	5.91	4.462
12					5.90	4.461
13					5.91	4.462
14					5.90	4.461
15					5.91	4.462
16					2.95	4.461
17						4.462
18						4.461
19						4.462
20						4.461
21						2.231

Bonus Depreciation

This is like a yo-yo. Some years, we have bonus depreciation. Other's we don't. Law-makers use this provision as a political toy. You will have to read the "What's New" section of IRS Publication 946 each year to see if you are entitled to any bonus depreciation. Typically, if there is bonus depreciation, it will only apply to the purchase of new, not used, assets. Sometimes, the bonus depreciation will only be available in designated disaster areas. Sometimes, it will be universally available.

TABLE 6.4 Residential Rental Property Mid-Month Convention Straight Line—27.5 Years

Year	Month Property Placed in Service											
	1	2	3	4	5	6	7	8	9	10	11	12
1	3.485%	3.182%	2.879%	2.576%	2.273%	1.970%	1.667%	1.364%	1.061%	0.758%	0.455%	0.152%
2–9	3.636	3.636	3.636	3.636	3.636	3.636	3.636	3.636	3.636	3.636	3.636	3.636
10	3.637	3.637	3.637	3.637	3.637	3.637	3.636	3.636	3.636	3.636	3.636	3.636
11	3.636	3.636	3.636	3.636	3.636	3.636	3.637	3.637	3.637	3.637	3.637	3.637
12	3.637	3.637	3.637	3.637	3.637	3.637	3.636	3.636	3.636	3.636	3.636	3.636
13	3.636	3.636	3.636	3.636	3.636	3.636	3.637	3.637	3.637	3.637	3.637	3.637
14	3.637	3.637	3.637	3.637	3.637	3.637	3.636	3.636	3.636	3.636	3.636	3.636
15	3.636	3.636	3.636	3.636	3.636	3.636	3.637	3.637	3.637	3.637	3.637	3.637
16	3.637	3.637	3.637	3.637	3.637	3.637	3.636	3.636	3.636	3.636	3.636	3.636
17	3.636	3.636	3.636	3.636	3.636	3.636	3.637	3.637	3.637	3.637	3.637	3.637
18	3.637	3.637	3.637	3.637	3.637	3.637	3.636	3.636	3.636	3.636	3.636	3.636
19	3.636	3.636	3.636	3.636	3.636	3.636	3.637	3.637	3.637	3.637	3.637	3.637
20	3.637	3.637	3.637	3.637	3.637	3.637	3.636	3.636	3.636	3.636	3.636	3.636
21	3.636	3.636	3.636	3.636	3.636	3.636	3.637	3.637	3.637	3.637	3.637	3.637
22	3.637	3.637	3.637	3.637	3.637	3.637	3.636	3.636	3.636	3.636	3.636	3.636
23	3.636	3.636	3.636	3.636	3.636	3.636	3.637	3.637	3.637	3.637	3.637	3.637
24	3.637	3.637	3.637	3.637	3.637	3.637	3.636	3.636	3.636	3.636	3.636	3.636
25	3.636	3.636	3.636	3.636	3.636	3.636	3.637	3.637	3.637	3.637	3.637	3.637
26	3.637	3.637	3.637	3.637	3.637	3.637	3.636	3.636	3.636	3.636	3.636	3.636
27	3.636	3.636	3.636	3.636	3.636	3.636	3.637	3.637	3.637	3.637	3.637	3.637
28	1.97	2.273	2.576	2.879	3.182	3.485	3.636	3.636	3.636	3.636	3.636	3.636
29							0.152	0.455	0.758	1.061	1.364	1.667

Nonresidential Real Property Mid-Month Convention Straight Line—39 Years

Year	Month Property Placed in Service											
	1	2	3	4	5	6	7	8	9	10	11	12
1	2.461%	2.247%	2.033%	1.819%	1.605%	1.391%	1.117%	0.963%	0.749%	0.535%	0.321%	0.107%
2–39	2.564	2.564	2.564	2.564	2.564	2.564	2.564	2.564	2.564	2.564	2.564	2.564
40	0.107	0.321	0.535	0.749	0.963	1.177	1.391	1.605	1.819	2.033	2.247	2.461

Section 179 Depreciation

It is called Section 179 depreciation because that is the Internal Revenue Code section that covers this. Section 179 depreciation may be used for new or used property. This tax code provision lets you write $250,000 or more worth of equipment or vehicles that are placed into business use each year. This limit changes constantly with the political wind. In fact, just as we were going to print, Congress passed the Small Business Jobs Act of 2010 increasing the limit to $500,000 for 2010 and 2011. Read Chapter 2 of IRS Publication 946 each year to learn the current limit.

There are strings attached to the Section 179 deduction.

- If more than a specific dollar amount of property is placed in service during the year, the allowable Section 179 expense must be reduced by the amount in excess of the limit. (This annual limit ranges from $400,000 to $800,000.)
- The Section 179 election can't cause income from all trades or businesses to be reduced below zero.
- Any amounts expensed under this provision reduce the depreciable basis of the assets placed in service during the year. In other words, you can't expense part or all of the cost of an asset and also depreciate the same costs.
- If the property is disposed of prior to the end of its useful life, you will be required to recapture some of the Section 179 deduction previously taken. *Recapture* means that a portion of your Section 179 deduction must be included as taxable income on your tax return.
- You can use Section 179 on vehicles over 6,000 pounds. But the deduction is limited to $25,000. (See Chapter 8.)

Large corporations have entire departments devoted to tracking assets and recording their disposal. Take the cost of administration into account when you discuss the value of depreciation deductions.

If the Section 179 deduction will take your business income to zero, cut back on how much of it you use. You cannot use Section 179 to take your business profit below zero. However, regular depreciation may be used to generate a loss. A good tax professional will play with the numbers to give you the highest deduction you can get without throwing you into alternative minimum taxes, or having you waste the deduction. When the Section 179 depreciation you take is too high, the rest of it gets carried forward to the next year; while regular depreciation might have given you a deduction. I've seen people totally waste this deduction. Remember, you may have to pay back the deduction if you stop using the asset for business, trade it in, or sell it. So do a careful analysis before using Section 179.

Affecting Pass-Through Entities

When using bonus depreciation and Section 179 depreciation for partnerships, LLCs, S-corps, or other pass-through entities, talk to the partners, members, or shareholders first. If you take the deduction on the business return, but they can't use it, they'll be forced to carry it forward. It might be wasted.

Depreciation is one of the most complex tax computations. So many forms, schedules, and limits are affected that it's like playing multidimensional chess. Even the best tax software doesn't always get this right. If you talk to your tax advisors, they'll admit they check their software's depreciation calculations to make sure all affected forms and limits are taken into account on your tax returns.

More Deductions Than You Can Imagine

We've just scratched the surface of how to use expenses, and we haven't delved deeply into the expenses you can't use. Some businesses are subject to passive loss limitations or alternative minimum taxes and the intricacies of net operating losses. These are things you'll need to have your tax professional explain if they pertain to you. After all, you need to have something to call your tax person about now that you've learned all you need to know to run your business.

Incidentally, a word to the wise—don't spend *all* your time learning to run the business. At some point, you have to take action—and start working.

Deduction Resources

- **Form 4562, Depreciation.** http://www.irs.gov/pub/irs-pdf/f4562.pdf.
- **IRS Publication 946, *How to Depreciate*.** http://www.irs.gov/publications/p946/ch01.html.
- **Per Diem Rates from the U.S. General Services Administration.** http://vur.me/taxmama/PerDiem.
- **IRS Audit Guides for Specific Industries from the Market Segment Specialization Program (MSSP).** http://vur.me/taxmama/IRS_AuditGuides.
- **McGraw-Hill's Construction Industry Resources.** http://www.construction.com.

- **Howrey's Construction WebLinks.** http://www.constructionweblinks. com. Wow! A wealth of links to resources, legal information, licensing, and more, for construction companies and construction workers, provided by a law firm (Howrey, LLP) specializing in the construction industry.
- **Small Business Taxes and Management.** http://www.smbiz.com. Tax updates, summaries, and news for small businesses.
- **Tax MiniMiser.** http://snurl.com/homebiz-tax. Tax MiniMiser allows you to log the usage of vehicles or mixed-use assets. You can use it to track income and expense as a complete accounting system—on paper.
- **Open, by American Express.** http://open.americanexpress.com. For discounts on business supplies and services.
- **TaxMama's Quick Look-Ups.** http://www.taxmama.com/quick-look-ups. You will find all kinds of useful reference materials, Webinars you can replay, e-books, the 100% Home-Based Business Tax Solution—and even More Quick Look-Ups at http://taxmama.com/family-member-resources.
- **Your Business Bible.** http://www.yourbusinessbible.com. Look for worksheets and updates to this book.

✔ CHAPTER 7 OFFICE IN HOME
To-Do List and Questionnaire

1. Do you have an office in home? ____Yes ____ No

    If no, and you are not planning to have one, skip this chapter.

    If yes, continue.

2. Do you have a distinct and separate area you are using for your business?

    ____Yes ____No–if no, you will probably lose your deduction, unless you operate a day-care center or your entire home IS your business

3. For day care, etc., keep a log of hours used for business. Date that the log was created and updated with YTD information _____

4. Create the schematic of your home or property, showing the distinct areas you use for business. Enter the square footage. Date _____

5. Take photographs or film each area, labeling what it is used for. Date _____

6. Do this again each year; keep a copy in your tax file for that year.

7. Homeowners, get cost split between land and building for depreciation purposes. What is your source (attach a copy)? What is the split percentage?

    • Property tax assessment _____

    • Written appraisal by _____

    • Other _____

Remember to put a copy of each document behind this page, folded in half.

OFFICE IN HOME

Wherever you wander, there's no place like home.

—SONG LYRICS

The Song Is Right! Let's Stay Home

In 2007, the latest year for which IRS statistics are published,[1] more than 32,887,081 business returns were filed, reporting over $34 trillion in sales. Of these businesses, over 23 million were "non-farm sole proprietorships." In other words, they were businesses like yours and mine. Businesses like ours produced $1,324,403,080,000 in revenues for this country—that's over $1.3 trillion! In total, those small businesses also reported a little more than $1 trillion in expenses. Although the IRS tracks information on various forms, there are no 2007 statistics for "office in home." Perhaps people are so afraid of the red flag it represents, that they have cut back on using Form 8829, the office-in-home deduction.

---

1. Table 1, "Number of Businesses, Business Receipts, Net Income, and Deficit," http://www.irs.gov/pub/irs-soi/80ot1all.xls, and Table 3, "Number of Businesses, Business Receipts, Net Income, and Deficit, by Form of Business and Industry, Tax Year 2007," http://www.irs.gov/pub/irs-soi/07ot3naics.xls.

For a new business, having your office at home is an excellent idea because it keeps your overhead low. You can get away with earning less, so you can concentrate on building the business instead of paying the bills. Not only do you save money on renting an office space, but you also save precious time by not having the distractions and office politics of a shared suite.

For me, moving out of the penthouse suite on Ventura Boulevard meant a savings in tangible dollars of more than $1,000 per month. I no longer paid rent, additional annual common-area costs, parking for staff and myself, parking validations for clients, tips to the valets, or utilities. I saved at least another $1,000 per month in my staff's increased productivity because they didn't have all the distractions that came with managing a suite with several tenants. Many tenants had too much free time and liked to hang around chatting with my charming staff.

Another advantage to working from home is that when your family needs you, you're there. Once all the interruptions end, or the family time is over, you can slip back into your office, perhaps late at night, without having to dress up and drive across town. You can step in for just a minute, even on days off, to take care of something quickly and conveniently.

Besides, you can take expenditures you're already making and use them to help reduce your business profit and the related self-employment taxes. Which expenses do double duty like this? Your rent. Or if you own a home, your mortgage and property taxes. You're already paying those bills, right? With an office in the home, a percentage of those costs will move to your Schedule C.

Of course, working at home may have some drawbacks.

It's a Red Flag; It's Just Asking for an Audit

Sure it's a red flag! So what? If you are operating a real business out of your house, shouldn't you be entitled to take legitimate deductions for it? True, having an office-in-home deduction and using Form 8829 will definitely increase your chances of an audit. But if you keep good records, you have nothing to worry about. You'll need to be able to prove exactly what part of your home you used for business. It's also important to define what the business use was for each area you're claiming as business space. But with the instructions that follow, you'll be able to prove to the IRS that you're entitled to the deduction. And if you're ever audited again, you'll have proof that the IRS accepted your evidence in the past.

Why does having a home office seem risky to many small businesses? Here's the background on the issue. It relates to the Pomarantz case[2] and the Soliman case.[3]

Until 1998, the IRS knew an office-in-home audit was one easy way to generate money for Uncle Sam's coffers.

Why? Until the end of 1998, the rules for in-home offices were dictated by the results of a court ruling against Dr. Pomarantz. He was a physician whose work took place in a hospital. But he did have a legitimate office at home where he took care of all his business transactions, planning, and calling and where he maintained his records. Since he didn't meet with patients at home, under a strict definition of the tax code, he was not permitted a deduction for an office at home.

Pathetic, isn't it?

The same treatment applied to such people as plumbers (they didn't fix their customers' pipes by bringing them to their own home and working on them there), Laundromat owners, traveling salespeople (a whole other problem), actors, and . . . you're getting the idea.

Looking at these businesses' returns, odds were in the IRS's favor to score some good money by auditing office-in-home returns. But no more.

Under the rules that took effect as of January 1, 1999 (based on a law that passed two years earlier . . . why it took so long, I have no idea!), you no longer have to meet customers in your home to qualify for the office-in-home deduction.

IRS Publication 587 outlines the present requirements:

1. Your use of the business part of your home must be:

   a. Exclusive
   b. Regular
   c. For your trade or business

---

2. The Ninth Circuit Court concluded that an *emergency* care physician's home office was not his "principal place of business" under §280A. See *Pomarantz v. Commissioner*, 867 F.2d 495 (9th Cir. 1988). The Ninth Circuit ruled that Pomarantz could not deduct home office expenses because he consistently spent more time on duty at the hospital than he did at home. The essence of his profession was the hands-on treatment of patients, which he did only at the hospital and never at home. Finally, he generated income only by seeing patients at the hospital, not by studying or writing at home.

3. *Commissioner v. Soliman*, 506 US 168—Supreme Court 1993. In this case, an anesthesiologist spent 30–35 hours per week working in the hospital. He performed his billing, management, and administrative functions at home. The U.S. Tax Court supported him. So did the Fourth Circuit Court of Appeals. The IRS took the case to the Supreme Court, which supported the IRS—there was no office at home since Dr. Soliman derived his income from the practice of anesthesiology.

and

2. The business part of your home must be one of the following:

   a. Your principal place of business
   b. A place where you meet or deal with patients, clients, or customers in the normal course of your trade or business

or

   c. A separate structure (not attached to your home) you use in connection with your trade or business

That little item you see in 2a opened up the door to you if your office in home is only used for administrative purposes, even if you generally work at customers' locations. But this must be the *only* business office you have. The office in home doesn't have to be a whole room; it may be part of a room. It doesn't have to be just a room; it may also include closet space, garage space, carport, or parking pad for your primary business vehicle or tools (tractors, cement mixers, clown cars, drill presses, whatever you use or store).

Under the present rules, pretty much everyone who operates a business from home will have a legitimate claim to an office in the home. Since 1999, the odds of the IRS finding fault with the office-in-home deduction on a tax return have decreased dramatically.

Oh, there's no doubt that many people who are taking the deduction are not really entitled to it. But it's no longer a sure thing that you'll get audited. These days, to get the IRS's attention, you need to have both an office in home and a loss on Schedule C. (See Chapters 5 and 6.)

Another Attractive Change to the Law Affecting Homeowners Only

Before May 6, 1990, there was a consideration even more daunting than IRS audits for people who planned to sell their homes within a few years. You would lose the $250,000 ($500,000 for couples) personal residence exclusion on the business portion of your home. As a result, when you had a large gain on the sale, you would have to pay tax on the business percentage of that gain. For instance, let's say you used 15 percent of your home as your office. Your home was worth $200,000, but you bought it for $100,000 several years ago.

In the past, when you sold the house, $170,000 would have been treated as sale of your personal residence. The gain would not have been taxable since it's less than the $250,000 exclusion per person. But $30,000 ($200,000 × 15 percent) would have been treated as the sale of business property. Without going through all the numbers, essentially, you would have had to pay $3,000–$5,000 in IRS and state taxes on the sale, depending on how much depreciation you had taken.

That additional tax is no longer an issue. Under the present law, you get to treat the whole house as your personal residence when you sell it. You only have to pay tax on the depreciation you've deducted. Since most people don't get to deduct more than $500 per year of depreciation, the tax doesn't usually amount to much. (See http://vur.me/taxmama/Sale_Home_Office.)

New computation complexities have arisen as a result of the Housing and Economic Recovery Act of 2008. They affect second homes used as rentals. They won't affect your office in home. So relax. It's all right to use office-in-home deductions if they apply to your business.

Inner Space

Now that you're comfortable taking the deduction, just how much of the home's area can you deduct?

Carefully measure out the square footage of the space(s) you use. You'll find you use substantially more of your home for business than you realize. After all, most businesspeople use their car for business more than 40 percent of the time. Have you ever noticed how much space your garage takes up? While you may have a 1,400-square-foot home, your two-car garage may add 800 square feet (about 20 feet × 40 feet). If half that garage is used for your 75 percent business-use car—that amounts to 300 square feet (800 × 50 percent × 75 percent). Add in the storage for your files, inventory, tools, and records (about 10 × 20 square feet), and that's another 200 square feet. You've just found 500 square feet in the garage alone!

Look at the space you're using in the house. You have that area at the back half of the living room. You have a desk (or two to make an L-shape), a bookcase or three, a cabinet for your printer, several upright or lateral files. You're talking about 12 feet × 15 feet = 180 square feet. Don't forget the closet filled with office supplies—another 6 feet × 4 feet = 24 square feet. So far we have 704 square feet! (24 + 180 + 500). Dividing that by the total square footage of

TABLE 7.1 The Home Office Spaces

Total Business Square Footage		
Area of your desk and main files		_____
Primary supply closet		_____
Additional in-house storage		_____
Office lavatory		_____
Vehicle parking area		_____
Garage or carport storage area		_____
Additional structures		_____
Total Business Square Footage	**(A)**	_____
Total Home Square Footage		
Area of primary residence		_____
Area of garage or carport		_____
Area of additional structures, if used in the business		_____
Total Home Square Footage	**(B)**	_____
Percentage of Business Use		
(A) ÷ (B) = (C)	**(C)**	_____ %

the house and the garage (1,400 + 800), which is 2,200 square feet, results in a business use of 32 percent of your home. You can use the worksheet in Table 7.1 to help you.

Just using your unimaginative desk area, you'd have had 180 ÷ 1,400 = 12.9 percent.

As long as the areas you're taking for the deduction are really used for business, you will have no problem in an audit.

Just remember one thing—you can't add in space that is not exclusively used for business. If you do your work on the kitchen counter and then clear it all away to make and serve family meals, that's *not* office space. On the other hand, if you use the dining room as your office and never use it for family meals—that is office space.

Isn't this exciting?

Two Critical Reminders

Let's pause for just a second here. Please do be careful about two things when claiming this deduction.

1. You really do have a business with a profit motive.
2. You really are using your home as your principal place of business.

While the IRS isn't chasing after office-in-home deductions per se, it is looking for fraud. So please don't be frivolous about this because the IRS really doesn't have a sense of humor in this area.

Incidentally, having gone through this exercise to see how much of your home you're using for business may get you to do some thinking about your business space. Is there really enough space to run your business the way you'd like? Would you be better off in a traditional business facility? Or would you be better off in a bigger house? Perhaps, looking all this over will help you realize not only that you need more space but also that your business can afford to pay for it.

Prove It, Baby!

Okay, you're comfortable using the home office. You've learned how to determine how much of the home is a business. Now, how do we prove it to the IRS in the event of an audit?

After all, if the IRS does audit you, it will be about two or three years after the year you used the area. You might have remodeled that area by now—or moved away. How do you protect your deduction? Simple: take photographs. Take lots of pictures of the office spaces in the house and remember to include the closets and storage areas. Take photos of the garage area and any business space out there.

I know you love your digital camera. It makes life so easy. But print those snapshots. Keep a hard copy in your permanent file for the house and another copy in your tax file. Who knows if you'll still be able to read the same digital medium in 2016?

Make a schematic drawing of the home. It doesn't need to be fancy. Just make an outline of the house, garage, and storage areas, putting lines in to separate each room. (Remember those old-fashioned things called rulers? They come in really handy for making neat, straight lines. If you don't have a ruler handy, use the edge of a book or your *TV Guide*.) Write in the lengths and widths of each room. Then add up the total square footage and list it neatly in a corner of the page. Next, identify all the areas you use for business and add up their measurements. Enter the total business square footage on the page. Finally, show the computation of the business percentage (business square feet divided by total square feet).

Do not use the number of rooms used for business divided by the total rooms in the house. It doesn't work that way. You must use square footage.

Set up a permanent office-in-home file. Put a copy of this schematic into that file and another copy in your tax file for each year that you operate from this home. That way, in case of an audit, you won't have to scramble to find a copy.

Now that you have the measurements, what can you deduct?

What Are Office-in-Home Expenses?

Don't get too carried away here. I've seen people drag in everything they spend money on and try to turn it into a business expense. Don't get greedy. If you don't have clients coming to your home, don't deduct things like your gardener, pool guy, or other outside maintenance expense. When it comes to your housekeeper, if you don't even let her set foot in your office, don't take that deduction. I'm not trying to spoil your fun—just trying to keep you looking good.

Rent Is Easy

If you don't own your home, multiply the business percentage (you've already computed it) times your total rent. For example, let's say you pay $12,000 per year for rent plus $500 for renter's insurance. Earlier, you computed your business use as 32 percent. Your deduction then is $4,000 (12,500 × 32 percent). That's it. Drop that number onto line 20—"Other expenses" on Form 8829.

If You Own, You Depreciate

Since the home area is being used for business, you'll need to use the nonresidential real property tables to look up your depreciation. Business property is depreciated over 39 years. If you can't get your hands on a depreciation table, just do the computation yourself. There are 468 months in 39 years (12 × 39). Divide your depreciable cost by 468. That gives you the depreciation per month. Then multiply the monthly amount by the number of months you used the space for business this year.

It's important to figure out the value or cost of your office in home. It's not quite as easy as it looks. The number might start with your purchase price of the

TABLE 7.2 Depreciation of Home

Lower of cost of home or fair market value		_____
Improvements to home before becoming office		_____
Less:		
Cost of land		_____
Casualty loss used		_____
Total Adjusted Basis	(D)	_____
Divide (D) by 468 (months)	(E)	_____
Multiply (E) by months of business use in current year		
Total Depreciation	(F)	_____

home. Or if the current market value of the home is lower than your purchase price plus improvements, that's your starting point. That will give you a basis (tax cost) for the home. You can't depreciate land. To determine the cost of the land, look at your appraisal, if you have a copy. Most professional appraisers include that information. If you're in the process of buying the home, or refinancing, ask for a copy of the appraisal. Be sure to ask the appraiser to define the land value. You can't get your hands on an appraisal? Use a copy of your property tax assessor's statement or annual invoice. It shows land and building value. Don't use the value shown. Use the percentage (divide the land value by the total value of the property). Apply that percentage to your basis to get the cost of the business portion of your home. Use the worksheet in Table 7.2 for guidance.

Add in any major improvements that weren't previously depreciated. Have you ever taken a casualty loss deduction on your home? If you live in a flood, a tornado, or an earthquake zone, you might have. Be sure to reduce your basis by the amount of the casualty losses you deducted. Line (D) in Table 7.2 will give you the adjusted basis. Table 7.3 will guide you on the rest of the depreciation calculation.

There are still more expenses you may take.

Utilities (gas, electric, sewage, trash, water). Rather than using the square-foot method, what I like to do is this:

- Start with your utility bills from before the office was in your home. Add up a year's worth. Take the average (divide by 12). That number is your

TABLE 7.3 Home Office Deduction Overview

Total Business Profit from Schedule C	(G)	_____
Indirect Expenses: Shared with Home		
Rent or mortgage interest	_____	
Property taxes	_____	
Home insurance	_____	
Utilities	_____	
Repair and maintenance	_____	
Other	_____	
Total Indirect Expenses	(H)	_____
Multiply this by the percentage in Table 7.1 (C)	(I)	_____
Direct Expenses: Business-Related Only		
Insurance	_____	
Repair and maintenance	_____	
Other	_____	
Other	_____	
Total Direct Expenses	(J)	_____
Depreciation from Table 7.2	(F)	_____
Prior year carryforward from Form 8829		_____
Total Office-in-Home Expenses		
(I) + (J) + (F)		_____
Deduct profit from	(K)	(_____)
Deductible Office-in-Home Expenses This Year	(L)	_____
If the result is negative, you have a carryover to next year.		

average monthly utility charge. Deduct this amount from your present monthly utility total. The difference is your business expense. For instance, before working from home, your electricity bill was $50. Now that you're working from home, with all the computers and air conditioning, your bill is $150. The $100 increase is your business expense.

- If your office was always at home, you're stuck using the same percentage as your square footage of business use. If you have a way of proving that your home office uses more power or water than is needed for regular living, use it. One way would be to get copies of a neighbor's utility bills for a year. Even three months would be great. Find someone who works outside of the home, has a similar number of people living in the home, and won't mind letting you use his or her utility invoices for your audit. Follow the instructions above.

• Generally, doing the calculation this way will result in a higher and more reasonable deduction. (Put this worksheet into your permanent office-in-home file.)

Keep logs for the following expenses! Even the courts are disallowing deductions when you don't maintain logs.

• **Internet access.** If your family is using the same lines, you'll have a hard time justifying the deduction. You might get away with deducting the difference between dial-up and a high-speed line, using the logic that you wouldn't have gotten the high-speed line if not for the business.

• **Cable TV.** To get this deduction, you'll need to keep a log of the shows watched and which were for business purposes. Keep a notebook outlining how that program related to your business. Deduct only the business use. (When I take this deduction, even for my entertainment folks, I know it's usually a giveaway—one of those things you're prepared to give up during an audit.)

• **Repairs and maintenance.** If you repaint or repair any part of your business space, naturally, 100 percent of those costs are deductible. For instance, if you install an additional bathroom just for your office, you can deduct all those expenses. However, if you make repairs or improvements to the whole house, such that it also benefits your business space, you'll only be able to deduct the business percentage we arrived at earlier. An example of such an improvement would be installing an air-conditioning system in the whole house.

• **Property tax and interest.** Deduct the business percentage on Form 8829. Use the rest on Schedule A.

• **Insurance.** Business liability insurance or business insurance just on your office space is fully deductible. You may use the business percentage of whatever you pay for homeowner's insurance or renter's insurance.

• **Household supplies.** You'll buy certain things at the supermarket or discount store for household cleaning or beverages or coffee. Some of those things may look like personal groceries. But if you are using them strictly for your clients or staff, they may be business expenses. Think about the expenses from this perspective: If you were in an outside office, you would have a "kitchen" area containing a coffeemaker, microwave, and refrigerator, and you would stock it with coffee, tea, cocoa, popcorn, and other supplies for visitors and staff. Are you doing the same thing at home? At the store, I like to separate out the groceries that are for the office from the ones for the house. The store doesn't mind ringing it up as two sales. If you keep separate receipts, it's easier to support your deduction. Be careful not to abuse this.

When You Can't Use Office-in-Home Deductions

If your business shows a loss, your office-in-home deductions are suspended. If your business shows a profit, but when you use the office-in-home expenses, your profit turns into a loss, you may only deduct enough expenses to zero out your profit. The unused expenses don't entirely go away. You carry them forward to next year's tax return. There's a line at the bottom of Form 8829 for carryovers.

Evaluate Your Options

You understand how to use the office in home. Now, the question arises, should you use it? There may be times when it's wise to just skip it.

These are some of the considerations I look at for my clients:

- Do you own or rent your home?
- If you own, will you still be living there two years from now?
- How soon *do* you plan to sell it?
- Will you have a gain or a loss if you sell it?
- Do you expect your business to show a profit after using these deductions?

If you are renting the residence, there are no long-term repercussions from using this deduction.

When you own your home, it has most likely appreciated since you bought it. You will have to pay taxes on the depreciation you've taken. Is it worth it for the small amount of depreciation deduction you get anyway?

It may be worth it if all the other office-in-home expenses really help reduce your taxable business profit. You don't get to use all the other office-in-home expenses without also using the depreciation. The tax code has a special rule about depreciation. It's called the "allowed or allowable" rule. That means if you should have taken depreciation, but didn't, the IRS will treat your tax return as if you had. It's complicated and nasty—and if you were in business for more than three years and didn't take the depreciation, but should have, it could cost you. This is definitely one of those areas that you want to discuss face-to-face with a good tax professional.

One of the questions above asks whether your business is profitable. I ask that for two reasons:

1. When your business shows a loss, your office-in-home deduction cannot be used. (Sure, it will carry over to the next year, but it's useless now.)
2. If you expect to be showing losses for several years, you may never get the advantage of the office-in-home deduction, but you will attract an audit for a hobby loss. (See Chapter 13.)

Generally, seeing a pattern like that, I avoid the deduction altogether. If you can stand the scrutiny and have a solid business plan that shows how and why your business will start being profitable five years from now, go ahead and use the office-in-home deductions.

Then there are times when you just want to throw out the whole deduction altogether. Which is what I did for one client, until I went all the way. Erica hadn't filed tax returns for a long time. I prepared seven years' returns for her, including her office-in-home deduction. It wasn't that hard because she was renting an apartment. As a self-employed publisher, she worked from home. You can just bet that a substantial portion of her home really was devoted to her business.

Erica had losses for the first six years. She could prove how deeply in the red she was by the very high balances on her credit card and bank loans. Seeing all those losses during the first years' returns and thinking of the added scrutiny the IRS gives to nonfilers, I went back and removed the office-in-home deduction. (I kept a printed copy of those pages in case I needed them again.)

Good thing, too. When I prepared the last year, she had $50,000 worth of profits. Suddenly, all those years with losses became very attractive. Putting the office-in-home deduction back in and carrying it forward each year wiped out most of Erica's $50,000 profit, including her self-employment taxes. In the end, Erica only owed a few hundred dollars for all seven years. (I love it when I can see the future like this, don't you?)

When I first removed the Form 8829, it was because she already had such high losses that it was clear her net operating losses (NOLs) would wipe out income for years to come. The trouble with NOLs is that they don't wipe out self-employment taxes. The self-employment tax is 15.3 percent of your business's current-year profit. Some people don't mind paying that money because it's for their own Social Security and Medicare coverage. Others are so broke or operating on such a tight budget that they can't look toward the future—only to keeping the lights on.

Working on this series of tax returns helped remind me that NOLs only have a limited use. It was also a defining moment for me. Preparing Erica's tax returns was how I came to understand that the office-in-home carryforwards are one of the few deductions that *will* reduce self-employment tax.

All the reading and education in the world doesn't help. You've got to go hands-on to understand the tax system.

A Final Note—and a Final Story

Working at home can be really grand. You are free to indulge yourself when you simply need a break. You can spend time with friends, children, and lovers. Or you can be interrupted constantly. How you separate work space and time from personal space and time is strictly up to you. But you will reduce your stress levels if you establish specific boundaries for your family and friends—and stick with them. When you work at home, people tend to treat you as if you're not really working. Or they will call you to service them at all hours of the day or night.

Personally, I set time boundaries. TaxMama's telephone hours are Monday through Friday, from 8 a.m. to noon. Outside of those hours, even if I am here, I will rarely ever pick up the phone. That is my time to write or to get other work done, without interruptions—or to give myself some *me* time. We all need time that we control. So remember, budget time for your own relaxation. Whether it's five minutes of meditation each hour or a half-hour nap each afternoon or a once-a-week bubble bath, *you* need time to recharge yourself. Or you will collapse.

Alex's Productivity Hat

Alex Mandossian is best known for his TeleSeminar Secrets course, which is, naturally, a course conducted as a teleseminar. Mandossian works from home, surrounded by a young, bright, inquisitive and active family. How does he get anything done with small children around? He turns it into a game. When Alex is wearing his Productivity Hat, he can work unmolested. Alex can even wander into the kitchen to pick up a sandwich or go out to the yard. His children might come running to him, then stop. They see Daddy's Productivity Hat, put their fingers over their lips, and tell themselves to shhh . . . Daddy's working. Try your own version of a Productivity Hat or scarf or sock or sash, . . . or whatever turns you on. It really works.

Office-in-Home Resources

You can get some help and support with the issues you're facing from an assortment of online resources. Many have articles and tools to help. Some also have forums where you'll find it a relief to talk to other people dealing with the same issues as you.

IRS Forms
- **Form 8829, Expenses for Business Use of Your Home.** http://www.irs.gov/pub/irs-pdf/f8829.pdf.
- **IRS Publication 587,** *Business Use of Your Home.* http://www.irs.gov/publications/p587/index.html.

Books
- *The Home Daycare Complete Recordkeeping System* by Brigitte A. Thompson. http://www.DaycareRecordkeeping.com.
- *Minding Her Own Business: The Self-Employed Woman's Guide to Taxes and Recordkeeping* by Jan Zobel. http://vurl.bz/taxmama/Jan-Zobel. My readers and clients have been using this book for years.

Online Support for Home-Based Businesses
- **SoCal Mom** by Donna Schwartz Mills. http://www.socalmom.net. Articles, e-books, tools.
- **Work at Home Moms** by Cheryl Demas. http://www.wahm.com. Resources, tools, message boards, a way to find local moms. There's also a forum for work-at-home dads at http://stayathomedads.about.com.
- **WomanOwned.com** by Christiana Blenk. http://www.womanowned.com. Articles, resources, forum, networking.
- **Alex Mandossian's TeleSeminar Secrets.** http://vur.me/taxmama/Mandossian. Eye-opening information about how to run your business from home, with sensible and practical ways to turn your own education and expertise into a variety of online or tangible products.
- **TaxMama's Quick Look-Ups.** http://www.taxmama.com/quick-look-ups. You will find all kinds of useful reference materials, Webinars you can replay, e-books, even the 100% Home-Based Business Tax Solution.
- **Your Business Bible.** http://www.yourbusinessbible.com. Look for worksheets and updates to this book.

✓ CHAPTER 8 VEHICLES: EVERYONE'S FAVORITE DEDUCTION
To-Do List and Questionnaire

1. List all the vehicles you use for business:

        Primary business vehicle–license and make _____

        Part-time business vehicle–license and make _____

2. What is the odometer reading today on each vehicle?

        Primary business vehicle _____

        Part-time business vehicle _____

3. Find the earliest repair or service receipt this year.

        What is the odometer reading on that receipt?

        Follow instructions in this chapter to reconstruct YTD mileage.

4. What are you using to keep a mileage log?

      • Tax MiniMiser _____

      • Spreadsheet software _____

      • Appointment book _____

      • Cell phone or PDA _____

5. How much have you already depreciated your vehicle?

      • Actual depreciation on Form 4562 _____

      • Depreciation component of mileage _____

Remember to put a copy of each document behind this page, folded in half.

8

VEHICLES: EVERYONE'S FAVORITE DEDUCTION

Leasing means never having to say you're debt-free.

—Eva Rosenberg

Autos, trucks, vans, minivans, trailers, SUVs, whatever you're using, it's probably one of your most costly assets. It's also your best source of business deductions, since you've got to have a set of wheels for personal use.

Vehicles are essential to your life and your business. Practically everyone has at least one car at home. You may have several, depending on your family size, hobbies, interests, and business requirements.

When it comes to using cars for business, select just one of those vehicles as the business vehicle. When more than one family member is involved in the business, assign one business vehicle to each person as a business vehicle, or have several family members or staff use one vehicle. Try not to keep switching around. Consistency of use makes it simpler to track business mileage. If you must use more than one vehicle, keep logs in each car to track total mileage and business mileage. Being able to track the actual miles may be more important for a "fleet" than for a single car.

When your business requires the use of a single-purpose truck or van, such as an outfitted plumbing truck or delivery van, you shouldn't have problems establishing that you used it 100 percent for business. That vehicle is not fit for personal use. Take a photo of the vehicle full of your usual equipment or inventory and put it in your tax file.

Clearly, certain vehicles really are used 100 percent for business by their very nature. But for regular vehicles, don't expect the IRS to allow you 100 percent business use. The IRS realizes that even if you have several cars, sometimes you're going to use your business car to shop for groceries, pick up your children, or run some personal errands. The IRS expects that you will record a reasonable amount of personal use.

Some of my clients have a separate business vehicle, or they work from home and practically all their driving is business. For them, it's easier to track the personal miles than the business miles. While they may not drive many miles during the year, the larger percentage of the miles they do drive will be business.

Deducting Auto Expenses

Table 8.1 shows you two ways to report auto expenses—the mileage method and actual expenses. Yes, it looks like three ways. That's because actual expenses are different for owned and leased vehicles. Please note that the mileage method isn't nearly as easy as you may have thought. You have four different rates, depending

TABLE 8.1 How to Deduct Auto Expenses and Mileage Rates

Mileage Method	Actual Expenses for Leased Vehicles	Actual Expenses for Purchased Vehicles
• _____ cents per mile	• Lease payments	• Interest on auto loan
• Parking/valet	• Parking/valet	• Parking/valet
• Tolls	• Tolls	• Tolls
	• Gasoline	• Gasoline
	• Repairs and maintenance	• Repairs and maintenance
	• Parts, washes	• Parts, washes
	• Insurance	• Insurance
	• License and registration	• License and registration
	• Parking/valet	• Parking/valet
	• Garage rent	• Garage rent
	MINUS	• Depreciation
	The lease inclusion amount	

on how you use your car. In addition, there's also a depreciation component built into each mile.

Actual expenses used to be simpler before depreciation got so complicated. Now you have such a varied menu of depreciation options that it really does take a computer to find the best treatment.

Regardless of which method you use to write off your auto expenses, you will need to know two mileage numbers for each car you use—total miles and business miles. The second page of Form 4562 still asks for the mileage breakdown. To make this as correct as possible, on January 1 of each year, note your vehicle's odometer reading on your calendar.

If you didn't make any notes during the year about your total miles, you can reconstruct the total miles. Find a repair invoice from early in the year and one from later in the year. Find the box showing the mileage when you brought the vehicle in for service. Deduct the miles shown on the earlier invoice from the miles on the later invoice (for example, the February 16 invoice shows 14,500 miles and the June 8 invoice shows 19,600 miles). Divide the difference by the number of days in between invoices (in our example, 5,100 miles ÷ 112 days = 45.54). Multiply the result by 30 to get the number of miles per month (returning to our example, 45.54 miles × 30 days = 1,366 miles per month). Then multiply by 12 to get the total miles for the year (1,366 miles × 12 months = 16,392 miles driven this year).

If you tracked the business miles, you'll easily be able to figure out your business use of your vehicle. If you only tracked your personal miles, deduct the personal miles from the total miles you drove to get your business miles (continuing our example, 16,392 total miles − 2,634 personal miles = 13,758 business miles). Divide your business use by the total miles to arrive at the percentage of actual expenses you're entitled to deduct (13,758 business miles ÷ 16,392 total miles = 83.9 percent business use of the vehicle).

Using the Standard Mileage Rate

Once you have the total miles and the business miles, enter them on the second page of Form 4562. If you're using the mileage rate, multiply the current year's rate by the total business miles (for 2010 using our example, 13,758 × 50 cents = $6,879), and pop it onto the "Car and truck expenses" line of your personal tax return's Schedule C or onto a schedule on your business return. Steve Hopfenmuller at the Small Business Taxes and Management Web site maintains a list of mileage rates from 2003 to the present, available at http://www.smbiz.com/sbrl003.html. Visit that site if you need the most current rates. Or log into TaxMama.com's Quick Look-Ups resource.

You can see a sample of mileage rates from previous years in Table 8.2. Built into the standard mileage is a certain amount of depreciation per mile. Don't worry about the number until you sell the car. Then add up the miles you've deducted each year and multiply the sum by the depreciation rate for each year.

Just a little note that no one seems to tell you—if you take advantage of any of the special depreciation methods, including the bonus depreciation or Section 179, you may not use the mileage method to deduct your car expenses for the life of the vehicle.

When using actual expenses, follow the guide in Table 8.1 to see what you can deduct for owned and leased vehicles. We'll examine the special vehicle depreciation rules later in this chapter.

Should I Lease or Buy?

Car ads make automobile leases sound awfully tempting. Before getting seduced by the temptation of driving a sleek Lexus for a low monthly payment, know

TABLE 8.2 Standard Mileage Rates

Cents per Mile	2010	2009	2008	2007	2006	2005	2004	2003
Business	50	55	50.5[1]	48.5	44.5	40.5[3]	37.5	36.0
Charitable	14	14	14	14	14[2]	14[3]	14	14
Medical	16.5	24	19[1]	20	18	15[3]	14	12
Moving	16.5	24	19[1]	20	18	15[3]	14	12

Note: The mileage rates may vary during the year. Always look them up!

[1]January 1–June 30, 2008	July 1–December 31, 2008
Business rate = 50.5 cents/mile	Business rate = 58.5 cents/mile
Medical/moving rate = 19 cents/mile	Medical/moving rate = 27 cents/mile

[2]For 2006 the Katrina-related charitable rate was 32 cents/mile.

[2]January 1–August 31, 2005	September 1–December 31, 2005
Business rate = 40.5 cents/mile	Business rate = 48.5 cents/mile
Medical/moving rate = 15 cents/mile	Medical/moving rate = 22 cents/mile
Katrina charity = 29 cents/mile -ONLY FOR August 25–August 31, 2005	Katrina charity = 34 cents/mile

that there are big-dollar tax ramifications lurking behind the small-dollar dealer hype.

The most frequent call I get is from business clients trying to decide whether to buy or lease a car. Being a number cruncher, I computed several test scenarios, coming to the conclusion that there are too many variables to generate general answers. Instead, let's highlight the questions you need to ask yourself when facing this decision.

Thoughts to Ponder
- Do you plan to drive more than 12,000 miles per year?
- How many miles do you drive for business?
- How many commuting miles do you drive? (Commuting is not deductible.)
- What percentage of the total use of that vehicle will be for business?
- Do you have a second car for personal use?
- How long do you normally keep your vehicles?
- Do you mind having payments for the rest of your life?
- How frequently do you service your vehicles?
- How much money can you afford to put down on a vehicle?
- If you lease, how much of a "deposit" does the leasing company require?
- How good are you at keeping detailed records?

All these issues will affect your long- and short-term operating costs and tax benefits.

Aside from my being nosy, how do my clients' responses affect my recommendation? Let's examine each topic more carefully.

Driving Issues

Most leases penalize you for driving more than 12,000 miles per year. Take into account the additional costs for the excess mileage. This is usually prohibitive. Some people, though, don't mind.

If you live in your car, getting your wheels serviced can be a problem. Look for a lease or purchase that includes free loaner cars. I discovered that whether buying or leasing an Infiniti from the dealer (even a used one), free loaner cars during scheduled service are included as a matter of company policy. For me, that's one of the most valuable accessories any car can offer. To be competitive, other car companies or dealers may offer the same deal if pressed—so ask.

Presently leases are advertised at very low, very tempting prices. But when you can buy a car with 0.0 percent interest and no down payment, buying may be better. Look closely at your options and compare them carefully.

To negotiate the best price, whether you lease or buy, you must be an informed shopper. You will find detailed instructions on how to buy a used car in an article on Edmunds.com by consumer advice editor Philip Reed and automotive editor John DiPietro. In the article, Philip Reed provides 10 steps to buying a new car.

The lease down payment is almost as much as (or sometimes more than) the down payment to buy the car. That makes the total cost over the life of the lease less attractive—especially since you must turn your vehicles over every two years under most lease agreements. That's a lot of "down payment" money for something you'll never own!

Tax Issues

When deducting the lease expenses on your tax return, even if you use the car 100 percent for business, there is a mandatory "lease inclusion cost," described later in this chapter.

Whether you lease or buy, you still must maintain mileage logs to track what percentage of the actual expenses to deduct. The best way to keep track of mileage is to keep a daily log in your car. Most people find that too onerous. I've found it's a good habit to record your mileage in your appointment book when you get into your car. Just put it at the top of the page or in your PDA calendar for that date. Use the record-keeping tips you learned in Chapter 4 to track all your time and expenses. Or keep a Tax MiniMiser envelope handy. Not only can you record your mileage, but you can also toss in receipts and make notes about cash payments (such as valets tips, parking meters, etc.).

You computed your business use percentage earlier in this chapter. In our example, it was 83.9 percent. Multiply your total expenses by that business percentage. Assuming you spent $5,400 on the lease, $250 for registration and license fees, $1,200 for insurance, $600 on gasoline, and $600 on car washes and routine service, the total expenses equal $8,050. Your lease inclusion was $120, and so net expenses are $7,930. Multiply that by 83.9 percent. Your total auto expenses are $6,653, plus parking and tolls.

The only expense that doesn't get hit by the percentage is parking. After all, you're only including your business parking receipts.

My First Rule of Thumb

If you drive very few miles each year (10,000 or less) and more than 80 percent of that mileage is directly business related, I recommend that you buy the vehicle, deducting the actual expenses.

Why? The numbers say it all.

The lease deduction based on a $450-per-month lease would be *over $6,600*:

> \+ $1,200 insurance
> \+ $350 license
> \+ $800 fuel
> \+ $500 repairs and maintenance
> \+ $60 washes
> × 80 percent business use
> − $18 lease inclusion on a $25,000 car
> = $2,310 + $4,320 (lease $450 × 12 × 80 per cent) = $6,630

After taking the tax benefit into account, how much cash have you spent for the year? Let's see:

> $450 × 12 = $5,400 (lease) + $2,910 (operating costs) = $8,310

> $8,310 cash spent − $2,000 tax benefit (IRS and state) = $6,310 spent for the year

The tax deduction for a similar car you purchase, based on the actual expense method, would be *$4,728*:

> $0 interest on a $25,000 loan
> \+ $1,200 insurance
> \+ $350 license
> \+ $800 fuel
> \+ $500 repair and maintenance
> \+ $60 washes
> \+ 3,000 depreciation (approximately)
> × 80 percent business use

After taking the tax benefit into account, how much cash have you spent for the year? Let's see:

$5,000 (loan payments) + $2,910 (operating costs) = $7,910

$7,910 cash spent − $1,400 tax benefit (IRS and state) = $6,510 spent for the year

At the end of 5 years, you will have spend $31,550 for the leased car, after taxes. At the end of 5 years, you will have spent $32,550 for the owned vehicle. Owning appears to cost $1,000 more over 5 years! Or does it?

At the end of 5 years, you still have annual lease payments of $5,400 or something similar. When you own at the end of 5 years, your annual payments are—*zero!*

Oh sure, you might have some repairs. But if you paid for an extended warranty on your car, you may not have to pay for anything but oil changes, tires, and brakes for the first 7 to 10 years. That means at least 2 years without a car payment or significant repair bills.

My Second Rule of Thumb

If you drive 20,000 miles per year for business, I usually recommend that you buy.
Why?
The deduction based on buying the car and using the actual expense method would be *nearly $6,200.*

    $0 interest on a $25,000 loan
    + $1,500 insurance
    + $350 license
    + $1,600 fuel
    + $1,200 repair and maintenance
    + $60 washes
    + $3,000 depreciation (approximately)
    × 80 percent business use

Your tax savings, if you're in a 28 percent tax bracket, is nearly $1,750.
The deduction based on a $450-per-month lease would be around $8,000, netting you approximately *$2,300* in tax savings.

    $450
    × 12
    + $1,500 insurance
    + $350 license

    + $1,600 fuel
    + $1,200 repair and maintenance
    + $60 washes
    × 80 percent business use
 − $18 lease inclusion on a $25,000 car

Excess mileage is generally charged at $0.15 × miles over 12,000 = 8,000 × $0.15 = $1,200.

Your real benefit would be only about $1,100 per year. Your tax savings are about $650 higher if you own the vehicle.

Hmmm. I think you are coming to the conclusion that leasing is not the best tax alternative for moderately priced vehicles. You're right! Frankly, I just can't figure out why people would lease a car and saddle themselves with payments forever.

The only time you really get a tax advantage from leasing is when you lease a hyperexpensive motorcar. Assuming monthly lease fees of $750 or more, plug your costs into the examples above.

When the depreciation deduction is limited, the tax benefits are far higher when you lease a BMW, Eldorado, Mercedes Benz, or other high-ticket car. On the other hand, wouldn't it be nice to have three to five years without a car payment? Buy it!

Lease Inclusion—Add It Back In

When you lease a vehicle, unless it is a commercial vehicle like a Mack truck, the IRS knows you will have some personal use. There is no 100 percent business use for leased personal vehicles. The IRS has established a formula to use, based on the value of the car. The agency publishes new tables each year. In fact, it has now added tables for trucks, due to the new rates. You can look them up in IRS Publications 463 and 946 or at http://www.irs.gov. Or you can do it more quickly and easily by using the online tables provided by the folks at Small Business Taxes and Management at http://www.smbiz.com/sbrl003.html. Their lease inclusion tables typically cover the last six years.

The Cons of Depreciation

Chapter 6 outlined how depreciation works. Now that you understand the principle, let me tell you how it's different for vehicles.

First of all, be aware that the rules for autos change slightly almost every year. Next, be aware that this aspect of taxes is a political football and also gets changed dramatically whenever Congress feels like it.

It's a really confusing area of tax law. It's not enough to know the numbers. You need to know when to use which numbers. Please have a tax professional set up depreciation for your vehicle(s)—at least for the year of purchase. You may also want to have your tax pro review the depreciation again in the fourth year when the limit drops to $1,775 to see if you can switch to mileage at that point.

Bonus depreciation is a political football. Some years it's there; some years it's not. It often becomes available for residents of disaster areas. Generally, when bonus depreciation *is* available, you may only use it on the purchase of new vehicles. You may only use bonus depreciation (if it is available in a current year) and Section 179 depreciation if your business use of the vehicle is more than 50 percent.

Once you've used up as much of the bonus depreciation and Section 179 as you can, it's time to take regular depreciation on your vehicle. When it comes to cars, you can forget everything you learned in Chapter 6 about depreciation methods. For vehicles, there are luxury auto limits, which brings us to special limits on how much depreciation you may use each year.

Luxury Auto Limits

It's getting harder and harder to find the IRS's minimum value (or cost) to determine what a luxury vehicle is. The last time I saw a report, in 2009, the IRS defined a *luxury vehicle* as anything costing more than $14,800. Have you looked at vehicle prices lately? You're not apt to find much in the $14,800 or less price class. Especially if you want luxuries like carpets, radios, even air conditioning (which is not a luxury in the hot South), you're not apt to find anything but a Kia for under that price, though the Chevrolet Aveo might still qualify. You can find low-cost vehicles at http://consumerguideauto.howstuffworks.com/new-cars-under-15000.htm.

Most cars you will use for business will fall under the luxury auto deduction limits. That means, regardless of what your total depreciation should be for the vehicle, you may deduct no more than the amounts shown in Chapter 5 of IRS Publication 946. Generally, although vehicles are considered 5-year assets, using the IRS passenger automobile depreciation rates, you will not be fully writing that car off in less than 10 years.

There are different rates for autos, trucks, and electric vehicles, so be sure to look up the rates for your type of vehicle. The rules were originally written to penalize owners of high-cost vehicles such as Mercedes, Jaguars, or Rolls-Royces. Back then, in 1984, an average person could actually buy a fully loaded car for about $5,000. Not anymore!

The SUV Craze

Despite the push to cut back on emissions and to discourage gas-guzzlers, there is a little loophole in the depreciation rules that rewards you for buying gas hogs. Intended to exempt trucks and commercial vehicles from the luxury auto rules, this loophole has been snapped up by clever planners to subsidize the cost of expensive cars.

Buying vehicles weighing more than 6,000 pounds provides dramatically better tax benefits. They are not subject to the luxury vehicle rules. You may be able to deduct as much as $25,000 plus regular depreciation costs in one year, using the Section 179 depreciation. (See Chapter 6 for more information about depreciation.)

Give Yourself Credit

When considering buying a vehicle, there is one more tax benefit to explore: tax credits for "green" vehicles—electric and hybrid cars. Form 8834 allows you a variety of credits for golf-cart-type vehicles, hybrid cars, and a variety of other engines that use little or no gasoline. The laws change regularly. And the credits phase out as the manufacturers' sales hit certain limits. So be sure to explore the IRS Web site (http://www.irs.gov) before you buy to see how much of a credit you could get.

Driving Home Conclusions

Remember, if you sell the car or stop using it for business within five years, you will have to pay back some of that depreciation. So don't get too greedy.

If you're going for the moneybags image—such as a Mercedes or Rolls-Royce—lease the car.

If you want a good value, give yourself a break from payments and buy the vehicle! At least you'll be able to have something to sell when the payments stop. Or better yet, breathe easy for a couple of years with no payments at all. What a concept!

Does all this confuse you? Me, too. Please, as I said earlier, don't try to figure this out alone. There are so many nuances to vehicles and depreciation. This is one of the easiest parts of your tax return to get wrong. To make the vehicle part of your business tax return work, here's what you need to do.

Give your tax professional a good summary of each of your auto expenses. Provide the total mileage and business mileage. Provide a copy of the purchase or lease contracts if you got a new car during the year. Be sure to provide copies of the sales documents if you sold the car.

With that information in hand, your tax pro can give you the best results.

Vehicle Resources

- **Bankrate.com.** http://www.bankrate.com/calculators/auto/buy-or-lease-calculator.aspx: Lease-versus-buy calculator.
- **"How to Get a Used Car Bargain,"Edmunds.com.** http://www.edmunds.com/advice/buying/articles/45310/article.html.
- **"How to Buy a New Car,"Edmunds.com.** http://www.edmunds.com/advice/buying/articles/78386/page001.html.
- **Tax MiniMiser.** http://snurl.com/homebiz-tax: Track vehicle mileage and expenses.
- **Standard Mileage Rates.** http://www.smbiz.com/sbrl003.html#smr. For the current year.
- **Cents per mile valuation for use of company vehicle.** http://www.smbiz.com/sbrl003.html#cmv.
- **Annual depreciation adjustment for standard mileage rates.** http://www.smbiz.com/sbrl003.html#dsm.
- **All other vehicle rates.** http://www.smbiz.com/sbrl003.html. Depreciation and lease inclusions.
- **Deducting Vehicle Expenses.** http://www.poznaklaw.com/articles/auto1.htm. Excellent summary by Poznak Law Firm Ltd. for owned and leased vehicles.
- **IRS Publication 463,** *Travel, Entertainment, Gift, and Car Expenses.* http://www.irs.gov/formspubs/page/0,,id%3D11531,00.html.
- **IRS Publication 946,** *How to Depreciate Property.* http://www.irs.gov/publications/p946/index.html.
- **Form 4562, Depreciation.** http://www.irs.gov/pub/irs-pdf/f4562.pdf.
- **Form 1040, Schedule C.** http://www.irs.gov/pub/irs-pdf/f1040sc.pdf.

- **Form 8834, Qualified Plug-in Electric and Electric Vehicle Credit.** http://www.irs.gov/pub/irs-pdf/f8834.pdf.
- **TaxMama's Quick Look-Ups.** http://www.taxmama.com/quick-look-ups. You will find all kinds of useful reference materials, Webinars you can replay, e-books, even the 100% Home-Based Business Tax Solution.
- **Your Business Bible.** http://www.yourbusinessbible.com. Look for worksheets and updates to this book.

✓ CHAPTER 9 EMPLOYEES AND INDEPENDENT CONTRACTORS
To-Do List and Questionnaire

1. Review your staff:
    - Does anyone work at your office who is not on payroll?
    - Does anyone work outside your office who is not on payroll?
    - If any of them should be employees, set them up on payroll ASAP.

2. Have you been issuing nonemployees 1099–MISCs? ____ Yes ____No

3. Get a Form W-9 from each nonemployee worker–NOW. Date _____

4. Get all documents on the Independent Contractor Checklist–NOW. Date _____

5. Get your employer ID # from the IRS. EIN _____ Date _____

6. Get your employer ID # from the state. EIN _____ Date _____

7. Have each employee fill out a Form W-4 and a Form I-9.

8. Have you hired members of your family?
    - Be sure they fill out time cards or keep accurate records of the basis of their compensation (time versus commission).

9. What employee benefits do you offer? _____ _____

   _____ _____

10. Meet with your tax pro and insurance broker to see what your tax savings would be for employee benefits. Date _____

11. Meet with your staff to discuss which benefits they can use. Date _____

Consider restructuring compensation to provide tax-free benefits for things they are already spending money on–or need:

☐ Health   ☐ Child care   ☐ Education   ☐ Retirement

Remember to put a copy of each document behind this page, folded in half.

EMPLOYEES AND INDEPENDENT CONTRACTORS

It's always easier to do it yourself. You do a much better job.

—TAXMAMA'S MOTHER

On your last job, you came to realize you did all the work but got paid only a fraction of what you're worth. You quit and ranged out on your own. Now, with your own business, you get to keep all the money. You're better off, it's true; only now you have to do all the work yourself.

You may decide that you need help; if so, it's time to hire your own staff. Excellent idea—many companies can grow to great heights with the right employees, and there are tax benefits to hiring employees. This chapter covers everything you need to know about categorizing employees, hiring family members, setting up payrolls, paying employee taxes, and much more.

Who Is an Employee?

Often, new small business owners are apt to think of people who work for them as temporaries or as freelancers. You may feel that since you haven't had employees until now, that you don't want to go through the hassle of setting up a formal payroll until you absolutely must.

You've got my sympathy. But not the IRS's.

Knowing the legal difference between an official employee and an independent contractor can be challenging. The following examples show just a small sampling of the wide range of possible employment situations:

- Nancy comes to Jackie's home to open mail, do filing, and pay bills. Nancy picks up a big stack of files and works on them at her own home. Is Nancy an employee?
- Joe hires Dan as his Webmaster and site developer. Joe is gearing up for a big marketing push, making it clear that Dan must devote all his time to the project. Dan agrees to work for Joe exclusively for 2010. Is Dan an employee?
- Perry is self-employed as a journalist. During the school yearbook season, Perry works for PhotoKiddie, snapping shots of schoolchildren for the yearbooks the company creates. Perry uses PhotoKiddie's film, contracts, and forms and also collects all the payments, which are made out to Photo-Kiddie. Is Perry an employee of PhotoKiddie?
- You do work for your corporation, but you have a full-time job. You're only working on corporate matters 10 hours a week. Are you an employee?

All right, which of these people are considered legal employees and how can you tell?

In actuality, the descriptions above don't provide enough information to make a decision. To determine if someone counts as an employee, you must ask more questions about each person you pay. As the positions are described above, it could go either way. With more information, however, there is an answer.

The IRS uses 20 common-law factors that determine a person's employment status, and the factors don't all carry the same weight. Without having experience facing employment audits, you won't know which factors matter. To make things more challenging, your state might have its own factors that don't match up to the IRS's. A tax professional whose practice specializes in small businesses and freelance work can evaluate the relative importance of each of the following factors for your business and industry.

The 20 Common-Law Factors the IRS Uses to Define Independent Contractors

1. Instructions are generally not given by the company that hires you.
2. Training is not essential and is not given by the company.
3. Your personal services are not required; you can assign the work to anyone.
4. The work you are performing is not essential to the company.

5. You set your own hours.
6. You have no continuing relationship with the company.
7. You control and hire your own assistants.
8. You are free to pursue other work.
9. Where you work is your choice.
10. You set your own work priorities.
11. No interim reports are required of you.
12. You work for more than one firm.
13. You pay your own business expenses.
14. You use your own tools and equipment.
15. You bear a risk of loss.
16. Your services are available to the general public (or industry).
17. You have a significant capital investment.
18. Right of discharge is limited by contract.
19. You are not compensated for incomplete work.
20. Timing of payment coincides with completion of the job, rather than in regular intervals.

Consider those 20 factors whenever you need to decide if someone you hire should be on payroll or not.

Do They Act Like a Business?

If you're unsure how the IRS definition of *contractors* applies to your situation, consider this when looking at someone you want to treat as an independent contractor—people in business must look and act like a business. They must have all the licenses and certifications standard for their profession and their city, county, state, province, or other government division. They don't need to have a business name, but if your contractor uses Susan Johnson Consulting instead of plain old Susan Johnson, she'd have to get a fictitious name filing.

People you consider freelancers who are working for you, on your premises, using your equipment, and following your instructions are typically employees. Did you give them a key? Or access to one, to get in when you're away? That sounds like an employee relationship. If they feel like taking off, going down to the beach for the day, and sending a colleague to do the work, may they? If not and you require that only the person you hired do the work, on your schedule—you have an employer-employee relationship. Essentially, it means that you control the person's work, hours, and staffing decisions. If people were in business for themselves, you couldn't do that, could you?

Now, if your new hire does fit the definition of an *independent contractor*, what should you do to prove it to the IRS just in case the agency ever asks?

Protecting Yourself from Independent Contractor Claims

Whenever the IRS audits a business return that shows independent contractors, the first thing it checks is whether the 1099s are filed. (You'll learn about them later in this chapter.) The second thing the examiner looks at is the worker's job duties. If the IRS decides you have an employee, not an independent contractor, it will create a payroll and assess you for payroll taxes you should have paid, plus penalties and interest.

To legitimize your claim of the independent relationship, use a checklist when hiring new vendors who provide rent or services of any kind. Simply hand the list to all new hires.

Alert: If needy friends beg you to hire them without putting them on the payroll, be wary. The biggest cause of employer audits is a nonemployee who is let go (even voluntarily) or gets sick. Suddenly, people in this situation realize they can't collect unemployment or disability insurance, but they file anyway—and turn you in. Yes, this could even be your best friend—someone who was really in need and begged you to hire him or her under the table. Here is a horror story from one of my clients.

Bennie the Barber

Bennie the Barber had a modest shop in Santa Monica that supported his family. Carlos came to him, begging for work. Bennie really couldn't afford it, but Carlos kept calling and coming by, telling Bennie how desperate he was for work. Relenting, Bennie gave him the second chair and turned customers over to Carlos. Bennie cut his own income because Carlos didn't bring in a single customer of his own. Then Carlos started coming in late. Some days, he just didn't feel like coming in—no explanations. After two years of being treated rudely, Bennie finally got smart and let Carlos go.

What did Carlos do? You guessed it. He filed for disability. Carlos claimed he didn't know why he wasn't an employee. Carlos accused Bennie of cheating him. The state disability auditor was no dummy. Under the circumstances she had no choice. She audited Bennie. Digging deeply and looking at the whole situation, the auditor was sympathetic and limited her assessment to only one year. With penalties and interest, the bill was more than $5,000. It could have been double, without her sympathy. IRS charges added another $10,000.

Tip

Insist that all independent contractors provide all the information on the checklist in Table 9.1 before issuing the first check. Make this a part of all contracts. It's easier to compel people to provide an address and identification number when they want their check than it is in January when you want to file 1099s.

If you encounter a situation similar to Bennie the Barber's case, there's a way to reduce the IRS assessments when it decides your independent contractor is really an employee. You can use a safe harbor, which we'll discuss in the next section.

Before moving on, though, there's one very important thing you need to remember about independent contractors. Don't call them employees when talking about them, describing them, or speaking to them. Especially, do not use the word *employee* during an audit. You'd be surprised how many people trip themselves up that way. It's important that you change the word you use to think of these people. Get your mind around a new word, depending on what they do. Some options are *consultant*, *expert*, *contractor*, or *advisor*.

Also, they are not your associates or your partners—that's a different relationship. How you think of the person will determine what you instinctively say. At

TABLE 9.1 Independent Contractor Hiring Checklist

Obtain These Original Documents from Independent Contractor
☐ Form W-9–Request for Taxpayer Identification Number
☐ Business card
☐ Flyer, advertisement, brochure
☐ Contract or proposal
Obtain a Copy of These Documents from Independent Contractor
☐ Current business licenses
☐ Professional license number, if applicable
☐ Sales tax certificate or license, if applicable

least, if the terminology is common in your industry, the safe harbors covered next may help reduce the damages.

Safe Harbor Rules

Section 530 of the Revenue Act of 1978 provides a safe harbor with special leniency toward certain employers.[1] Barbers and beauty salons are among those protected by Section 530.

Congress decreed that you had a reasonable basis for treating your staff as independent contractors if you can pass a test. You pass the test if you relied on:

- Judicial precedent, published rulings, technical advice, or letter ruling to the employer
- A past IRS audit in which no assessment was made on account of improper treatment of workers (even if the audit was not related to employee issues)
- A long-standing recognized practice of a significant segment of the industry in which the individual worked. (The IRS used to require the practice to span more than 10 years, before 1979, or more than 50 percent of the industry. The new law requires no fixed amount of time and no more than 25 percent of the industry.)

Earlier, we posed some situations. The PhotoKiddie example would fit the safe harbor rules. Why? When an industry (photographers) treats its freelance workers as contractors, it can get the penalty reduction.

When the IRS decides you should have had an employee, the agency charges you for both halves of the Social Security and Medicare taxes that should have been withheld from the worker's wages. It also charges you for a certain amount of the withholding. Then the IRS adds various penalties and finally tops off the whole thing with interest on the combined total. The final balance due may be hefty enough to shut down your business.

When facing an employment tax audit, be sure to ask your tax pro to invoke the Section 530 safe harbor rules. You'll be relieved of a substantial part of the Social Security taxes and IRS withholding you should have taken. Hopefully, you'll never need this rule.

---

1. Full text, plus amendments, of §530 of the Revenue Act of 1978 can be found at http://vurl.bz/taxmama/IRS-530. (*Note:* This is not Code Section 530 of the Internal Revenue code.)

What Are 1099s?

You're familiar with W-2s. Think of 1099s as the same thing for people without full-time jobs. Form 1099 is also the IRS's way of catching tax cheaters. Before the program started in 1980, there was a huge under-the-table economy. It's still large, but getting smaller as enforcement improves. Using 1099s, the IRS can ensure free-lancers report all their income. Knowing you'll be reporting their earnings to the IRS, freelancers have two choices:

1. They can refuse to work for you, which has happened. If someone refuses to provide the requisite information, you're better off knowing this when the project starts while you have time to find someone else. You don't want to find out that this person may not be ethical after giving him or her access to sensitive information or clients.
2. They can do like everyone else—earn the money and pay taxes on it.

OK, there's always a third option—where they collect the fees and don't file. When they do that, the IRS sends out notices to companies that filed 1099s, insisting the companies withhold 28 percent of all checks to those individuals as backup withholding. You'll rarely face this issue. If it comes up for you, you'll find instructions and explanations in IRS Publication 1281, *A Guide to Backup Withholding on Missing and Incorrect Names/TINs.*

Some states realized that waiting until 1099s are filed and processed means the tax evader can stay on the job before being caught until July or August of the following year. To shorten the time, many states are coming up with solutions. California created Form 542, which companies must file with the state as soon as they pay anyone $600 or more. Since this is working for California, expect other states to request it, too.

Who Gets 1099s?

IRS instructions on the 1099 forms require you to send them out to people you've paid in the course of your trade or business. As of 2010, issue Form 1099-MISC to any person or business that provides a product or service to your business. This includes all corporations, LLCs, partnerships, and individuals.

Starting with 2012, you must issue 1099s for the purchase of products or supplies. Issue 1099s for reimbursed expenses you pay to independent contractors even if they give you a copy of the receipts for their purchases. Since this is such an excessive standard, these requirements may be repealed.

When your own business pays you for your work, without putting you on payroll, you'll need to issue 1099s to yourself. The only exception is if you're filing on a Schedule C. When you are an LLC filing on Schedule C, you may need to issue yourself a 1099 if your business is taking a deduction for payments to you.

Tip

Here's a 1099 secret. Hardly anyone knows this, but if you need extra time to file those 1099s, you can get another 30 days using Form 8809. If you're really in trouble and need still more time, you can get a second extension using the same form.

Looking at the boxes on the form, even without reading the tax code or the instructions, you can readily get an idea of who gets 1099s. Let's review only the boxes that are apt to affect your business.

- **Box 1: Rents.** This is for payments to your landlord. Also, use it for equipment leases from private parties. If you pay for storage and the company is a partnership, it gets one, too. If your business pays you rent, you get one.
- **Box 2: Royalties.** This applies if you have a graphic artist, you're licensing technology, you have a coauthor or ghostwriter, or you're a publisher. If you are licensing something to your entity, issue this to yourself.
- **Box 3: Other income.** Be generous with this. If you're paying someone for something that clearly is not self-employment, use this box instead of Box 7. Anytime you're not sure how to categorize payments to people and have no one to ask, use Box 3. Leave it up to them to decide how to report it on their own tax returns.
- **Box 4: Federal income tax withheld.** Some of your vendors may want withholding (rarely). Usually you will withhold taxes when the IRS garnishes their incomes. Incidentally, having the company take withholding from their compensation is a convenient way for partners or LLC members to avoid making quarterly estimated tax payments (more on this in Chapter 11). When you do withhold, be sure to issue the 1099s early so recipients can file their tax returns on time.
- **Box 6: Medical and health care payments.** When individuals are not your employees—when they are independent contractors—if your company has paid their medical or health care, this is self-employment income to them. They will report this on their Schedule Cs.
- **Box 7: Nonemployee compensation.** All remuneration to anyone performing a service to your business gets reported here, including your

tax pro, consultants, freelancers, Web designers, outside services, virtual assistants, trainers, advertising agency, public relations firm, landlord, and equipment rentals. *Attorney fees go into Box 14.*

- **Box 9: Payer made direct sales of $5,000 or more of consumer products to a buyer (recipient) for resale.** This is for network marketers and MLM participants. The company you represent will report the gross sales you've made. Remember, the IRS knows you also use the products. So when receiving a 1099 in this case, be sure to deduct your personal usage of the purchases.

- **Boxes 16 and 17: State income tax withheld and State/Payer's state number.** When you have withheld money for state taxes, remember to fill this again. See the notes for Box 4 for instances where this might be necessary.

The other boxes won't affect the average small business. If they do, you need to have an accountant on staff to help you.

To the recipient, it's very important that you get the boxes right. Income reported in Box 1 and Box 2 is not subject to self-employment taxes. Taxpayers pay self-employment taxes on all income in Box 7. When they don't, the IRS sends them nasty letters (we'll discuss this in Chapter 13). Box 3 is a gray area. Generally the income in that box is not self-employment taxable—but it could be. The IRS's computers won't be looking for a match on Schedule SE for amounts in Box 3.

When Are 1099s Issued?

1099-MISC forms must be issued when paying $600 per year or more to anyone for services rendered or rents. The forms must be distributed to payees by January 31. You then have until the last day of February to file them with the IRS. Folks filing the forms electronically have until March 31 to file. (Forms may be filed on the following Monday when the due date falls on a weekend.)

I recommend that you mail out all the forms in January. Then hold off filing them until you get the address corrections back from the post office or the payees. During this time, you'll probably hear from people if their earnings records are different from your records. This will give you the time to reconcile the amounts before you send in the final 1099s.

When you find errors, naturally, you may send in corrected 1099s, but those attract attention. Try to get it right the first time.

Oh, and if you're holding them until the end of February, don't forget to mail them in.

Payroll and Payroll Taxes

To avoid complications and painful audits, once you start using regular help, go ahead and put them on payroll. In the short run, this may cost you a little more than using contractors. In the long run, though, you'll be better off. Depending on the form your business takes, you may even end up putting yourself, your spouse, or your children on payroll.

Payroll across Entities

Before we get into the mechanics of payrolls, you'll need to know whether or not you're required to be paid wages. Let's look at a quick outline of personal and family compensation for the different forms of businesses you learned about in Chapter 3.

- **Sole proprietorships.** The owner may never be on payroll. The spouse and children may be—if they perform services for the company and are not owners of the company. Watch out for community property states with laws that say each spouse owns whatever the other spouse owns. You can overcome community property rules with contracts. Be careful; make sure you have a solid marriage. Otherwise, in the event of a divorce, one spouse will have signed away valuable ownership rights just to gain some short-term tax benefits.
- **Partnerships, LLPs, and LLCs taxed as partnerships.** The rules are the same as for sole proprietorships. However, partners may receive guaranteed payments. These are specific allocations, such as a monthly stipend. Partners may receive different amounts, based on the time or resources they contribute to the business. Be sure to allocate reasonable guaranteed payments to working partners. If you don't, as explained in Chapter 3, the IRS will assign a compensation level to you.
- **Corporations and LLCs taxed as corporations.** The shareholders and officers must be on the payroll, and reasonable compensation must be paid based on profits, time devoted to the business, and industry standards. Family members may be hired. Children's payroll is fully taxed. Officers are entitled to receive benefits like any employee. When it comes to profit-sharing and retirement plans, there are special rules to avoid discriminating in favor of highly compensated employees. Those rules won't affect you if you have no employees outside your family. If you have employees outside your family, this is where your advisory board will

become really helpful. We won't be covering the details in this book—
that's advanced tax planning. I just wanted you to be aware of the issue.

- **S-corporations.** Working shareholders must receive wages. The IRS has just started an audit campaign to catch omissions in this area. People who own more than 2 percent of the company are excluded from benefits. Legislation has been proposed to require 100 percent of profits to be treated as wages for S-corporations where the income is generated primarily from the services of three or fewer shareholders. Although this legislation may not pass, it's wise to show reasonable, market-level salaries for the owners. And no, taking the compensation in the form of fees instead of wages will not allow the shareholders to escape IRS penalties for lack of payroll. (This is an area of discussion with the IRS and tax professionals lately. The IRS has come down solidly on this issue.)

With these points in mind, let's start with the very touchy issue of hiring family members.

Hiring Family Members

Your e-mail is likely full of messages from scamsters wanting to sell you tax-cutting kits. One of the tax loopholes they push most aggressively is the practice of hiring family members. The IRS has shut down a number of operations whose primary focus is encouraging people to take fraudulent deductions for home and family expenses, including The Tax People and Tax Toolbox. The IRS has filed civil and criminal charges against tax professionals promoting this practice fraudulently.

Does that mean you should completely avoid hiring your spouse and children? Nonsense! There would be no Rothschild dynasty, or Ford Motor Company, or Disney, or Wal-Mart, or Harry and David, or any number of great companies if people had been afraid to build family businesses. To the contrary, many founders nurture dreams of having their children take over the family business. Some of today's major corporations started out as family businesses. Many publicly traded companies still have significant family leadership and ownership.[2]

So please, don't let fear of the IRS prevent you from establishing your own dynasty. Besides, so much good comes from getting your family involved—and some of the benefits have nothing to do with taxes.

---

2. The Institute for Family-Owned Business lists 100 of the world's top family-owned businesses grossing over $1 billion each. (Information courtesy of *Family Magazine;* see http://vurl.bz/taxmama/FamilyBiz.)

Intangible Benefits of Hiring Family

- Your spouse and children understand the time requirements and pressures you face. This reduces familial conflict.
- You see your children more often. You don't just see them rushing out in the morning or wolfing down dinner on the way out to the library or to meet friends.
- You have things to talk about together, rather than the vacuous, "So how was your day?"
- Being in the same office or business location, you're apt to overhear your children's conversations with their friends and be more tuned in to the good and bad things in their lives.
- Working with you, your family members have less time to get into the kind of trouble that comes from boredom or from too much time and money.
- Your children actually earn their "allowances." This is so important in eliminating that attitude of entitlement. You see other people's children growing up rude and demanding, without consideration for their parents. Your children won't act this way if they work for their spending money.
- When you are your family's employer, you know how much money your children have available to spend. If they suddenly come home with something unreasonably expensive, you won't fall for "I got a bonus at work." You'll know it's a warning sign.
- Your family knows the details of your business and where the important files and documents are. If anything happens to you, they can carry on.
- Each of your family members develops marketable skills. If your business fails, your spouse and kids will be able to get jobs and earn decent money. When your children head off to college, they'll be able to score higher-paying jobs because of their skills and experience.
- Maintaining all the records and time sheets needed to prove your family members are working in the business develops discipline, organization skills, and reporting skills—all of which will be important in the business world.
- Finally, growing up together in the business, your children may become passionate about getting an education they can bring back home to enhance the family's business.

Oddly enough, doing everything right, doing things just the way the IRS demands, could be the glue that holds your family together.

See, it *is* in your best interest to avoid the temptation to take shortcuts and to pay your family members from the business without their earning the money.

Think about the kind of message you will be sending them if you cheat. You would be telling them it's all right to lie; to operate outside the rules; to avoid your responsibility to your community; to shrug off authority. Teaching them to lie or cheat will tell your children they may behave that way toward you, too. Children do not see the difference.

Sure, we could get into long arguments about what your tax money pays for and how often it's wasted. And it *is* wasted! The bottom line: your taxes do go toward maintaining a measure of sanity, safety, comfort, and predictability in a community of millions of passionate individualists.

Tax Benefits of Hiring Family

In Chapter 10 you'll learn all about the health-care, insurance, and retirement benefits available to small business owners and their families. Right now, we're going to cover the payroll tax and compensation benefits available to you.

Special Tax Benefits of Hiring Your Child(ren) for Proprietorships and Partnerships

- Wages paid to your children are fully deductible to your business. Allowances are not. You can give your children more money than you give them now—but have them earn it. All of it will be deductible to you.
- If you are a sole proprietorship or partnership, the wages you pay your children who are under 18 are not subject to Social Security, Medicare, or federal unemployment taxes. Most states also waive payroll taxes—but not all, so be sure to check with your state's payroll tax authority. The Web site http://www.taxadmin.org/fta/link/forms.html has more information. On wages of $7,000, this strategy would save you nearly $1,100 (15.3 percent) worth of your self-employment taxes and $2,100 (30 percent) of federal and state income taxes. You've just cut nearly $3,200 off your tax bill.
- If you had hired a nonchild employee, you'd be paying half the Social Security and Medicare, all the federal and state unemployment taxes, workers' compensation insurance, holidays, sick days, and, possibly, benefits. Those additional expenses would add more than $1,000 to your business overhead. Paying your child, you're just converting money you'd give to your child anyway into a deduction. Even when you spend twice as much on your child as before, the government pays for nearly half the money you give him or her.

Tax Benefits of Hiring Family in General

- For jobs requiring the use of cars, you may pay your spouse, your child, or yourself a mileage allowance or auto expenses. Be sure to get a mileage report and a copy of auto expenses to support your checks. The U.S. Tax Court just issued a ruling in support of the IRS's position. The IRS determined that payments that Continental Express, Inc.,[3] made to its drivers were subject to the meals and entertainment rules. Continental Express didn't require substantiation of the expenses from its drivers. That ruling cut the company's deduction by 50 percent. Expect this same logic to be applied to other businesses. Warnings aside, paying your child $100 per month for deliveries and errands cuts your taxes by about $550 per year (15.3 percent self-employment taxes, 30 percent federal and state taxes). If your child submits expense reports, he or she doesn't report this income at all. You don't have to pay your spouse or child's auto upkeep from your own pocket.
- The money you pay your spouse and child doesn't need to go into their pockets. Arrange to set up IRAs, Roth IRAs, or other retirement plans, to save $3,000–$5,000 of those wages each year. They will get a deduction for the contribution. Your child may end up paying no tax at all on that money, and your personal taxes are reduced. Chapter 10 describes the types of plans available.
- Chapter 10 explains how medical expenses may be deducted by small businesses. This could convert $5,000–$10,000 of unusable deductions into business deductions.

The financial and emotional rewards of hiring family members are substantial. Only don't push it. If they resist, don't force the issue relentlessly. You'll only take a good thing and turn in into something nasty. Knowing that you're doing it for their own good won't make them resent you less. Know when not to push. Just leave the door open for whenever they're ready to join you.

Better yet, sucker them into it. Just ask for a little help with some minor thing. Be sure to thank them and praise them. Once they get used to doing that, add one more little thing. As they do the small things automatically, and well . . . gradually

---

3. *Boyd v. Commissioner*, 122 T.C. No. 18 (4/24/04)—an S-corporation's shareholders were not entitled to a 100 percent deduction for the portion of the per diem allowance paid to drivers for nonmeal expenses, including mileage. It all boils down to establishing clear accountability.

add a few more tasks. Pretty soon, they'll be working by your side. Shhh, don't tell them I told you.

Now it's time to work on the payroll.

Paying Payroll

First of all, whenever you hire someone, have the person fill out two forms *before starting working.* The first is Form W-4, Employee's Withholding Allowance Certificate. You've seen W-4s before—get a new one filled out by each employee every January. The second form is the I-9, which you can access at http://www.uscis.gov/files/form/i-9.pdf. It's important that all your employees fill out this form for the benefit of immigration, even if they are citizens. Make a copy of each identification document used by the employee to substantiate his or her right to work. Keep it with the signed I-9 in the person's permanent employee file.

Compensation Methods

You may pay your employees in a variety of ways. Each one is acceptable, as long as you're consistent, using the same method for all people in the same position. If you pay people doing the same job at different rates, or using different methods, it won't be the IRS you'll have to face. Most likely it will be the wrath of the employee, in front of a labor judge. So if you're going to discriminate in favor of friends or family members, give them a higher title or additional duties to justify the higher pay rate.

Note: Be sure to look up the latest rules relating to hiring employees on the U.S. Department of Labor's Web site, http://www.dol.gov/elaws/flsa.htm. Look up minimum wage rules, overtime rules, etc. Also, check with your state to see if it has specific rules and rules for your industry.

These are common compensation methods:

- **Hourly.** Your employees keep a time sheet or punch a time card. Multiply their hours worked by their hourly pay rate. If they work overtime, multiply the pay rate by 1.5 to get the overtime rate. For example, if the base hourly rate is $10, overtime is paid at $15 (10 × 1.5). A weekly payroll for 50 hours of work including 10 hours of overtime would look like this:

  Base pay: 40 hours × $10 = $400
  Overtime pay: 10 hours × $15 = $150
  Total wages: $550

- **Salary.** Your employee gets paid the same amount each pay period, regardless of the hours worked. For instance, Nancy gets $50,000 per year, paid every 2 weeks. (*Note:* That does not mean twice a month. Twice a month is 24 pay periods.) Divide 52 weeks by 2 weeks, and the result is 26 pay periods. Now divide $50,000 by 26 weeks. That gives Nancy $1,923 per pay period. Often, people who are paid salaries get no overtime.
- **Commission.** Employees are paid on a percentage of their sales or unit's revenues. Often, to equalize the compensation, they are paid some fixed rate against commission. That means they get a base pay of, let's say, $1,000 per month, before they earn commissions. That $1,000 per month should be treated as wages, with all the usual withholding. When they earn the commissions, their advance payments get deducted from their commission checks. Josey had her first big sale at the end of December. It netted her a commission of $25,000. She had been with the company since June and had received $8,000 in advances. When she gets paid her commission in December, her employer will deduct the $8,000 from her net check, before taxes are taken out—since she has already paid taxes on the first $8,000. The payroll taxes will be computed on the $17,000 ($25,000 − $8.000).
- **Bonus.** Regardless of the other compensation methods, there is nothing to prevent you from giving your employees bonuses at any time you choose. Bonuses may be rewards for individuals or teams hitting targets or goals. They may simply be split among all employees because you had a great month. Even small bonuses, given to everyone to celebrate, can really boost morale and build team spirit. The bonus is fully taxable, just like payroll.
- **Employee gifts.** Except for minor gifts worth $25 or less for the whole year, the value of a gift is fully taxable. Include the value of all gifts in the employee's wages.
- **Employee achievement awards.** When the award is part of a written plan with defined targets, you may give an employee an award worth up to $1,600, without including it in the employee's income. Unfortunately, the award must be a thing, not money. There are very specific rules about who qualifies. Read Chapter 2 of IRS Publication 15-A (at http://www.irs.gov/publications/p15a/ar02.html) for more details.

Payroll Taxes

Along with a payroll come payroll taxes. When you cut the check to the IRS at the end of each payroll period, it looks like you're paying the IRS a ton of money. Actually, your payroll taxes are lower than you think. Most of the money you're sending to the IRS is the employees' own money, deducted from their paychecks. The only things the employer pays are:

Social Security, up to an annual limit (which changes each year):	6.2 percent
Medicare, no limit:	1.45 percent
Federal unemployment, up to $7,000 in wages:	.8 percent
Total federal employer taxes:	8.45 percent

Add in your state unemployment taxes and other minor local taxes as well as mandatory workers' compensation, and you're paying about 10 percent of the employees' wages.

Note: While the percentages haven't changed in decades, the limits on Social Security wages increase each year. See the "What's New" section of IRS Publication 15 (http://www.irs.gov/publications/p15) for the new Social Security limits each year.

Preparing Payroll: Checks, Journals, Reports

You have several options when it comes to the accounting involved with payroll. You can do it the old-fashioned way, by hand, on paper, on columnar pads, or by using journals. You can do it by hand using preprinted manual systems. One-Write is a very popular manual system. You also can use software that either integrates into your accounting system or stands alone, like QuickBooks. Or you can do the really smart thing—*turn it all over to a professional!*

Payroll record keeping is fraught with danger. There are so many little things that go wrong all the time, due to errors on your part, program glitches, or tax law changes you didn't get. Messing up on payroll tax forms unleashes a gusher of notices. Your time is worth more than that. Worse, most really small businesses end up with huge IRS payroll tax debt because they don't do their payroll reporting properly and don't pay their payroll tax deposits.

Make all the problems go away. Turn your payroll processing over to a tax professional or a professional payroll service. It will cost $50–$100 per month for a small company, but it's really worth it. A good payroll processing house will make your life so easy. Once you set up your employees, all you have to do is call in with their hours or enter the hours online. All the major companies have toll-free customer service centers.

They prepare your payroll, cut payroll checks on your account, file all the tax returns, issue the W-2s, and—for a small extra fee—arrange to make your tax agency payments directly from your account. This will give you proof your payments were made on time. If they make an error, the payroll services must pay any penalties incurred, not you. (But if you don't have funds in your bank account on payroll day—that's your error, not theirs.)

The best thing about payroll services is that if the IRS sends correspondence, they will handle all the responses. You don't need to be bothered. If you're the kind of person who cringes every time you see one of those white envelopes with the IRS eagle . . . a payroll service is for you.

Here are the top two companies in the industry:

- **Intuit's QuickBooks Payroll.** If you request the Complete Payroll Service, you can get additional services, including background checks before hiring, integration into QuickBooks, cafeteria plans, and retirement plans. Reach the company at http://vurl.bz/taxmama/QB-Payroll.
- **Paychex.** Though geared toward companies with 50 employees or more, it will still work with mom-and-pop businesses. The service reps are a joy to work with. Check the company out at http://www.paychex.com.

For more options, visit the IRS's list of payroll providers, available at http://vurl.bz/taxmama/IRS_P-R.

Tips on Using Payroll Service Bureaus

- Be sure to get yourself assigned to a local personal account manager. He or she will be a big help to you any time there is a problem or you have a question.
- Give your tax preparers online access so they can look up information and print out forms and reports when working on your business return, without ever bothering you.
- Some payroll services, or your bank, will enable you to offer direct deposit to your employees' bank accounts, so you never have to cut checks or mail them.
- You will be able to offer employee benefits economically, even if you're a small company.

Alert: Set up an IRS EFTPS (electronic federal tax payment system; see http://www.eftps.gov) account and a similar state account, if available, so your payroll tax deposits can go directly from your own bank account to the IRS and your state (see Chapter 1). That way, your payroll service will not be holding your funds. Unfortunately, there have been instances of payroll companies going bankrupt while holding client funds. You don't want that to happen.

Regardless of who prepares your payroll, it pays for you to get educated about it. The IRS provides detailed information on its Employment Taxes for Small Business Web site, available at http://vurl.bz/taxmama/IRS-EmploymentTax.

The IRS, SCORE, and your state government frequently offer free workshops on how to handle payroll and employee issues. Take advantage of the free information. It's important that you understand what your responsibilities are and how things work. It also will help you catch errors or oversights on the part of your staff, service bureau, or tax preparer. It's important that you know what forms must be filed and when.

Reporting Payroll

Payroll tax returns are filed quarterly and annually. Table 9.2 provides the due dates and lists the forms that are due. For the final quarter of the year, you must file both the quarterly reports and the annual summaries, for both the IRS and state, along with the W-2s and 1099s. These days, as much as possible, the IRS wants to see payroll tax forms filed electronically. That's another benefit of payroll services.

Form 941 is the quarterly report. You can also find this form on the IRS's Web site at http://www.irs.gov/pub/irs-pdf/f941.pdf.

On Form 941, do you see that box on line 4, where it says if no wages or compensation are subject to Social Security or Medicare tax? If you've hired your children who are under age 18 and they are your only employees, check that box.

TABLE 9.2 Quarterly Payroll Tax Return Due Dates

When the last day of the month falls on a weekend or holiday, the forms and payments are due on the following business day.

Quarter	Due Date	Forms Due
1st (Q1)	April 30	941 and state
2nd (Q2)	July 31	941 and state
3rd (Q3)	October 31	941 and state
4th (Q4)	January 31 of following year	940, 941, 1099s, W-2s, and state

That alerts the IRS that you didn't omit the Social Security and Medicare wages by accident. Remember, your children's wages are *not* subject to those taxes. If you have other employees who are subject to Social Security and Medicare, leave that box empty. You will be using lines 6a-6e to enter your children's and other exempt payroll. Be prepared to get a flurry of mail from the IRS. It usually takes the agency three letters before it accepts your explanation about having hired your child. But keep replying to the letters. In time, you will get the IRS to accept it—and next quarter the letters will start again.

You must send in your payroll tax payments within three business days after each payroll. (Some people have more time, but it's a good habit to get into.) When you file the returns at the end of the quarter, you should owe no more than $2,500. If you do owe more than that, you will be required to establish that EFTPS account I mentioned. The IRS has phased out the Form 8109 vouchers in that thin yellow book the IRS used to send you when you got your employer identification number.

Form 941-V is the payment coupon for Form 941. If you are making payment by check, fill in the coupon and send the check with it. Be sure to include FYTIN (form number, year, and taxpayer ID number). If the balance due is more than $2,500, pay it online via the EFTPS.

Form 940 is the annual unemployment tax return. The final tax rate only ends up being 0.8 percent if you file the return on time and pay your state unemployment taxes on time. If you default on the state tax, you end up paying 6.2 percent for federal unemployment. So make sure you always pay the state unemployment taxes first.

W-2s must be mailed out to employees by January 31. No payment goes with these forms. They must be mailed to the Social Security Administration by February 28 or 29, if applicable. If you file online, you have until March 31. Do the same thing you did with the 1099s. Mail the W-2s to the employees on time, but hold off filing them until the last minute. That way, you'll have time to update addresses and correct any errors employees find.

Form W-3 is the summary of all the W-2s. Be sure all the boxes on the W-2s add up to the totals on the W-3. Included on the W-2 is the information about employee benefits, which we'll discuss in the next section.

Employee Benefits

Companies may offer their employees an array of benefits. Owners can only participate if they are incorporated. On the other hand, S-corporation shareholders who own 2 percent or more of the company are excluded from most benefits.

Two of the common benefits employees receive are sick pay and vacations. Were you aware these benefits are not a legal requirement in all states—particularly for small companies? Paying for these for employees is more custom than law. Check with your own state's labor commission to learn the standards in your state.

You can offer some fringe benefit plans for employees that they pay for themselves—and would gladly. When it comes to medical and insurance plans, even if you don't pay the premiums, your employees could get some terrific tax savings. You pay a small administrative fee, offset by the tax savings from the plan, and for your employees it's like a small raise. They save nearly 38 percent of the amount they spend anyway on things such as medical insurance, medical costs, or dependent care (7.65 percent Social Security and Medicare, 25 percent federal tax, 5 percent state tax). For the average family paying $3,000 in medical premiums, that's nearly $100 per month into its pockets, perhaps double if it has dependent care. As the employer, you save about 12 percent of the cost of those premiums because the employer's taxes don't apply to that money either. That savings will more than cover your administrative costs for the plan.

Plans Where Employees' Money Is Spent

Here are two popular fringe benefit plans employees pay for:

- **Premium-only plans (POPs).** The employees pay their medical insurance premiums. Premiums are deducted from their wages before taxes are computed.
- **Flexible spending accounts (FSAs).** These accounts let your staff deduct their medical, dental, optical, and therapy costs, as well as dependent-care expenses (child or elder care). Dependent care is limited to $5,000 per year, but may increase with inflation. Employers, or your payroll service, set up limits on the medical spending. The FAQs page on the FSA Feds site (https://www.fsafeds.com/fsafeds/SummaryOfBenefits.asp) provides a comprehensive set of answers to most FSA questions.

Plans Where Your Money Is Spent

Setting up employee plans for small companies has been complicated and expensive. Now that the payroll services are offering complete administration packages, even a small employer can offer these benefits. It only costs a few extra dollars per employee per month for the administration.

- **Group term life insurance.** Employee benefits up to $50,000 are free to the employee. The premiums for coverage exceeding $50,000 are added back to their wages. Have the insurance expert on your advisory team help you find the right plan.
- **Education benefits.** You may reimburse employees for up to $5,250 per year. It's tax-free to them and a full deduction to you.
- **Employee death benefits.** Employee death benefits may be paid to the employee's family to help out with the funeral and other related costs. It would be a deduction to the employer. And it would be income to the employee if the benefit is based on the employee's past service or other economic benefit due to the employee.
- **Meals and lodging.** Some companies set up a cafeteria offering free meals to all employees to save time off from work or to ensure they get some nutritious meals. When you offer it to all employees, the company may deduct the costs without charging the employees. I'd be careful about this if you're working from home and it's just you and your family. Lodging is a bit more interesting. When your employee (such as an apartment manager) must live on the premises for the benefit of the employer, so he or she is available full-time, the lodging is free, without tax consequences to the employee.

Companies providing fringe benefits to qualified employees may deduct the costs of the benefits and administration. You'll want to think carefully about setting up these plans, because once you start, employees expect them. To keep employees for the long term, you need to be generous. But it's worth it to keep terrific employees. Be sure to build the costs of the perquisites into your product or service costs. On the other hand, many of these benefits reduce your tax and insurance costs, and you can use that savings to pay for the benefits.

There are a variety of retirement plans and profit-sharing plans you can offer your employees. Chapter 10 describes most of them as they apply to business owners and related parties. The spreadsheets in Tables 10.1 and 10.2 in Chapter 10 will give you an overview of each plan, with the limits, setup dates, and funding dates as well as the pros and cons of each plan.

Employee Ownership and Stock Options

Whether for tax planning or retention, employee ownership is an appealing option. Since the IPO craze of the 1990s, highly skilled employees are starting to expect a share of the equity and growth of a company.

Using stock is an excellent lure to hire an employee whose price you couldn't otherwise afford. Giving up stock, you can offer a salary you can presently afford, with a promise of riches as the company grows. The right highly talented employee, who isn't also highly strung, will make the difference between growing slowly or explosively. Which is better, giving up 5 percent of a company worth $10 million or owning 100 percent of a company worth $250,000? That's the kind of difference the right employee(s) can make.

You can also use employee stock ownership plans (ESOPs)[4] to avoid paying taxes. When you turn over 100 percent of the company's stock to an ESOP, the ESOP pays no taxes on the company's profits. It does mean giving up stock to each employee as he or she becomes eligible, and so you will own less of the company. But you will also own a share of the ESOP. However, with all the tax money available to the company for growth, what you've given up may earn you a greater reward—allowing you to build a bigger company.

Companies such as JetBlue and United Airlines have substantial employee ownership. You don't have to be a large company to do this. Kinko's started out quite small and was entirely employee-owned. With great employee training and participation, the company grew dramatically. In February 2004, Federal Express paid $2.4 billion for the company. You can just bet those Kinko's employees' retirement plans look healthy. All the profit is sitting in their ESOP accounts, ready to be drawn whenever they want to retire.

You can also offer stock options.[5] The rules on when the options are taxable, when the employee can exercise them, and what taxes get paid when are very complex. I prefer to leave all that in the hands of the tax and labor attorneys. If you want to study this in depth, you'll find a feast at the National Center for Employee Ownership's Web site at http://www.nceo.org.

Summing Up Employees

Overall, you and your family can gain great benefits by having eligible family members go on the payroll. The trick is to pay wages only for valuable services performed on behalf of the business. Do what the IRS asks of you—your family will be closer knit, and your business will grow in leaps and bounds.

---

4. The National Center for Employee Ownership (NCEO) has an extensive ESOP resource section, available at http://www.nceo.org/main/publist.php/id/1.

5. NCEO also provides an extensive stock options resource at http://www.nceo.org/options/option_articles.html.

Just as the benefits are good for your family, think of how treating your employees well affects them. Seeing you extend yourself to provide them with ways to make their money go further will increase their loyalty to you.

At tax educational seminars I often hear the presenters speak about how to devise retirement and benefit plans that cut the employees out. Isn't that the silliest thing you've ever heard? Why would you not want to give your employees benefits? Cost? Sure, cost is a factor. But think of the cost of hiring, training, and teaching a new employee because you didn't value the previous employee enough. Cheap labor is not cheap! New hires make mistakes—sometimes mistakes big enough to cost you important clients.

So as you prosper, see to it that your employees do, too. Get some good planning with the help of the employee benefit specialist on your advisory team—and you'll ensure being able to retire in style.

Employee and Independent Contractor Resources

- **Form I-9, Employment Eligibility Verification.** http://www.uscis.gov/files/form/i-9.pdf.
- **Form SS-8, Determination of Worker Status.** http://www.irs.gov/pub/irs-pdf/fss8.pdf.
- **Form W-4, Employee's Withholding Allowance Certificate.** www.irs.gov/pub/irs-pdf/fw4.pdf.
- **Form W-9, Request for Taxpayer Identification Number and Certification.** http://www.irs.gov/pub/irs-pdf/fw9.pdf.
- **Form 940, Employer's Annual Federal Unemployment (FUTA) Tax Return and Form 940-V Payment Voucher.** http://www.irs.gov/pub/irs-pdf/f940.pdf.
- **Form 941, Employer's Quarterly Federal Tax Return and Form 941-V Payment Voucher.** http://www.irs.gov/pub/irs-pdf/f941.pdf.
- **Form 8109, Federal Tax Deposit Coupon.** http://www.irs.gov/pub/irs-pdf/f8109b.pdf.
- **Form 8809, Request for Extension of Time to File Information Returns.** http://www.irs.gov/pub/irs-pdf/f8809.pdf.
- **Section 530, Safe Harbor Information.** http://vurl.bz/taxmama/IRS-530. See the article "Section 530: Its History and Application in Light of the Federal Definition of the Employer-Employee Relationship for Federal Tax Purposes" (February 2009) by the National Association of Tax Reporting and Professional Management.

- **IRS EFTPS (electronic federal tax payment system).** http://www.eftps.gov. Set it up for your payroll tax deposits.
- **U.S. Department of Labor's Web site.** http://www.dol.gov/elaws/flsa.htm.
- **Links to state tax agencies.** http://www.taxadmin.org/fta/link/forms.html.
- **Intuit's Complete Payroll.** http://vurl.bz/taxmama/QB-Payroll.
- **Paychex.** http://www.paychex.com.
- **IRS's list of payroll providers.** http://vurl.bz/taxmama/IRS_P-R.
- **Service Corps of Retired Executives (SCORE).** http://www.score.org.
- **Institute for Family-Owned Business.** http://vurl.bz/taxmama/FamilyBiz. Provides support to Maine's family-owned businesses. Perhaps, in time, it will expand nationwide.
- *Family Business Magazine.* http://www.familybusinessmagazine.com. An excellent collection of articles, resources, and information for small family businesses intending to become major businesses.
- **National Center for Employee Ownership.** http://www.nceo.org. A private, nonprofit membership and research organization providing unbiased information on employee stock ownership plans, broadly granted employee stock options and related programs, and ownership culture.
- **TaxMama's Quick Look-Ups.** http://www.taxmama.com/quick-look-ups. You will find all kinds of useful reference materials, Webinars you can replay, e-books, even the 100% Home-Based Business Tax Solution.
- **Your Business Bible.** http://www.yourbusinessbible.com. Look for worksheets and updates to this book.

✓ CHAPTER 10 OWNERS' FRINGE BENEFITS, RETIREMENT, AND TAX DEFERMENT

To-Do List and Questionnaire

1. What business entity are you using? _____

2. What are the legal limits to your deductible benefits, if any?

   _____   _____   _____

3. Do you have children under age 13?

   • Do you pay for child care?

   • Do you have an employer-provided child-care facility?

4. Do you have medical coverage? _____ Yourself _____ Family

   What tax-deductible methods are you using for medical coverage?

   • Section 105 plan _____

   • Section 125 plan _____

   • HSA _____

   • Small business health-care tax credit _____

   • Other _____

5. Do you have a retirement plan? ____ Yes ____ No

6. Does it cover your employees? ____ Yes ____ No

7. Are you funding it regularly and properly? ____ Yes ____ No

8. Schedule a meeting with your tax pro and retirement administrator to review the plan for compliance.

   Date _____

9. Schedule a meeting with your tax pro to see if there are any owner benefits you have overlooked.

   Date _____

Remember to put a copy of each document behind this page, folded in half.

10

OWNERS' FRINGE BENEFITS, RETIREMENT, AND TAX DEFERMENT

Income tax is the fine you pay for thriving so fast.

—TOM ANTION

There are wonderful benefits to being in business for yourself. You may spend as much as you like, to improve yourself, educate yourself, care for your health, and plan for your ultimate triumphant retirement. While I won't cover all the potential benefits here, I will include some options you won't find anywhere else. For the ones everyone covers—you know the usual suspects—simply go to an Internet search engine (such as http://www.google.com) and type in "fringe benefits."

Fringe Benefits and Reimbursements

When you're an employee in a responsible position, you are always offered an array of fringe benefits to induce you to take the job. You get vacation, sick time, bonuses, stock options, medical plans, and various reimbursement plans for things like child care, education, auto, and meals. Your employer pays for all that.

Having your own company means you may offer those things to your employees. (See Chapter 9.) But if you get them, the cost for them comes out of your own pocket. On the other hand, if you handle the benefits properly, Uncle Sam will pick up a nice part of the freight.

Health Insurance

The form of business you've chosen (see Chapter 3) will govern whether or not your insurance expenses are deductible in your business. C-corporations get to deduct all employee fringe benefits, and as an employee of your own C-corporation, you're treated the same way as other employees. On the other hand, when you're self-employed, in a partnership, or in an S-corporation, you don't get a business deduction.[1] You may deduct your family's health insurance costs on page 1 of your tax return, as an adjustment to income. If you have an S-corporation, this doesn't matter as much, because you're not paying self-employment taxes on your profits. But when your income is on your Schedule C or through a partnership (or LLC filing as a partnership), all your profit is subject to an extra 15.3 percent levy for Social Security and Medicare taxes.

Not being able to deduct your family's medical insurance costs of $650 per month from your Schedule C business costs you nearly extra $1,200 extra in taxes each year. Toss in the cost of routine out-of-pocket medical expenses (braces, contacts, eyeglasses, annual checkups, co-pays), which might average another $1,500 for a family of three. Your overall extra taxes are nearly $1,500 per year from self-employment taxes alone.

You may provide insurance coverage for your dependents until they reach age 26, as a result of the Health Reform Act of 2010. More about that in a moment.

Health Savings Accounts

Congress voted health savings accounts (HSAs) into law on December 8, 2003. By now, coverage is easy to find. To help you find insurance carriers for these plans in your state, eHealthInsurance.com put a special section up on its Web site at http://www.ehealthinsurance.com/hsa.

What's so special about these accounts? Your medical insurance costs are cut because your deductible must be at least $1,200 (revised annually for inflation). Your medical expenses drop for two reasons:

1. Premiums decrease when your deductible increases.
2. No co-pays are permitted, and so you have no out-of-pocket expenses

---

1. You may have seen a company pay the officers' medical insurance or expenses in an S-corporation. The money is added to the wages as additional compensation. Or it is treated as dividends or as repayments of loans to the officers.

A health savings account is something like an IRA. The money you deposit is deductible in the current year. You can draw that money out to pay for medical expenses, tax-free. Or if you and your family are generally healthy, you can leave the money invested for years. Draw it when you really need the money to cover medical expenses, or wait until you get old and infirm and need to spend money on in-home care or long-term care. Or just draw it out and pay taxes on it, like an IRA. For more information, refer to my Web site at http://taxmama.com/insurance/hsa.

Code Section 105 Medical Reimbursement Plans

Created for farming families whose lives are so closely tied to their businesses, this is a special provision of the tax code. It provides a way for family businesses to deduct all the medical insurance and medical expenses for family members from their business returns, just the way you can for your employees. The plan is based on the premise that you can hire your spouse, paying him or her a salary. The family medical plan is part of the compensation. There are stringent rules to follow, including having a plan document and keeping records of all the expenses and reimbursements. You could do it yourself or with the help of your tax professional. You can also contact the Agri-BizPlan folks at (866) 690-2929. They pretty much own this niche, so they are quite efficient and reasonably priced. For more information, go to http://taxsavings105plan.com/agribiz/index.html.

If you prefer to do it yourself, you will need a plan document. You may adapt the one on A/N Group, Inc.'s Web site for your own company (http://www.smbiz.com/sbfrm002.html). Make sure you don't issue reimbursement checks to your spouse or your employees unless you have a copy of the medical receipt in your hands—and it qualifies as a medical deduction.[2] Keep separate files for each employee and separate each year—either with tabs or using different folders for each year.

Since Section 105 lets your business deduct all the family medical expenses, not just the insurance premiums, the savings are substantial.

The Section 105 Plan in Action

Ward Cleaver is self-employed by his California business. He hires his wife, June, to answer his phones at his office. He pays her a modest salary, so she has some spending money—$500 per month. In addition to the salary, he sets up a Section 105 plan, giving his entire family full medical coverage. The

---

2. For medical expenses, see IRS Publication 502 at http://www.irs.gov/publications/p502/index.html.

insurance premiums are $400 per month for the family of four ($4,800 per year). Ward and June pay another $125 per each family member for dental and visual insurance ($500 per year). Even with the dental insurance providing $1,500 toward Beaver's braces, the Cleavers are still paying $3,000 out of their pockets. Beaver's scrapes and Wally's sports activities usually result in a few hospital visits, generally at least $500 per year. Ward and June's annual checkups and co-pays usually add up to $500 per year. And they spend an additional $500 on Ward's eyeglasses and prescription sunglasses and June's contacts each year. The medical benefits added $9,800 to June's compensation. Since the $9,800 was not subject to employment tax, it saves the Cleaver family $4,860 in taxes (15.3 percent self-employment tax, 25 percent IRS tax, 9.3 percent state tax = 49.6 percent).

Without the Section 105 plan, they would only have been able to deduct the medical insurance, on page 1 of Form 1040. This reduces the Cleavers' taxes by $1,650 ($4,800 × 34.3 percent, rounded). As for the other $5,000 of medical expenses, Ward's income was too high (more than $66,000) to itemize any of it. The Section 105 plan saved the Cleavers more than $3,200.

The Health Care Reform Act of 2010

Starting in 2010, as a small employer, you may take a tax credit if you are paying at least 50 percent of your employees' health insurance costs. The credit is as high as 35 percent (50 percent after 2013). If your spouse or children are your employees — or if you are employed by your corporation—this may apply to you. Watch out, though; the average annual wages of your employees, including yourself, must be under $25,000.

Adoption Credits

As an employer, your may pay all or most of the adoption expenses of your addition to your family. The limits change each year. The Health Care Reform Act raises the adoption credit to $13,170 through 2011. It also allows employers to pay this benefit to their employees. So it can be an employee benefit for a spouse in a sole proprietorship or partnership, if a spouse is an employee. Or it may be an employee benefit to a shareholder-owner in a corporation.

Employer-Provided Child-Care Facilities Credit

Hardly any small businesses even know about this excellent way to reduce your taxes if you have a child. The IRS will give you up to 25 percent of the cost of a qualified child-care facility for your children—or your employees' children—to a maximum of $150,000 per year. Unused credits may be carried to the future for up to 20 years. That doesn't mean you have to set up your own child-care facility. You can get the credit for paying an existing facility for child care, as long as it's licensed and meets all the IRS's rules for such facilities. The employer must pay the facility directly; reimbursements are not permitted. Use Form 8882, available at http://www.irs.gov/pub/irs-pdf/f8882.pdf.

You can get another 10 percent credit for the cost of having your child evaluated by an expert to help determine the appropriate child-care facility for your child. This need will usually come into play if your child seems to have trouble learning or adapting to other children.

Your state might have similar credits. For instance, California has a 30 percent credit. Just think, if you lived in California and paid $300 per month for your child's care, your tax credit would be $1,080. In addition, the business gets the deduction of $2,520 (total cost of $3,600, credit of $1,980). That's worth about $1,250 more (15.3 percent self-employment tax, 25 percent IRS tax, and 9.3 percent California tax). You've just saved over $2,300 of the $3,600 costs of your child's day care.

Life Insurance

Typically, life insurance is not a deductible expense—certainly not when it is for the benefit of the owner of the business. In a C-corporation, though, you may deduct the cost of up to $50,000 coverage for each employee, including the primary shareholder. Check with your tax professional to see if there are other ways to include life insurance in your business and make it deductible.

Employee Leasing and Trusts

There are ways to use trusts and employee leasing arrangements to generate substantial deductions, but that's advanced tax planning, with both benefits and pitfalls, often requiring the services of a sophisticated tax attorney.

Education

Naturally, your business may deduct the cost of all courses you or your staff takes to increase your professional or trade expertise related to your business or industry.

Management and business courses and seminars are deductible. When it comes to courses taken in order to get a college degree, you may have to fight to win those deductions. Individual courses related directly to what you need to know for your business can probably be deducted. But those anthropology courses? For a plumber . . . well, I don't think so. You get the idea.

A Tax Court case in 2010 has clarified some of the issues that determine whether or not you can deduct your education. Lori Singleton-Clarke, a nurse, objected to the IRS's decision in her audit and presented her own case to the Tax Court—and won an impressive decision. You can read about the logic used by the court in TaxMama's AccountingWeb.com blog (http://vurl.bz/taxmama/Deduct_MBA).

Your company may offer an education assistance plan, reimbursing employees for up to $5,250 of annual education expenses.[3] Since January 1, 2002, graduate-level courses qualify. In the past, only courses up to a bachelor's degree or a certificate program were included. If you are a C-corporation, the cost of your education expenses for a degree may be reimbursed, along with those taken by other employees. However, in an S-corporation or other entity, nope. You may, of course, deduct the cost of specific seminars or workshops for your industry—just not the cost of courses leading to a degree. You may hire your spouse or children. If they legitimately work for the business, like any other arm's-length employee, you may be able to reimburse their education expenses as part of their employee compensation. This may be iffy in an S-corporation. Since your family members are related parties, the IRS treats them as owning the business, too. Definitely clear this with your tax professional before including it in your business plan, especially because this is an area of tax law that may change soon.

What expenses are deductible when it comes to education? The cost of books, tuition, fees, tools, and supplies related to the course. Sometimes, even computers are deductible. Travel to the course or seminar is also included as well as meals, if you are gone overnight. There's a broad definition for *tools*. But if you're studying construction and your class project is to build a house and you build one for yourself . . . I don't think you'll be able to deduct the costs as education expenses. So be reasonable when you take deductions on your tax return.

Courses to qualify you for a new business or a new profession aren't deductible. For instance, if I were working for a certified public accounting firm and wanted to take a CPA review course, that wouldn't be deductible for me. Even if I took the course and passed, and I continued to do exactly the same job as before, as

---

3. See IRS Publication 970 for education fringe benefits: http://www.irs.gov/publications/p970/ch12.html.

if nothing changed, it would *not* be deductible. The IRS considers CPAs a different profession than simply a degreed accountant. However, individual courses relating to accounting and tax topics would be deductible. Look at your industry and see how that relates.

In addition to being able to provide up to $5,250 worth of reimbursements to your employees (including family employees), as an employer, you may pay for courses directly related to your business. For instance, I pay for continuing education courses for my long-term staff. When appropriate, I also pay for their travel and lodging. For instance, you will find us in Las Vegas each year at the IRS Tax Forums.

Education deductions can be lucrative—or they can be dangerous. However, for the next few years, even if you can't use the deductions as business expenses, you have education credits and above-the-line-deductions available to use. The American opportunity credit is worth up to $2,500; the hope credit, perhaps $2,000, etc. Publication 970, which you can access at http://www.irs.gov/publications/p970, provides current information.

Retirement Plans

The good news is, if your business follows your business plan, you'll be making lots of money and living well. The bad news is, you won't die young. At least, so says the Centers for Disease Control (CDC).[4] The CDC's 2006 projections say you'll live until age 77.7. That looks like a long time from now, doesn't it?

News flash. It sneaks up on you faster than you can imagine. I was just 24 last week. Or so it seems. I blinked and more than two decades passed. Looking around at friends, family, and clients, many are living well into their eighties and nineties. In fact, have you seen Raquel Welch doing those Foster Grant sunglasses commercials lately (2010)? At age 70, she is looking stunning! May we all look that good and be that healthy at her age. If we're going to live a long, healthy life, we'd better look toward saving for our own longevity.

Retirement Basics You Must Know

Each investment vehicle has contribution limits based on your income, except the SIMPLE-IRA. In general, if you (or your spouse) have a job with a retirement plan, your contribution to any plans related to an IRA (individual retirement account) will be limited.

---

4. Fast stats on average life expectancy can be found at http://www.cdc.gov/nchs/fastats/lifexpec.htm.

You may contribute $1,000 to $2,500 extra per year if you're age 50 or over, depending on the plan. These contributions are called catch-up contributions. All contribution amounts, catch-ups, and income limits change based on inflation or congressional rules.

You may not put money into all these retirement vehicles at once. Putting money into one will generally conflict with your right to fund one of the other retirement options—so pick the optimum retirement plan(s) for your business.

A common misconception is that these plans are investments. They are not. They are vehicles into which you put money. You may open these plans with banks, brokerages, perhaps even with insurance companies. Brokerages and mutual fund companies let you diversify and manage your investments. You control the rate of the return by watching the appropriate market. You may move the funds from one company to another—as long as they stay within the same investment vehicle.

All the plan descriptions assume you have no employees. If you have any, please see a good local tax professional who understands qualified and nonqualified plans. And if that person doesn't know what those terms mean, go somewhere else.

Tax-Free Retirement

Tax-free means you'll never have to pay tax on the money when you take it out. You also don't generally get a deduction for your deposits when you make them, though. Table 10.1 provides an overview of the tax-free plans. Here are the details of some plans available to small business owners.

Roth IRAs. For any year, contributions to Roth IRAs must be deposited by April 15 of the following year. For 2010, for example, you may contribute up to $5,000, plus a catch-up of $1,000 by April 15, 2011.

There is no deduction for the amount you contribute to a Roth IRA. Obey the rules—you'll get all the money out tax-free when you retire. You may only draw the money out of your own account when you and your spouse are each over age 59½ and you've left the money in the account for 5 years. In times when investments do well, this is a very appealing investment. For young people, whose money will grow in these IRA accounts for 15 or 20 years, this option can yield a generous source of tax-free money in the future.

Why doesn't everyone use it? Several reasons:

- The contribution allowed is low.
- The income limits to qualify are low.
- Roths are a nuisance to fix if you contribute when your income is too high.

TABLE 10.1 Tax-Free Retirement and Savings Plans Available in 2010

Tax-Free	Roth IRA	Municipal Bonds in Your State	Sec. 529 College Plans	Employee 401(k)s 403(b), 457, SAR-SEP
Basic contribution 2010	$5,000	No limit	$13,000	$16,500
Age 50 catch-up	$1,000	N/A	N/A	$5,500
Income limits—single	$105,000 – $120,000	No limit	No limit	
Income limits—joint	$167,000 – $177,000	No limit	No limit	
Date account must be opened	April 15 of following year		December 31 of plan year	
Date contribution is due	April 15 of following year	N/A	December 31 of plan year	
Pros	Qualified withdrawals are not taxable.	Earnings are not taxable. Draw money anytime.	Earnings are not taxable if funds are spent on courses, supplies, or room and board, including travel or hobbies.	
Cons	People who deposit early may face penalties if they don't remove the funds when they prepare their tax returns and don't qualify. Requires planning.	Low interest rate. Tax-free interest may be subject to alternative minimum tax.	This isn't really a retirement fund. It's an education fund.	

continued

TABLE 10.1 *continued*

Tax-Free	Roth IRA	Municipal Bonds in Your State	Sec. 529 College Plans	Employee 401(k)s 403(b), 457, SAR-SEP
Special Rules				
Contrib: 2005–2007	$4,000		Tied to gift tax limits.	2005 is $14,000.
Contrib: 2006 forward				$15,000
Age 50 catch-up 2005	$500			$4,000
Contrib: 2008 forward	$5,000			$5,000
Age 50 catch-up 2006 forward	$1,000			
Age to draw	59 1/2			
Holding term minimum	5 years			
Investment's annual income limit	N/A	$100,000	N/A	
First-year maximum contribution			$65,000	
			It replaces 5 years of gifts.	

Section 529 College Education Plans. You may contribute up to $13,000 per beneficiary, per year.[5] Or in the first year, you may deposit up to $65,000, using up 5 years' contributions at once. Contributions must be made by December 31 of the plan's year. Section 529 plans are unique because, although you are gifting a fortune to your child, relative, or friend, you still have control of this asset. At any time you choose, you may pull it back into your own estate and keep the money. Or if your beneficiary doesn't use up all the money, you may either transfer it to another student or take it back. The money may be spent on tuition, fees, books, supplies, room, and board—as long as the school is on the approved list.

You're saying 529s are not really retirement plans? My approach is indeed novel. No one else has written about this—but it was cleared with the IRS on May 13, 2004. The IRS agrees it's legal. If you are related to the beneficiary, you may transfer the money to yourself as the new beneficiary, even if you're a senior citizen. Once in your name, you're free to use that money to get educated—taking courses on cruise ships, traveling across Europe or wherever, including most expenses and course supplies for accredited schools. Just think—gourmet cooking school, scuba training, professional golf college . . . what have you always wanted to learn?

Your Home: A Tax-Free Strategy. Buy a home and build equity. You may sell a home every two years and keep up to $250,000 ($500,000 for couples) tax-free. Use the proceeds to buy the next home in a rapidly appreciating area. Repeat every few years. Ten years before you plan to retire, accelerate the mortgage payments so you pay off the loan entirely. If your profits look as if they'll be more than $500,000, add your children, living at home, to the title. Each owner gets that $250,000 exclusion. Along the way, you collected lots of money to use either toward a better house or toward funding your retirement plans, or both. Once retired, you'll have no mortgage payments, so if anything goes wrong with your retirement accounts (as happened to many in April 2000, and again in 2009 and 2010), you'll still be fine. If you ever need money, simply make sure to establish a home equity line of credit (HELOC). A home equity line costs little or nothing to have. You only pay interest on any money you borrow—usually at favorable rates.

Tax-Deferred Opportunities

Tax-deferred means you get a deduction or credit for your contributions now, when you deposit the money. But you'll pay tax on all the money when you take it out.

---

5. The annual contribution limit is the amount of the annual gift tax exclusion—the amount of money you may give a person as a gift without paying a gift tax on it.

There is a whole menu of retirement savings opportunities, but they're deceptively complicated. Many have income limits and strings attached. Use Table 10.2 as a starting point. Discuss the options with your own tax pro. Table 10.2 provides an overview of tax-deferred plans. Here are the details of some plans available to small business owners.

Savings Incentive Match Plan for Employees (SIMPLE-IRAs)

You may contribute up to $11,500 plus $2,500 catch-up in 2010. You may contribute your entire profit, or wages from your own corporation or LLC, up to those limits. The money must be deposited by December 31. As your own employer, you must also make a matching contribution of 3 percent of your wages or profits. The matching contribution may be funded when you file your tax return. The plan must be opened by September 30, 2010, to use it in 2010.

Simplified Employee Pension (SEP-IRA)

You may fund 25 percent of your net profits or wages from your own business, up to $49,000, into an SEP-IRA. You may set up and fund SEP-IRAs until the due date of your tax return, including extensions.

KEOGH Plans

KEOGHs are similar to the SEP-IRA, but with two differences: (1) they must be opened by December 31 of the tax year being deducted, and (2) you may contribute up to 100 percent of your business's net earnings—or up to 25 percent of all participants' compensation, to the same $49,000 limit as for the SEP-IRA.

Solo 401(k)s

These are like the regular 401(k)s you might get from an employer—only much better. You have the same contribution limits as the SEP-IRA—$49,000 (plus the $3,000 catch-up). But the percentages are more generous. At lower levels of income, you may contribute 100 percent of your wages. The best part about these plans is that you may roll over your IRA funds into a solo 401(k) account. Then you may borrow up to 50 percent of the account balance, or up to $50,000. This is the only account that lets you and your spouse (and even your children if they are employees) get the maximum tax benefit—but still gives you access to your money. If each of them works for you and owns shares in the company, they may each have their

TABLE 10.2 Tax Deferred Retirement and Savings Plans Available in 2010

Tax Deferred	IRAs	SEPs and KEOGHs	Simple IRAs	Solo 401(k)s
Basic contribution	$5,000	25% of income up to $49,000	11,500	Up to $49,000
Age 50 catch-up	$1,000		2,500	$3000
Income limits–single	$55,000 – $66,000 (1)	$245,000 (2)		
Income limits–joint	$89,000 – $109,000 (1)	$245,000 (2)		
Defined plan limits		$165,000		
Date account must be opened	April 15 of following year	SEP–Due date of your return KEOGH–December 31 of plan year	September 30 of plan year	December 31
Date contribution is due	April 15 of following year	Due date of your tax return, including extensions.	30 days after the end of the month for which you're making contributions.	Due date of your tax return, including extensions.
Pros	Contributions are deductible.	Contributions are deductible May be funded by employer or employee.	3% matching may be paid on due date of return, including extensions.	You may transfer over your IRA balances and borrow up to 50% or $50,000.
		Employer may match with profit-sharing contributions.		

continued

TABLE 10.2 *continued*

Tax Deferred	IRAs	SEPs and KEOGHs	Simple IRAs	Solo 401(k)s
Types of Plans Available		Money purchase, profit sharing, defined benefit		
Cons	Withdrawals are taxable.	Withdrawals are taxable.	Withdrawals are taxable.	If you close the business or the plan, you must pay back the loans or pay penalties and taxes.
Special Rules				
Phase-out	(1) Applies only if covered by qualified plan at work or from your own business.	(2) Income is net business profit or wages per person.		
Contrib: 2005–2007	$4,000	N/A N/A	Increases annually by $1,000 until reaching $10,000.	
Age 50 catch-up	2005–2006 is $500. 2007 forward is $1,000.		Increases in increments of $500 annually Indexed.	
Special Rules		Lets you contribute up to 100% of business earnings or up to 25% of all employees' earnings.	Employer must also match 3% of employee's wages, if employee participates, and/or owner's profits – for Schedule C.	

200

own plan. That means, in a couple of years, you could have access to $100,000 or more easy capital. You may borrow the money without penalties or taxes, as long as you honor the payment plan—and don't shut down the business. Otherwise, you will face early withdrawal penalties and taxes if you don't pay it back.

Defined Benefit Plans

Defined benefit plans are a different animal and require some long-term planning. The concept is to provide you with a specific monthly payout when you retire. To get that payout later, how much do you have to put away now? The older you are, the more you get to put away. The computation is predicated on the three highest consecutive earnings years based on income or wages from your business. The annual benefit limit for 2010 is $165,000. You may contribute as much as 100 percent of those wages to achieve the benefit limit. The plan must be opened before December 31, but it may be funded until you file your tax return, including extensions.

This is an excellent option for anyone wanting to build up plan assets quickly. The biggest objection to these plans is that once you set them up, you are obligated to make the annual payment, even if your business doesn't have the money to cover the costs. So what do you do in lean years? Suspend the plan. But be very careful how you handle this. If you get your timing wrong, the whole plan is invalid and may be subject to penalties. Work with a tax planning professional who really understands this area well. Not all do.

A good tax professional, whether it's an attorney, an enrolled agent, or a certified public accountant, can help you devise the best way to set aside money for the future by letting Uncle Sam give you tax breaks. This will cut the financial pinch so you can live well now—and when you're age 77.

Two last notes:

1. Various tax provisions are designed to sunset (disappear) on December 31, 2010.
2. Your legislature may change all the rules at any time, without warning.

So if you build a retirement plan, be sure to get your professional or trade organization, friends, contacts, chamber colleagues, and family to lobby Congress to keep the provisions intact.

Using the IRS to Your Advantage

Clearly, with the right kind of planning, you can practically wipe out your present tax obligation or at least move much of it to your retirement years, when your earnings are likely to be lower; although I'm finding that many of my clients' earnings are higher during their nonworking years than they were when they were struggling. A nice surprise.

One of the nice surprises they've gotten is Social Security. They didn't really expect it to still be there for them. So let's just address that for a moment. In all our efforts, we've done our best to reduce or eliminate the self-employment taxes paid in. You may want to rethink that strategy.

For those of you who have not built up your Social Security account, you may want to pay in for a while. This may be especially important to immigrants who don't have their 40 quarters paid in through jobs. Have your tax professional help you develop a balanced strategy that cuts your taxes, increases your retirement income— and also ensures that you get the most out of Social Security when you retire.

Benefits Resources

- **U.S. Treasury Resource.** http://www.ustreas.gov/offices/public-affairs/hsa. All about health savings accounts.
- **Section 105 Medical Reimbursement Plan document.** http://www.smbiz. com/sbfrm002.html.
- **Agri-BizPlan.** http://taxsavings105plan.com/agribiz/index.html, (866) 690-2929.
- **Explanation of health savings accounts (HSAs).** http://taxmama.com/ insurance/hsa.
- **eHealthInsurance.com.** http://www.ehealthinsurance.com. Look at the special section for health savings accounts at http://www.ehealthinsurance. com/hsa.
- **Employer-provided child-care facilities credit.** http://www.irs.gov/pub/ irs-pdf/f8882.pdf.
- **IRS Publication 970,** *Tax Benefits for Education.* http://www.irs.gov/ publications/p970/. For education fringe benefits.
- **Pioneer Funds.** http://www.pioneerinvestments.com/default.jhtml. The Pioneer Funds' chart compares contribution limits to various plans for self-employed and incorporated businesses.
- **CNNMoney.com retirement calculator.** http://money.cnn.com/ retirement/tools/index.html.
- **Merrill Lynch.** http://www.businesscenter.ml.com. Click on "Retirement and Benefits" for current information on a variety of plans.

- **TaxMama's overview of the Health Reform Act of 2010.** http://taxquips.com/1/Summary_TaxMama.xls. You will find a breakdown by year for individuals and businesses. This is updated as changes occur.
- **TaxMama's Quick Look-Ups.** http://www.taxmama.com/quick-look-ups. You will find all kinds of useful reference materials, Webinars you can replay, e-books, even the 100% Home-Based Business Tax Solution.
- **Your Business Bible.** http://www.yourbusinessbible.com. Look for worksheets and updates to this book.

✓ CHAPTER 11   ESTIMATED PAYMENTS
To-Do List and Questionnaire

1. Is your business profit over $5,000? ____ Yes ____ No

2. Are you making estimated tax payments? ____ Yes ____ No
   Or have you adjusted your or your spouse's payroll withholding?

3. For ES tax payments, date you set up EFTPS account. _____

4. Date you set up your state e-pay account (if applicable) _____

5. List your estimated tax payments for the year:

Refund applied: IRS amt. _____   State amt. _____ Local amt._____

Date _____ IRS amt. _____   State amt. _____ Local amt._____

Date _____ IRS amt. _____   State amt. _____ Local amt._____

Date _____ IRS amt. _____   State amt. _____ Local amt._____

Date _____ IRS amt. _____   State amt. _____ Local amt._____

Remember to put a copy of each document behind this page, folded in half.

ESTIMATED PAYMENTS

I love giving IRS lots of money. It means I have made a huge fortune!

—TaxMama

Estimated Payments Overview

You're in business now. Cool, isn't it? But your safety net is gone. If you're not on payroll, you don't get any W-2s. For the first time, you have to make your own tax deposits. Your mind is filled with questions.

- When do you make them?
- What forms do you use?
- Where do you send them?
- How much should you pay?
- What's the big deal if you don't make the payments?

Not making payments can cost you big-time! That's one of the two ways to destroy your business and drain your cash flow. (The other way is to skip paying payroll taxes. See Chapter 9 to learn about this important topic.) While it may hurt your wallet a little to make the payments each quarter, it might wipe you out, or worse, to try to pay all the taxes on April 15.

If you want to succeed in business, set the money aside and pay the tax.

What's in It for You?

When you have a system to guide you, life is much less stressful. There's a comfort to knowing how much to budget each month for each of your expenses. Taxes are no different.

If you're a numbers freak, like me, you like to see a nice, steady monthly cash flow statement, with all the numbers being consistent. Knowing how much you'll need to pay the IRS each quarter, you can put a fixed-dollar amount aside each month. You won't have to panic, wondering if you must make up for last quarter and pay a large amount all at once.

Best of all, if you do come up short, the IRS will go out of its way to help you because you've established a consistent history with the agency. It's like a credit history. The IRS is used to dealing with people who are contentious and belligerent. You'll be a breath of fresh air.

Think how easy it will be to get bank or venture capital financing once people see how responsibly you've handled your tax obligations. Lenders and investors get skittish when business owners come to them after having gotten themselves into tax trouble. Naturally, if you're totally brilliant and have a killer product, the "angels" might overlook your financial failings. Of course, they'll charge you more for the money.

Then again, not everyone needs to be paying estimated taxes. After all, if you don't have a profit, you don't need to pay taxes, estimated or otherwise.

Who Should Be Making Estimated Payments?

There are four categories of people who should be paying estimated payments:

1. People who are self-employed
2. People whose nonwage income is increasing (or expected to increase) in the current year
3. People who have done well on the stock market
4. People who have gotten a healthy inheritance (or other windfall), with assets that produce income

Anyone else? For business owners receiving wages, if you expect to owe extra taxes, simply have your tax professional manipulate your payroll tax withholding before year-end. That way, you never have to make estimated payments.

TABLE 11.1 Estimated Payment Schedule

When the 15th falls on a weekend or holiday, it's due on the following business day.		
Quarter	Due Date	Number of Months
1st (Q1)	April 15	3
2nd (Q2)	June 15	2
3rd (Q3)	September 15	3
4th (Q4)	January 15 of following year	4

When Should You Be Making Those Payments?

When we talked about payroll quarterlies in Chapter 9, you learned that "quarterly" means every three months, right? Not when it comes to estimated payments. We're dealing with the tax code here. Some extremely clever lawmakers decided that *quarterly*, for tax purposes, breaks down as indicated in Table 11.1. Notice that sometimes you've got to pay within two months; other times, the quarter is four months long.

How Much Must You Pay?

Before we get into any payment specifics, let's start with some fundamental tips about making estimated tax payments. Keep handy the link found at the end of this chapter to the online version of IRS Publication 505, which is about withholding and estimated tax payments. Changes in the rules will appear there.

You will be using Form 1040-ES (and your state's equivalent). For the current year, look up the instructions to Form 1040-ES—http://www.irs.ustreas.gov/pub/irs-pdf/f1040es.pdf.

Typically, you must only pay estimates *if*

1. You expect to owe $1,000 or more beyond any payroll withholding

and

2. Your withholding or other tax credits (education, children, and so on) will be less than 90 percent of the tax you expect to owe on your current year

tax return. (If your income falls into the "wealthy" or "high-income" levels for the year, you must pay 100 percent of what you expect to owe.)

or

3. Your withholding or other tax credits (education, children, etc.) will be less than 100 percent of the tax shown on your prior year's tax return. If you expect to have losses from the business, don't worry about making estimated tax payments on the business.

Wise heads feel that it is best to pay the minimum required taxes in advance. You can put your money to better uses than the IRS can.

My Short Method

Use this shortcut if your expected taxable income will be the same as or higher than it was last year. It's so simple. Everyone loves using it.

Start with your last year's return.

Look at page 2 of your 1040, where it says—total tax. Let's say it was	$10,000
From that, deduct any withholding you have from any sources (wages, interest, dividends, unemployment). Let's say,	$3,000
Deduct the withholding you expect to have from last year's taxes	$7,000
Divide the result by four quarters ($7,000 ÷ 4)	$1,750

Ta-daaaa! That's how much you should be paying each quarter. That's it. That's all there is to it. Read no further.

That Makes You Nervous? You Want to Pay More?

You'd rather pay just enough to owe nothing next April? OK, increase each of those payments by a couple of hundred dollars.

You don't have to. All you have to do to avoid the penalties is to pay the minimums. Some people prefer to have a small refund. That's fine. Uncle Sam can surely use your money.

You're well within your rights to open a savings account or investment account to hold those funds until it's time to pay. But in today's economic climate it may not be worth going to all that trouble. Earning 1.5 percent interest on my money doesn't excite me. On $5,000, that's $75 of interest for the whole year. Of course, when interest rates rise—or if your additional tax due is much larger—you may have an incentive to hold on to that money.

Cash Flow Strategy: Yes or No?

Some businesses feel they can make better use of this money to grow their operations, so not making estimated payments is part of their strategy. This is not a good idea.

Take the example of the Klaus Company (not the real name), which had a steady stream of work. Klaus's bids were generally accepted for large-ticket jobs. He was able to subcontract some of the work, so he didn't need a payroll. He worked more than 15-hour days on the jobs, usually hundreds or thousands of miles from home. He'd be gone for months at a time. It's not that he didn't want to make the estimated payments. He wasn't home long enough to take care of bookkeeping or administration or to cut the checks. Besides, every time he'd get a job, little disasters beyond his control would occur, wiping out most of the profit on the job. (In one case, he and his crew were not permitted to work during office hours. No one mentioned that when he bid the job.) Often, he'd be working for nothing. While he felt there was no profit at all, the rent and family expenses were being paid. That means he always had lots of self-employment taxes due. Since he didn't set any money aside each quarter, in April there'd be no money. And so he didn't pay the estimates, and he didn't get the bookkeeping done—and he hasn't filed tax returns. He's been behind for the last three years, and the IRS is about to attach his bank accounts.

In another example, Matt and Jamie Garrison of Aluria Software LLC, considering what it would cost them to borrow money, decided to hold back much of the money from their estimated taxes as their business grew. That money could be better used for payroll, payroll taxes, or advertising. As part of their strategy, they knew at the end of each year they had to save money, quickly, to cover the tax debt by April. They didn't always make it. By filing an extension, the Garrisons were able to keep the late-payment penalties to 0.5 percent per month. With IRS interest rates at the lowest in my lifetime, the penalties and interest paid to the IRS were lower than interest rates charged by traditional lenders.

I bring you the story of Aluria Software LLC because Matt and Jamie successfully built it into a million-dollar business. Their strategy did not get them into big trouble. Aluria is one of the few companies that managed its funds successfully using this strategy, until it got bought out—for millions of dollars.

Generally, when companies start tapping into the tax coffers, they're signing the death knell for their business. They end up like Klaus, whose business and marriage are both in jeopardy.

Worst-Case Scenario

Did I forget to tell you? Getting behind on your estimated taxes may destroy your marriage.

There's this whole snowball effect. First last year's estimates. Then this year's taxes. Then the IRS is attaching your bank account or levying your spouse's wages. Then your children start noticing that you're afraid to answer the phone or get the mail. You start losing sleep. Then you start quarreling with your spouse—usually over nothing. I cringe when I get calls from certain clients. I know they're into this loop. They're depressed. They can't work through their problem. They won't follow my advice, and their business starts going down the tubes. Then the spouse calls.

While people are most afraid of going to jail over their tax troubles, that's not the worst thing that can happen to you. After all, in jail you get room and board, plenty of exercise, and a library to use. You won't work any harder than you do now—probably fewer hours, even. The worst thing isn't going to jail. No, the worst thing is staying home—watching your home, family, and reputation fall apart.

Am I scaring you? Well, I'm trying to.

Sorry, my friends, but I've been doing this for a long time, working with people who think the rules don't apply to them. Your tax professional probably isn't dealing with this—he or she is sending those failures to people like me. There are a few of us in each town who work with taxpayers in trouble. We're not the ones running those ads on the radio or television, collecting huge fees. But the pros know who we are. People only come to us by word of mouth. It's a gut-wrenching business. I hate this part of my practice, and all of us in it want to do less of it. The only way for that to happen is to convince you not to get into trouble. So . . . don't monkey with your tax obligations.

If you can't afford your estimated payments now, what makes you think you'll be able to pay them in April? It's time to look at your budget and see what's wrong.

The only solid reason to delay those payments is when your business is cyclical. If much of your income comes in over the Christmas shopping season, for instance, or during the first quarter—you know you'll have the money in time.

Computing Your Estimated Installment Payments

Ideally, at this point in the book, you should sit down with the tax advisor on your team (see Chapter 1 to review). Figure out your payments, project your income, and estimate your profits, from all sources. Prepare for the meeting by making a list of your investments and how much income you expect. Do a realistic projection of your business profits. Your business plan from Chapter 2 and your accounting records from Chapter 4 should come in handy now. Run those numbers through one of the free handy online income tax estimator tools. Use the tax estimator calculators at TurboTax.com, H&R Block, or 1040.com.

Have your tax professional review the results to determine whether to revise your tax projections.

The main reason to use electronic brains like the online calculators is to compute self-employment taxes, Schedule SE (which you learned about in Chapter 9), and alternative minimum taxes, Form 6251. Whenever I see people guesstimating their tax liability, those are the two big surprises they get on April 15. You think you have no taxable income because your mortgage, property taxes, and child tax credit swallowed up your taxes. Then these two taxes rear their ugly heads.

Self-employment taxes amount to 15.3 percent of your business profits from Schedule C or your Schedule 1065 K-1.

The alternative minimum tax limits and rules have changed several times during each presidential administration, and Congress is always talking about changing them. All you need to know is that if your itemized deductions are too high or your income reaches certain levels, you will owe taxes you didn't anticipate. You can easily look up the alternative minimum tax levels by scrolling down this page on the Small Business Taxes and Management Web site—http://www.smbiz.com/sbrl001.html.

The original concept of the alternative minimum tax was to ensure rich people didn't get away without paying taxes. Instead, it's hitting the folks struggling to make ends meet.

There is one bright note about the alternative minimum tax. If you pay it this year, next year it generates an alternative minimum tax *credit* (Form 8801). That might reduce next year's tax—unless you have another alternative minimum tax. Chapter 32 of IRS Publication 17 can tell you more.

These are the kinds of questions and issues to submit to the National Taxpayer Advocate. If you have a solution or a viable suggestion, Nina Olsen, the advocate, is open to your input. She writes an annual report to Congress, outlining problems taxpayers have had with the IRS and the tax system. She proposes fixes, which sometimes become legislation. The submission form is on the IRS Web site at http://www.irs.gov/app/samsnet/IssueQualification.jsp.

Paying the Tax

Naturally, if you have the money, make the payment. Always put the form number, the tax year, and your Social Security number (and your spouse's) on each check. (See the section on FYTIN in Chapter 13.)

The IRS is pushing its electronic federal tax payment system (EFTPS). Once registered, you can make all your estimated payments online. It's actually a great idea. You can make your payment at the last minute, and you'll get proof that you paid it. The input form asks you all the pertinent questions. You're likely to get the payment applied for the correct tax year and to the correct account.

Is that important? You bet. If you don't put the correct information on the check, the IRS doesn't know to which form or year to credit the payment. This comes back to haunt you. It's such fun having the IRS locate your payment and apply it to the right account and year. You'll learn the IRS coded it wrong when you get a CP23 notice of underpayment (discussed in Chapter 13) for a year you thought you'd paid. So, yes, if you have access—pay online.

If you didn't set up an EFTPS, you may pay by credit card. Chapter 13 tells you how. Since the information about how and where to pay changes so rapidly, it needs to be maintained online.

Tips to Reduce Penalties for Underpayment of Estimated Tax

The IRS bases its penalty computation on the date and amount of your payments. Here's a way to make a December payment look like it was paid on time. Change it from an estimated payment to withholding.

Withholding

Did you know that when your taxes are taken out of your paycheck, the IRS treats all the withholding as if it had been paid in evenly throughout the year? Even if you had a total of $1,000 withheld from January through November and then paid in $20,000 in December, the IRS doesn't blink. This is something doctors and lawyers have been doing for decades. But it's not the greatest idea. It means scrambling during the most expensive gift-giving time of the year to come up with big chunks of cash to cover taxes.

While I really don't recommend that you handle your payments that way, it does give you a way to avoid late-payment penalties when you get behind in your estimated payment schedule. After all, if you're reading this book late in the year, there's a chance you haven't kept up with estimated payments until now. You didn't realize how important they were. Now you want to catch up and avoid the penalties.

How does this help when you're in business? If you have a spouse with a job, arrange to increase the withholding for his or her last paychecks of the year. You may even need to deduct everything except $1, so your spouse still gets a check. Will he or she be angry? Not if you hand over the money you would have mailed in for withholding.

When your spouse has a job, it's much easier just to increase his or her withholding all year long. We did that with my husband's paycheck when I operated as a partnership. I didn't need to pay as much each quarter. Now that I am an S-corporation, I am on payroll—and taking withholding out.

Another Withholding Option

When being paid as an independent contractor by your own company or a customer's, you have the option of requesting withholding from your fee. There's even a box on the Form 1099-MISC to allow for this. (See Chapter 9.) Take advantage of this option and deduct withholding from each remittance, if it can make your life easier.

Note: Beware! If you have a tendency to be behind on your tax payments, the IRS can mandate that your clients and customers take withholding from your fees and checks.

Annualized Payments Method

When you file your tax return, use the worksheet on page 4 of Form 2210, Underpayment of Estimated Taxes by Individuals. With good bookkeeping software, getting the information you need is easy. You must be able to compute your net profits from January through the end of these months: April, June, September, and December. Armed with this information, you or your tax pro will have to allocate your deductions to each period. You'll need to know when you paid big medical bills, made large charitable donations, or bought the expensive employee tool. Apply all the deductions to the appropriate time frame. Then follow the computations. Better yet, have a computer do it.

I'll tell you right now, unless you owe tens of thousands of dollars' worth of tax, the time investment to fill in this page is prohibitive. Remember, you might save $100 in penalties and pay your tax pro $150 to work out the numbers. (It's not that bad, but it should be.)

This is only worth doing if the substantial part of your income was received in the last three months of the year—or your big expenses happened in the beginning of the year. Otherwise, it won't save you much.

Don't Overpay Your Estimates If You're in Trouble

Perhaps in the past you got into trouble with the IRS or a state. Perhaps you have a former spouse chasing after you for support. Or suppose you've defaulted on your student loan or ignored traffic tickets. Until you clear up those problems, the IRS will be grabbing your refunds. In your case, you're better off owing a little bit, rather than shooting for a big refund. You won't get it.

The best idea, however, is to clear up those old debts or get on a payment plan (which we'll discuss in Chapter 13) so the IRS doesn't embarrass you in your business. The last thing you need is for your employees or vendors to get wind of your tax woes.

Basically, though, if you just follow the guidelines at the beginning of this chapter, the whole process is easy.

Estimated Payment Resources

- **Form 1040-ES, Estimated Tax for Individuals.** http://www.irs.gov/pub/irs-pdf/f1040es.pdf.
- **Form 2210, Underpayment of Estimated Taxes by Individuals.** http://www.irs.gov/pub/irs-pdf/f2210.pdf.
- **Form 6251, Alternative Minimum Tax—Individuals, Estates, and Trusts.** http://www.irs.gov/pub/irs-pdf/f6251.pdf.
- **Form 8801, Credit for Prior Year Alternative Minimum Tax—Individuals.** http://www.irs.gov/pub/irs-pdf/f8801.pdf.
- **IRS Publication 17, Chapter 32.** http://www.irs.gov/publications/p17/ch32.html.
- **IRS Publication 505, *Withholding and Estimated Payments*.** http://www.irs.gov/publications/p505/ch02.html.

- **Links to all states' tax forms.** http://www.taxadmin.org/fta/link/forms.html.
- **TaxMama's payment and installment agreement information.** http://taxmama.com/?s=payment+and+installment.
- **The Taxpayer Advocate's Suggestion Page.** http://www.improveirs.org/default.shtml.
- **Thomas, the Library of Congress's searchable legislation database.** http://thomas.loc.gov.
- **TurboTax Income Tax Liability Estimator and other tools.** http://turbotax.intuit.com/tax-tools.
- **H&R Block Tax Liability Estimator and other calculators and tools.** http://www.hrblock.com/taxes/tax_tips_calculators/index.html.
- **Small Business Taxes & Management Web site quick lookup for AMT, and other annual limits.** http://www.smbiz.com/sbrl001.html.
- **TaxMama's Quick Look-Ups.** http:// www.taxmama.com/quick-look-ups. You will find all kinds of useful reference materials, Webinars you can replay, e-books, even the 100% Home-Based Business Tax Solution.
- **Your Business Bible.** http:// www.yourbusinessbible.com. Look for worksheets and updates to this book.

✓ **CHAPTER 12   SPECIAL CONSIDERATIONS FOR ONLINE BUSINESSES**
To-Do List and Questionnaire

1. Do you have an online business? ____ Yes ____ No

2. Where is your nexus?

   Home state _____ Fulfillment state _____

   State incorporated _____ Affiliate states _____

   States with virtual workers or consultants _____

3. In which states must you register your business?

   _____   _____   _____

4. With what agencies did you register in each state?

   ____ Secretary of state (for LLC or Corp)

   ____ Sales tax department

   ____ Employment tax department

   ____ Income or franchise tax department

   ____ City business license(s)

5. Do you need to revoke any affiliate relationships in states where laws are too stringent or expensive to comply with? ____ Yes ____ No

6. Dates notices went to affiliates—by state:

   _____   _____   _____

   _____   _____   _____

Remember to put a copy of each document behind this page, folded in half.

SPECIAL CONSIDERATIONS FOR ONLINE BUSINESSES

Internet Riches Made Easy! How I made $30,000 in 42 days

—Spam e-mail

WWW = Who, What, Where?

In 1996, when talking to radio and television talk show hosts about an Internet site I had created, I had to devote most of that precious on-air time to explaining what the Internet was, how to get on it, and how to use the site's address to find the site.

We've come a long way, baby! We've learned the jargon. We can find Web sites, with or without their www's. We can tweet, post on Facebook, IM our friends, or text all day.

Today, no business is complete without a Web site. Even if you sell nothing, it's vitally important to establish a Web presence. You certainly want to secure ownership of the uniform resource locator (URL) that is your business's name.

Your Web site provides information about your business for your clients or customers to access when you're not available. We are all faced with questions our customers ask over and over again. You can easily provide the information online. With the right software and security, even a small company can arrange for clients, vendors, and customers to look up their own accounts, make corrections, and find information.

The Web offers many time-saving tools. It's easy to set up an online database with your clients' contact information. In fact, many accounting programs integrate with MS Word or Symantec's ACT!, Outlook, or your iPhone, Blackberry, or favorite portable communications device. You can e-mail all your clients instantly when something important happens. Or you can target just a few—just those with children, for example. You simply write the message and click—and they have it. They can respond instantly.

Compare that to the time and cost of writing to a hundred people. You print out all the letters, stuff the envelopes, add postage, and get everything to the post office before the last pickup. The Internet offers so many time-saving applications that you can kill a lot of time, saving time. In fact, you can get lost for hours, can't you?

All kidding aside, once you stick your toe into the Internet's web, you're stuck forever. And all kinds of new tax issues and questions surface.

What? I Thought There Was No Internet Tax

You're so right. For now, no one may assess you taxes for your use of the Internet.[1] In fact, the Internet tax moratorium bill (HR 3678) passed in October 2007, extending the moratorium on Internet taxes for another seven years.[2]

Unfortunately, though, that doesn't mean you don't have to pay taxes on the Internet. The legislation only refers to communications activities—being connected to the Internet—access, online services, and hosting services. You can't pay a separate Internet tax for that. But you are paying taxes, nonetheless.

Have you looked at your phone bill lately? You know, the bill for the phone line you use to be connected—even if it's a DSL line or cable.

One of my recent phone bills shows:

Federal Subscriber Line Charge	$8.98	
9-1-1 Emergency System	.29	
CA High Cost Fund Surcharge—A	.08	
CA High Cost Fund Surcharge—B	.98	
Universal Lifeline Telephone Surcharge	.48	
Rate Surcharge Credit	2.54	(no explanation)
State Regulatory Fee	.05	
CA Relay Service and Communications Devices Fund	.13	(no one asked if I wanted to donate this!)
Federal Universal Services Fee	.78	

---

1. The Internet Tax Freedom Act, available at http://en.wikipedia.org/wiki/Internet_Tax_Freedom_Act.

2. Internet Tax Freedom Amendments Act of 2007 at http://thomas.loc.gov/cgi-bin/bdquery/z?d110:HR03678:

Federal Taxes at 3.00 percent	1.49
Local Taxes at 10.00 percent	4.96
Total Taxes and Surcharges	$17.68

Holy baloney! That adds 17 percent to each of my phone bills. Are you telling me there are no Internet taxes?

Also, nowhere does any federal law say anything about not taxing income earned online or prevent charging taxes on sales of products and services.

The question is, of course, where will you be taxed? To answer that, you must know your nexus.

Nexus

What an odd word—*nexus*. What is it? A car? A telephone company? A quickie photo shop? No! *Nexus* means a place where you have a business presence. It sounds pretty simple, doesn't it?

Not according to Diana DiBello, formerly director of product development at SpeedTax Inc. (http://www.speedtax.com), formerly with Vertex Inc. DiBello is one of the top people in the country who have seen the broad picture. She used nearly 80 PowerPoint slides to explain the complexity of this question to an audience of tax professionals. While the average small business owner doesn't need to know *that* much information, he or she does need to understand the information that typically affects small businesses.

Start by answering this question correctly: Where is your business located?

- Is it in your home?
- Is it at your office?
- Is it where your Web site's server is located?
- Is it where your Webmaster is located?
- Is it where your post office box is located?
- Is it where you've incorporated?
- Is it where you're drop-shipping your products?
- Is it where your salespeople are?
- Is it where your affiliates (commissioned sales force) are?
- Is it where your related companies are?
- Is it where your merchant account receives your money?
- Is it where your virtual assistant is located?
- Is it where your online shopping cart is hosted?

- Is it where your mailing list is hosted?
- Is it where your advertising agency or public relations agency is?
- Is it where you're running your ads?
- Is it where your shoppers or customers are located?

Are you starting to get the picture? A business's nexus can be widespread. But the good news is that with the advent of the Internet, home-based businesses can have customers all over the globe. Literally.

Why Do We Care about Nexus?

Nexus costs money. Even when you don't think you have a physical presence in a state, that state might believe it has the right to your money. State governments are hungry. With the slump in the economy after the wild ride in the 1990s and again in the early 2000s, state revenues have dropped dramatically. With more people shopping over the Internet, states are also losing the sales taxes they used to count on.

Having to make up the money somewhere, states have tapped into anyone they feel is operating within their reach. And they've won. There are solid legal precedents for states to assess income and sales taxes from people and companies that lightly brush the boundaries of their domain.

Perhaps you remember that infamous day in 1991 when Michael Jordan, playing for the Chicago Bulls, was hit by the state of California for a share of his earnings. David Hoffman, Tax Foundation economist and author of the "jock tax" report, explains: "The jock tax began with California trying to get back at Michael Jordan for beating the Lakers in 1991 and Illinois fought back with a retaliatory tax the next year. Ironically, if Jordan rejoined the Bulls in any capacity, he would find himself paying double taxes."[3]

Once other states learned that California had succeeded in taxing a transient, they too started to see this as a lucrative new means to replenish their depleted treasuries. The "jock tax" now affects all performers traveling across state lines, traveling sales folks, even Internet businesses. Many of my clients are affected. These days, their employers routinely provide W-2s with all the states' incomes and withholdings. Some of my film industry clients get three or four W-2s from the same employer for the same show.

As I predicted in the first edition of this book, this has become a major issue for online retailers. In particular, this is affecting the affiliate marketing community—

---

3. Tax Foundation report—Washington, D.C., July 14, 2003: "'Jock Taxes' Spread as State and City Governments Try to Maximize Revenue from Nonresidents," available at http://www.taxfoundation. org/research/topic/1.html.

companies that sell their products online with the help of people like you, who put links on your Web site to promote companies. You do this with Amazon.com, VistaPrint, the *Wall Street Journal*, and more. New York was the first state to get really aggressive about forcing online retailers based out of state to start charging sales tax if they had affiliates in New York. Now you have Colorado, too. California is considering it. Commission Junction is keeping tabs on the situation, since it is one of the major players in the affiliate marketplace. You can find the Commission Junction Internet tax map at http://www.cj.com/news/internet_tax.html.

Once you start making a lot of money online, if you're not aware of how the nexus rules and definitions affect your business, you might find yourself paying taxes to a state you've never visited.

For now, most likely, state income taxes on your earnings won't be your big problem. But sales taxes will be. You'll also face a problem with those 1099s we discussed in Chapter 9. We'll talk about both these issues now.

Where Is My Nexus?

I sit here in my living room; it is my principal office. I have several Web sites. One of the servers is in Colorado. I don't even know where the other one is. One of my mailing list servers is in Minnesota, or at least the company I pay is. The company may be hosting its server in China, for all I know. My Web designer is in Arizona. One of my corporations is in Nevada; the other is in California. My partners for various ventures are in India, New York, and Portugal. I have mailing addresses in Nevada and California, but my sites' shopping carts are in England and Missouri. The payment-processing center is in Utah. My tax returns are electronically transmitted to the IRS from a company in Maine. My tax clients are in Africa, Asia, South America, North America, Europe, Australia, New Zealand . . . My affiliates, those people who get a commission for selling my products or referring clients to me, are all over the world.

With all this information, where is my nexus? And what part of it is affected by tax laws?

You're beginning to see how unclear this can be, even for a small home-based business, once you take it online.

Internet Sales Tax Issues

Many people believe because the Internet is so new—and the topic of online taxes is so new—that new ground will have to be broken to establish guidelines for when and how taxes are paid.

Actually, that's not really true. It's only new to you, because, suddenly, your local business is selling nationwide or even internationally.

The sales tax issues involved with online transactions are the same ones the mail-order industry has been facing for decades. Currently, domestic sales tax issues are governed by your state's sales tax department. But what will happen in the long run? The states are getting together to create a system and software that collects sales tax from shoppers, remits it to the correct state automatically, and doesn't require the vendor to file forms in those other states. For more information on how states are working together, take a look at the Streamlined Sales Tax Project (http://streamlinedsalestax.org). It's still a long way from being implemented. Actually, what the states really want is for the federal government to mandate that companies, nationwide, charge sales taxes based on the destination state. DiBello suggests that even if a law like this passes, it's only practical for the large national companies. There will be thresholds designed to exclude small businesses.

I have no faith in that threshold level. These are the same legislators who think that a luxury auto is any car that costs more than $14,800 and that $100,000 is high income.

What do you do now? DiBello recommends that you stay tuned in to the status of the legislation so that when it does affect you, you're prepared.

In the meantime, should you simply ignore sales taxes for out-of-state shoppers?

Sales Tax Case Law

DiBello recently cited interesting situations where states went after companies that have no business presence in a state. Connecticut, for instance, sued Dell Computer for unpaid sales taxes because Dell contracted with a company to provide local service on customers' computers. The Connecticut Superior Court ruled against the state only because of the low volume of service calls. If the volume of repairs were higher, Dell would be paying sales tax in Connecticut.

Dell got hit because it simply had a contract with a local company.

What about your business?

Perhaps you're using an affiliate program or agents to sell your products on their own Web sites or in their own locales. You might just have created an "agency nexus" in their states. An agency nexus occurs when you have a representative in a state. Exactly what constitutes an agent depends on how aggressive the state is.

In another instance, the Scholastic Corporation was hit by California. You're familiar with Scholastic products. The *Junior Scholastic* magazines are in every dentist's office. We all got Scholastic books and publications in school, even preschool. That's how the publisher got into trouble. Scholastic sold books to students by having their teachers give them order forms and collecting the money. The California

Supreme Court held that because the teachers in California schools sell Scholastic's products, Scholastic does have nexus.

Think about how your business and sales avenues are structured. Will agency nexus affect you?

Sales Tax Nexus and Your Business

Because online sales tax is such a hot issue, I want to make sure you receive the best information possible. Until speaking with DiBello, I took a conservative approach to sales tax collections. I had been advising clients and readers that if they started shipping a high volume of sales to a state, it would be wise to register with that state's sales tax authority.

After all, you don't really pay the sales taxes. You collect them from your customers and pass them along to the state. The money only comes out of your pocket if you don't collect but should.

DiBello clarifies a common misconception about your nexus. Just because you ship a lot of merchandise into any state does not mean you have to collect the sales tax. Under the current status of U.S. sales tax laws, to be required to collect sales tax, you must have "physical nexus" in that state. What do the physical nexus rules mean?

1. You must have a physical presence in the state.
2. There must be sufficient benefit to the merchant from the taxes.
3. The taxes can't interfere with interstate commerce or give the merchant unfair advantage.

This basically means that unless you have an office or store in that state, you don't need to worry about collecting sales taxes on your out-of-state sales.

But hiring a contractor or agent in another state to represent you, along with the agent's other companies, falls under the rules of agency nexus. Of course, if you place your own agent in a state and that person represents you exclusively, you've just established a physical presence in that state. For instance, the state of California has a tax collections office in Florida, where many former Californians have retired. California has nexus in Florida. Do you think the state of Florida should be taxing California on the taxes it collects?

You do have to comply with your own state's rules, but you already know that. You registered with your state's sales tax department for in-state sales when you went through your checklist in Chapter 1.

You have nothing more to worry about, right?

Not so fast. There are still those services you're using. What about them?

Rents and Services — Domestic and Abroad

Since I started operating on the Internet in early 1995, it became clear to me that federal tax issues were going to emerge. As early as 1998, IRS spokesman Ed Mieszerski ruefully admitted, "Some of these questions [dealing with online taxes] will only be dealt with when they come before us as a result of an examination or court case."[4]

To date, I haven't seen an IRS case addressing these issues head-on. But we will, and you need to make sure you have protection in place when these issues start to arise. To avoid problems, you need to be aware of the issues. Following are some real-life scenarios and some points to ponder.

Incorporated in Nevada (no state income tax), Starry-Eyed, Inc., is based at home in California and receives money from sales of products. The company's inventory is stored and shipped from a fulfillment house located in Pennsylvania. The Web site is hosted on a server in New York. Starry-Eyed encountered the following questions—the answers should help you stay legal, too.

Q: *As a corporation, can it deduct office-in-home costs? (As a proprietor it can, so . . .)*

A: Treat your office at home the way you would if you weren't doing business online. Chapter 7 explains the rules.

Q: *In which state is it conducting business? All work, including design, artwork, search engine placement, etc., is often done by people working from their homes, often across the country. Under what circumstances would those workers be employees? Will the company have to file income, sales, or property tax forms in each (or any) state?*

A: Consider your business nexus to be only those states where you have a physical presence. Comply with all local rules.

---

4. In a memo to the author, in response to Internet-related tax questions, for use in the 1998 Insiders Series Workshops for tax professionals in Burbank, California.

Q: *Should the company be sending a 1099-MISC to the Web hosts (those hosting the actual site) for rent?*

A: The Web server rent is unclear. If you want to be safe, send the 1099-MISC for rent.

Q: *Some work is being done by foreign nationals in their own country. Since payment is being made for services rendered, how does the company "1099" a foreigner? Must it issue a 1099? Must the company take any backup withholding?*

A: Don't send 1099s to foreign individuals or companies outside the country that do work for you. If you knowingly hire a U.S. citizen or someone who holds a green card who works overseas, issue the 1099-MISC. Don't withhold taxes unless the IRS sends you a withholding order on that person. Review the 1099 instructions in Chapter 9 for guidance.

Roger B. Adams, an enrolled agent in Portugal (http://vur.me/taxmama/ International_Expert), answered a similar question in the TaxQuips Forum (http://taxmama.com/forum):

Ingrid's question: What do I do with the affiliates that are in Canada, Australia, or any other foreign country? Is there a set form like the W-9 that they need to fill out?

Roger's answer: Essentially this is a treaty issue. The income you are paying these people is characterized as commission, and they are performing "independent personal services"; thus the treaty article covering that type of payment is the one that applies. That kind of income can only be taxed in the country of residence of the person you are paying. Rita is absolutely correct; they need to send you a W8-BEN claiming the appropriate treaty article.

On the other hand, if they are U.S. citizens or green card holders, they submit a W-9 to you, and you send them the 1099-MISC.

However, if no treaty exists between the United States and your affiliate in another country, you as "payor" must withhold 30 percent of the payment and send that off to the Treasury and the balance to the "payee."

To make things just a little more complicated, they must get an ITIN to claim the treaty benefit. That is where the real problem will present itself, as this is no easy task for those abroad.

Let's look at another company with some different issues.

I Can Sell Anything to Anyone (ICSATA) is based in the United States, and its Web site also is hosted here. The company operates an associate or affiliate program. Other Web sites link to ICSATA's site—and ICSATA pays the linked companies a commission on whatever sales arise from those links (this is similar to how Amazon.com operates). Many of the companies that are linked are overseas businesses. The questions to consider here include:

Q: *Is this a commission, referral fee, royalty . . . what?*

A: When someone is a contributor to the design, content, or substance of your product or services, and he or she is contractually entitled to a share of the sales, it's royalty. Otherwise, you're paying commissions. Chapter 5 explains why we care about the distinction.

Q: *Is any of this subject to self-employment tax?*

A: When regular salespeople receive commissions, it's self-employment income. Why shouldn't this be? Chapter 11 explains self-employment taxes.

Frequently, when you ask the IRS these types of questions, you'll receive a vague answer. The above answers provide the most sensible approach for you to use until the IRS issues formal guidelines.

Legal Issues on the Internet

Once your business touches the Internet, you're going to be hit with some powerful legal issues, and you won't realize it until you get into trouble. The best guide to this topic is attorney Jonathan I. Ezor's book *Clicking Through: A Survival Guide for Bringing Your Company Online*.

So many things can affect you, even if you're just minding your own business:

- **You face copyright issues.** For instance, did your Web designer give you a written release for all the graphics and design? Or does he or she own your site?
- **You face liability issues.** You have affiliates marketing your product or service. They say something that isn't true, without your permission. You're the one getting sued.

- **You face spam issues.** You think you're sending out a simple newsletter. But one recipient becomes violently upset and decides he or she never subscribed. What do you do?
- **You have liability issues.** You are running someone's ads on your site. Perhaps you have banners through an affiliate program. You might be using Google's Adsense service. Someone clicks on an ad and is unhappy with the product. Are you liable?
- **You face privacy issues.** Issues with privacy can become very nasty. Suppose someone hacks your site or telephone book and steals client information. Or suppose you do something with a sponsor that results in the sponsor gaining access to your clients' e-mail. Your members can get really unpleasant if they feel invaded.

Overall, we're just scratching the surface of Internet issues. But don't let the worries get to you. Resources like Ezor's book will keep you safe.

The World Wide Web is an exciting environment. It can make your dreams come true. It did for me and for many of the people I know. The streets are virtually paved with gold. As I've said before, the Internet has the pioneering spirit and excitement of the Old West—law just hasn't been established yet. Getting there is lots of fun.

In the End

Most issues related to Internet taxation are unclear and apt to change. You now know you don't have to worry about sales taxes across borders. For all the other areas, when questions arise, treat them the way you would if you were not doing business online. If you're not sure, check with your advisory team for guidance. And if your advisory team can't give you reliable guidance, you can always try Tax-Mama's TaxQuips Forum. One of our tax professional members will either have an answer or be able to point you to a resource that can help you.

Online Business Resources

- **Vertex Inc.** http://vertexinc.com. This authority on all sales tax issues—and other business tax issues—publishes software and reference materials for companies engaged in interstate commerce. Sign up for a free newsletter.

- **The Tax Foundation.** http://www.taxfoundation.org. Find tax facts, statistics, and in-depth analyses of federal and state governments.
- **Streamlined Sales Tax Project.** http://streamlinedsalestax.org. This is a cooperative effort by most U.S. states to create a universal sales tax system to allow them to collect sales taxes on Internet sales.
- **Senate Finance Committee.** http://finance.senate.gov. See it before it becomes law.
- **Performance Marketing Association.** http://performancemarketingassociation. com. This is a not-for-profit trade association founded in 2008 by the leaders of the performance marketing industry to connect, inform, and advocate on behalf of this rapidly growing field. It is an excellent source of information about the sales tax issues related to nexus.
- **Commission Junction Internet tax map.** http://www.cj.com/news/internet_ tax.html.
- **TaxMama.com.** http://taxmama.com. The Ask TaxMama feature is free. Pose your question. If it hasn't been asked dozens of times before, you'll get an answer.
- **Google's Adsense.** http://adsense.google.com. If your Web site provides useful information, Google can provide advertising revenues for your site. Once accepted, you simply paste Google's code on your site, and Google sells the advertising. The software reads the content on your page and serves advertisements related to the content. People are excited, saying it adds value to their articles or information. The income is terrific—and you never have to sell an ad or give out information about your demographics.
- **Google's AdWords.** https://adwords.google.com/select. Use this to advertise and to test your advertising campaigns.
- **Ingenio-Live advice.** http://www.ingenio.com/categorylist/Taxes/41. Seek out a tax professional, based on the person's area of expertise and satisfaction rating. Please note that this site offers advice for a low fee and that satisfaction is guaranteed—expertise is not. There are more than a hundred tax professionals with all levels of expertise. Ingenio allows you to call the tax professional directly and pay only for your time online.
- **The National Association of Tax Professionals.** http://www.natptax.com, (800) 839-0001. Professionals will provide written responses to your tax questions, with citations supporting their answers. Like the site above, the advice on this site is also offered for a low fee, and satisfaction is also guaranteed.
- **Jest for Pun.** http://www.workinghumor.com/jfp/index.htm. The source of some humorous quotations used in this book.

- *Clicking Through: A Survival Guide for Bringing Your Company Online* by **Jonathan I. Ezor**. http://www.clickingthrough.com. You can read an excerpt of the book here.
- **Nolo.com.** http://vur.me/taxmama/Nolo_Internet_Sales_Tax. Legal books, articles, and information, including information about Internet sales tax issues.
- **TaxMama's Quick Look-Ups.** http://www.taxmama.com/quick-look-ups. You will find all kinds of useful reference materials, Webinars you can replay, e-books, even the 100% Home-Based Business Tax Solution.
- **Your Business Bible.** http://www.yourbusinessbible.com. Look for worksheets and updates to this book.

✓ CHAPTER 13   TAX NOTICES, AUDITS, AND COLLECTION NOTES
To-Do List and Questionnaire

1. Do you get IRS notices after you file your tax return? ____ Yes ____ No

2. To understand them, find your usual notices using the notice numbers in this chapter. (The notice number is at the top, right side of letter.)

3. To avoid audits, take these steps—review your business now:

   a. ____Make sure your address is current. If not, file a change of address, Form 8822.
   Date filed _____

   b. ____ Report ALL your income, even if you did not receive a Form 1099-MISC. *Note:* You are responsible for your own bookkeeping.

   c. ____ Remember to report all cash and barter income. Date entered on books _____

   d. ____Use separate a bank account and credit card for your business and personal activities. Date accounts set up _____

   e. If this is your only source of income, review your PROFIT to see if it makes sense compared with your lifestyle. If not, explain why when you file your tax return—what is your source of support? (Be prepared to prove it, if audited.)

      • Credit cards and loans

      • Savings and investment income

      • Family and friends

Remember to put a copy of each document behind this page, folded in half.

TAX NOTICES, AUDITS, AND COLLECTION NOTES

Blood's not thicker than money.

—Groucho Marx

This chapter will walk you through some of the routine or terrifying interactions you will have with the IRS. Whenever you get notices about audits or owing money, don't just ignore the notices. Always address them. If you are afraid or uncomfortable about dealing with the IRS alone, engage the services of a good local tax professional who understands how to handle audit or collections issues. Not all tax pros do. Ask them to tell you how much experience they have—and if they're successful. If they complain about all their problems with the IRS, move on. The real pros know how to get right to the key people who can help you.

Dealing with Basic Tax Notices for Individual Returns

When you file a tax return—or don't file—sometimes, there may be errors or you will have a balance due. The IRS has a series of standard notices it sends you. Each notice has a little CP code on the top right-hand corner of the first page of the letter. *CP* stands for "computer paragraph."

The notices are issued in a particular timed sequence by the IRS computer. If you don't respond in time for someone to receive your response and key it into the computer, it will automatically spit out the next one. If you are mailing a response right at the end of the response period, call the IRS immediately. Ask the agency to put a hold on any collections actions until it receives your information. Let me repeat—*call the IRS*. Don't just hope it will get your response in time. And when you call, always be sure to write down the name of the person you speak with, his or her IRS employee number, and the date and time of the conversation. (The person will give you that information at the beginning of each conversation. But he or she will say it quickly, so don't overlook it. If necessary, ask the person to repeat the name slowly—and to spell it for you.) Follow up with a written note to the IRS or that employee, summarizing your conversation.

Incidentally, if you get the right person (or the right group), he or she may be able to accept your information over the phone and the fax. If a person has helped you, it's always nice if you send a thank you letter. Remember, even though the agency is the big, bad IRS, you are dealing with real live people who have jobs and families. A nice letter in their file does two things. First, it could help them get a raise or a promotion. Second, a copy stays with your file, too, and alerts the IRS that you are a nice person. In the future, that could work in your favor.

The IRS has added many more notices to its repertoire. It has also been redesigning its notices. A *San Francisco Chronicle* journalist and I were puzzling over the changes. We weren't sure they were really improvements. But the IRS is trying.

A Key to Certain IRS Notices

- **CP 08—Additional Child Tax Credit.** You may qualify for the additional child tax credit and be entitled to some additional money.
- **CP 11—Changes to Tax Return, Balance Due.** Generally based on the math in your return. You probably owe this. Pay it.
- **CP 11A—Changes to Tax Return and Earned Income Credit, Balance Due.** Generally based on the math in your return and information the IRS has cross-referenced about your dependents. Or you have not provided information about the dates of birth of your dependents. Call the IRS to see if you can provide better information about your dependents to save your earned income credit.
- **CP 12—Math Error—Overpayment of $1 or More.** You still have a refund coming, but it may be lower than you expected. Look for child tax credit adjustments or disallowed dependents because of a Social Security number mismatch. *You have 60 days to respond or pay.* Compare the numbers on the notice with those on your tax return. The IRS's adjustment may be wrong. Or you may never have gotten a check from the IRS. Respond in writing before the deadline, with your explanation.
- **CP 14—Balance Due, No Math Error.** This is the computation of the underpayment penalties and interest to your tax return. It may also include

late filing or payment penalties. *You have 21 days to respond or pay.* You can reduce the underpayment of estimated tax penalty if most of your income was received toward the end of the year. Use the annualized income installment method of computing your penalties, found on page 4 of Form 2210, Underpayment of Estimated Tax by Individuals, Estates, and Trusts.

- **CP 23—We Changed Your Estimated Tax Total, You Have an Amount Due.** Perhaps one or more of the checks you thought were estimated payments were something else (perhaps payments for last year's tax). It's also possible that you sent a check but didn't write the correct year, form number, or Social Security number on it. The IRS may have your money but hasn't applied it to any specific year. Find your canceled check and make very clean photocopies of both the front and back. Send the check to the IRS with the notice and your explanation. *You have 21 days to respond or pay.*

- **CP 24—We Changed Your Estimated Tax Total, You Are Due a Refund.** Quite often, you either haven't recorded a payment to the IRS or didn't remember that you applied last year's refund to this return. The second page of the notice will show a list of the payments and dates the checks were received by the IRS. *There is no need to reply.* By the time you get the notice, the IRS will already have sent the check. However, it may be giving you credit for a payment you intended for a different year. Since you're getting the money back, you might not care. But it may involve an estimated payment that you had made on time for the current year—and now you'll get hit with underpayment of estimated penalties. To avoid this problem in the future, make sure you always write the following three pieces of information on each check you send to any government agency. TaxMama's acronym FYTIN may help you remember:

- *F.* The form number.
- *Y.* The tax year you're paying (use a separate check for each year).
- *TIN.* The taxpayer identification number (TIN)—your Social Security number (SSN) or employer identification number (EIN)—to credit with this payment. If you are paying money in toward a married filing joint return, list both SSNs.

   If the IRS sends you a refund for a payment that was intended as an estimate and you shouldn't have gotten the refund, do this: (1) Write "VOID" on it. (2) Make a copy. (3) Send it back with a letter explaining that you want that money applied to your account. Specify the tax form and year. This will prevent penalties for a tax you did mean to pay.

- **CP 31—Your Refund Check Was Returned to the IRS.** Contact the IRS immediately with your correct address. File Form 8822 to report your change of address formally.
- **CP 45—Unable to Apply Your Overpayment to Your Estimated Taxes.** The IRS found math errors in your tax return; or you included withholding or estimated tax payments that were not on record. That means your estimated taxes will be underpaid. Check your records to see if you made a payment last year that the IRS does not show. If so, contact the IRS and send copies of the canceled check or other proof of payment. If it is not an IRS error, make additional payments using Form 1040-ES.
- **CP 49—Overpaid Tax Applied to Other Taxes You Owe.** The IRS will send you this notice if you owe money for prior years. You might also get one of these if you owe back child or spousal support, state income taxes, or motor vehicle fines. The IRS will also grab your refund if you've defaulted on student loans or owe money to the Social Security Administration. The notice will spell out which years or debts are being paid. Often, the money isn't staying with the IRS. When the money is sent to another agency, you'll have to get a release from that agency. When that's the case, don't even waste your time trying to get more information about the outstanding debt from the IRS. It won't have it. You'll have to go to the source, for instance, the motor vehicle department, the district attorney's office, and so on. You'll need to contact the agency that initiated the lien on your refund. Sometimes you get an unpleasant surprise, learning about an old IRS balance you didn't know about or forgot. Track down the details. While the IRS may have only grabbed $39 this year, don't just shrug it off as being too small to matter. It might take $3,000 next year.
- **CP 90/CP 297/CP 297A—Final Notice—Notice of Intent to Levy and Notice of Your Right to a Hearing.** You will only get this notice if you have ignored all the other notices. *You have 30 days to respond or pay.* If you know you owe the money, call the IRS to work out a payment plan or an offer in compromise (OIC). Ask the IRS to put a hold on the collections activity until you either file the OIC or start the payment plan. Once you're on the plan, the IRS will hold off as long as you're current on your payments.
- **CP 91/CP 298—Final Notice before Levy on Social Security Benefits.** See CP 90/CP 297/CP 297A above.
- **CP 161—No Math Error—Balance Due.** This is the business version of CP 14.
- **CP 501—Reminder Notice—Balance Due.** *You have 10 days to respond or pay.*
- **CP 504—Urgent Notice—We Intend to Levy on Certain Assets.** Respond within 10 days or lose your state tax refund. The IRS will also start locating

and levying bank accounts, wages, or other funds it knows where to find. (If you have a government contract or 1099s have been filed under your Social Security number—watch out.) *Note:* If your bank or employer calls to tell you your wages or bank account has been levied or garnished, don't panic. The bank and your employer must hold those funds for 20 days to give you time to fix the problem. How can you solve the problem? First get a copy of the levy notice they received. Then call the IRS *immediately*. If you can set up a payment plan or get the agency to agree to give you some time (typically 30 to 45 days), you'll be able to get the IRS to release the levy.

- **Good news.** The bank levy only lets the IRS grab the money in the account on the day it receives the levy. Any money deposited afterward is safe—until the next levy.
- **Bad news.** If wages are garnished, that deduction continues until you get the IRS to release the garnishment or until you pay the balance in full.
- **CP 523—Notice of Default on Installment Agreement.** When you signed the IA, you gave the IRS your bank account numbers and the permission to levy if you didn't make your payments. Now it will. *Call immediately.* (See CP 90/CP 297/CP 297A above.) You have 30 days to sort this out. If you have a problem, the IRS is willing to help you modify your IA or put it on hold if you are unemployed or disabled.
- **CP 2000—Notice of Proposed Adjustment for Underpayment/ Overpayment.** This notice results from the IRS's computers matching up all the W-2s, 1099s, 1098s, and K-1s issued under your SSN. Quite often, the notices are wrong. Or they are reporting stock sales on which you had losses anyway. The information is reported somewhere on your tax return. Review the notice carefully. If the IRS is wrong, call the phone number on the form immediately and ask for another 30 days to respond. That way, if it takes a while for your response to reach the IRS, it won't already be billing you. When the IRS is right, it's because you left off employment income (perhaps a brief job early in the year) or dividends you forgot about. If the IRS is correct, just pay the bill. You don't need to file an amended return. *You have 30 days to respond or pay.*
- **Letter 1615 (LT 18)—Reminder—We Have Not Received Your Tax Return.** The IRS's records show payments or credits for this year. Prepare and file the return. (See CP 515.) Or if you have already filed it, clearly, the IRS doesn't have it. So send it again. Be sure to stamp it as a copy (or write "Copy" over it). Sign it, dating it the same date that you originally filed it. If you never filed a return—prepare one and file it now.

More Notices

We don't have room to list all the notices. You will find the current list on the IRS Web site at http://vur.me/taxmama/IRS-Notices.

Anytime you get a notice, the IRS recommends you call the phone number listed on the letter within the deadline shown on the letter. Yes, sometimes you only have a few days because the notice was mailed late. The IRS computer doesn't know when it was mailed, so it will take the next action on schedule. Don't argue with the IRS staff person who answers the phone. He or she isn't at fault. Be pleasant and polite, and the person will be more apt to help you.

IRS Audits

Sooner or later, just about all businesses get audited. Not that often though. The IRS does happen to be behind on its audits. But it released an announcement in April 2004 about rolling out its new, more aggressive audits of businesses.

During the IRS's fiscal year 2002 (covering your 2001 tax return), the IRS audited less than half a percent of all tax returns filed.[1] That makes you feel great, right? Think again. In fiscal year 2009, IRS audit activities have increased and become more focused due to the tax gap. Over 4 percent of tax returns with an adjusted gross income of zero or less were audited.[2] Over 5 percent of tax returns showing over $1 million in income were examined (10 percent over $10 million). In between? About 2 percent of tax returns with incomes in the $200,000—$1 million range. The average tax return, between $0 and $200,000 was hit about 0.5 percent—1 percent of the time.

With the tax gap being in the hundreds of billions of dollars, the IRS believes that a large part of the unreported income, or underpaid taxes, is coming from small businesses. In 2009, the small business audits on both individuals and S-corporations have increased dramatically. Over 3 percent of small businesses are being audited. That's two or three times the past rate.

Why am I boring you with these statistics? Because it will help you with two areas of your business. First of all, it will help you determine what business format

1. IRS Statistical Reports—Table 10. Examination Coverage: Recommended and Average Recommended Additional Tax after Examination, by Size and Type of Return, Fiscal 2002, available at http://www.irs.gov/pub/irs-soi/02db10ex.xls.

2. Table 9b. Examination Coverage: Individual Income Tax Returns Examined, by Size of Adjusted Gross Income, Fiscal Year 2009 (http://www.irs.gov/pub/irs-soi/09db09bex.xls).

you want to adopt. Second, it will help you understand just how much risk there is of your transactions being scrutinized. So if you're thinking of doing something questionable—you know the risk.

What Is Most Apt to Attract the IRS's Attention?

As a small business, inconsistent information on your tax return will generate an audit. For instance:

- You have an office in home, but you are also taking a deduction for rent. You can't have both. At least not without an explanation. (See Chapter 7.).
- You are an S-corporation with a profit, but no officer wages. Major red flag! (See Chapters 3 and 9.)
- Your adjusted gross income is very low, but you are able to afford to live in a high-rent district (Zip code), with expenses that substantially exceed your reported income.

Anticipating an Audit: Laying the Groundwork

Knowing you're being audited is usually simple. You get an audit notice. If you've moved frequently and haven't updated your address with the IRS by filing Form 8822, you might not have gotten the notices. If this happens, some nice Fed in a dark suit will come knocking on your front door. You'll go running out the back door to call your tax professional. (Yes, one client of mine really did that. It's not a good idea.)

Whether you deal with the audit yourself or turn it over to a pro, you need to understand the process. After all, you'll be gathering all the documents. Following the guidelines here will save you hundreds of dollars off your professional's invoice.

Your Return Is about to Be Scrutinized

What will the IRS want to know? The primary goal is not to see if you have receipts for the expenses you reported on your tax return. What the agency is really looking for is unreported income. You're about to get some insider information on how to handle audits.

Unless you have a simple tax return, don't handle the audit yourself. Send a seasoned tax professional to the audit instead. In addition to the paperwork, the auditor will be looking you over during the audit. He or she will focus on five fundamental audit issues:

1. Your financial lifestyle
2. Your standard of living and reasonableness of business operations costs
3. Your spending habits and new purchases (conspicuous consumption)
4. All your bank deposits
5. Whether you reported all income from 1099 or W-2 reports

If these factors don't match your tax return (or industry practices), the IRS will suspect unreported income, inflated expenses, or worse, though your source of funds may simply be nontaxable income. When you've done nothing wrong, you don't want your intermingled accounts to get you into trouble.

Remember, the IRS is the nation's tax collector. It knows that people will do anything to reduce their taxes—even something illegal. The IRS's main focus is no longer on substantiating expenses. The IRS is serious about identifying unreported income and making the audits profitable.

With so many electronic tools and information-sorting technology, it has become easy to pinpoint the right tax returns for audit. Before it sees you, or your representative, the IRS can run a search of your name or your company name on the Internet.

The IRS can find your press releases or newsletters, puffing your company's successes. It can find your marriage, engagement, birth, and death notices. If you throw a really big confirmation, bar mitzvah, or wedding, chances are your pictures and announcements are online. You may even have a Web site. Consider this: You're probably giving the IRS the information yourself. So make sure that the information you've put into the public arena matches what the IRS sees on your tax return.

Don't believe me? Google your name. Now Google your business name. See?

Where Else Will the IRS Look for Information about You?

Take a look at Table 13.1. You'll find a whole list of sources the IRS can use to find out about you and your industry if the agency is uncomfortable with your audit. Typically, before an audit, the examiner will pull all the information the IRS has on you internally. (See the first section of Table 13.1.) Sometimes, the examiner doesn't have time to get everything, so he or she asks you to bring things—like

TABLE 13.1 How the IRS Knows More About You Than Your Return Shows

Inside Info: Within IRS Records

W-2s	IRP (Information Returns Program)
1099s	Market Segment Spec Program (MSSP)
Audits of other people's returns	National Research Program (NRP)
Audits of related or pass-through entities	Prior audit(s)
Collections	Prior examiners
Currency and Banking Retrieval System (CBRS)	Tax returns

    Casinos
    CTRs (Currency Transaction Reports)
    Customs
    F-Bar (report—foreign bank accounts)
    Form 8300

Data from Everywhere Else

Agencies	Law enforcement
Bankruptcies	Liens
Better Business Bureau (BBB)	Mortgages
Bureau of Labor Statistics (BLS)	OSHA
Court records (amount/holder)	Permits
Department of Agriculture (DOA)	Probate
Department of Motor Vehicles (DMV)	Property records
Department of Social Services (DSS)	Small Business Administration (SBA)
Department of Transportation (DOT)	Social Security Administration (SSA)
Divorces	U.S. Post Office (USPS)
Fictitious Name Register	

City and State Information

Employment/unemployment	Permits
Licenses	Sales tax

Other Sources

Banks/S&Ls/credit unions	Informants
City directory	Insurance providers
Corporations (charters, etc.)	Internet searches
Credit applications/reports suppliers	Landlord
Dun & Bradstreet	Legal databases
Employees/contractors	Neighbors
Employer	Newspaper articles
Employer's personnel records	Public utilities
Ex-spouse/children	Third-party contacts—various
Former personal contacts/relationships	Trade associations

prior-year returns. If you notice errors, don't fix them. Sooner or later the examiner will pull the actual return that was filed—and you want them to match. Right?

The IRS will only dig into the sources in the second section if it feels you're holding back information. If the examiner doesn't believe your story about that $10,000 deposit being a loan from Dad, he or she will start digging into city, state, or credit resources to see if there is evidence of a business you're not reporting.

Remember, the IRS is the arm of the U.S. government that caught Al Capone, Wesley Snipes, Christina Ricci, and Richard Hatch (from the TV show *Survivor*). The agency has access to substantial internal and external resources about people—especially in today's computer age.[3]

How Do You Overcome the IRS's Advantage?

In order to be the most successful in an audit, make sure your representative knows as much about you as the IRS knows. You never want your representative going to an audit only to have him or her learn that the IRS has communications from you that your pro is ignorant of, or that the IRS knows about income or bank accounts that your tax pro doesn't know about.

Be sure to disclose all income sources to your pro. Pull a copy of your own credit report to see what the IRS will find.

If you have unexplained or suspicious transactions, you may want to consider hiring an attorney instead of hiring an enrolled agent or certified public accountant.

Keep in mind: Your reputation and credibility with the IRS are your best assets if you want to minimize audit damage. If you're caught in a lie, the IRS won't help you reduce the impact of your errors.

If you have inadvertently not reported income, there may be a good reason for your oversight. If the IRS understands it wasn't intentional, the agency may help you avoid fraud and other penalties.

What Will Happen during the Audit?

First, you should have received a letter telling you what items on your tax return will be examined.

Look carefully at the pages that outline what the IRS wants to see. If you don't understand the letter, you may call the IRS office before you get there and ask for

---

3. Love gossip? For more stars in tax trouble, see http://vurl.bz/taxmama/Celebrity_Tax_Trouble.

clarification. That ought to shock the office. Few people ever do that besides tax professionals.

During the audit, your examiner will ask a series of questions about you, your past audits, your personal circumstances, and so on. Answer the questions as honestly as you can. Never lie and don't argue or evade the questions. The examiner is just filling out a form. If you don't know an answer, say so.

Once finished with the general questions, the auditor will focus on the tax return. The first concern is how much income you received. After that number makes sense, then he or she will look at your expenses or the other areas under consideration.

The auditor will have a printout of the 1099s issued to you. Those 1099s show interest-bearing bank accounts and money market accounts, with account numbers. The IRS will already know about your accounts, so bring all the bank statements requested to the audit.

The Most Important Item to Prepare—Proof of Cash

The auditor will look at your income first. To see what the auditor will see, prepare your own proof of cash. When overlooked by taxpayers or tax professionals, this one step can cause more trouble in audits than any other.

When the IRS takes all your bank statements, from all your accounts, and adds up the deposits, what will it find? If you're as casual about what goes into your bank accounts as most people, the IRS will find much more money showing up as deposits than you ever earned.

The total deposits will include loans, gifts, cash advances, inheritances, repayments of loans by family or friends, insurance proceeds . . . Are you getting the picture? In fact, one of the biggest sources of bank statement inflation is transfers from one account to another. If you leave it up to the auditor, it will look as if you didn't report income.

What happens if you leave it up to the IRS? Let me tell you about George.

George owned about 25 low-income residential buildings when he got audited one year. He went to the audit without any real preparation. When the auditor did the proof of cash, she discovered more than half a million dollars of unreported income. The tax, with penalties and interest, was more than $300,000. His tax preparer went back to the IRS and requested an audit reconsideration. While the tax preparer didn't do a great job preparing his second audit, he did get the balance cut by $20,000. That still left $280,000 due. Worse, the state of California would probably add another $100,000 when it was notified about the audit results.

George got lucky. He ran into a sympathetic IRS collections officer—Marta— who had audit background, too, and listened to George when he insisted that he never had that kind of income. Marta helped us to find the obvious transfers and nonincome items. We found several, including proceeds from mortgages when he refinanced two buildings and pulled cash out. Unfortunately, there was still $300,000 to identify. George was adamant it wasn't income. We found the answer when George remembered that he had borrowed money from the bank using his certificates of deposit as security. We couldn't provide records of the transactions. He had none. George's bank had burned down in the Rodney King riots in April of 1992.[4]

How did we convince the IRS that the $300,000 wasn't income? We located his old bank manager and had her write a letter saying that she knew he made a regular practice of borrowing against those certificates of deposit. The IRS dropped the rest of the assessment.

In George's case, if he or his tax pro had simply done the proof of cash, they'd have known about the large discrepancy before the audit. They could have rescheduled the audit until he tracked down all the nonincome items. It would have saved him thousands of dollars of professional fees. More important, George would have avoided the stress and fear that comes when the IRS keeps trying to attach your bank accounts, wages, and investment accounts for a year or two.

So how do you prepare this nifty proof of cash? It's really easy. See Table 13.2 for step-by-step instructions.

Now, take a look at an example in Table 13.3. Prepare it yourself on paper or using spreadsheet software. It makes no difference. Just do it neatly.

Looking at the "Total" column, the IRS would have determined that your income was $141,960 based on adding up all the deposits to all the accounts. Look at the actual income in the "Total" column. You can see that the net paycheck amounted to $40,140.

Now you understand how the IRS can think you have $100,000 more income than you really do. That's why it's so important to be prepared.

Okay. You've established that you didn't deposit more money than you reported on your tax return. What's next during your audit?

Time to Work on Expenses

In ideal situations, when you have a business, you have a profit and loss statement and a balance sheet, along with a detailed general ledger printout. Or you could go in with an accordion file with all the receipts neatly arranged into categories—with each batch of expenses totaled with adding machine tapes attached. You can prob-

---

4. Los Angeles reporter Stan Chambers of television station KTLA writes about the Rodney King and Watts riots, available at http://www.emmytvlegends.org/interviews/people/stan-chambers.

TABLE 13.2 Proof of Cash

Add all the deposits on all the bank statements for all 12 months. Use a spreadsheet like the one in Table 13.3. Make a separate column for each bank account and a "Total" column.

Deduct the following items from the "Totall" column:

☐ All personal loans

☐ Gifts or inheritances deposited to the account (get paperwork to prove it's a gift)

☐ Credit card cash advances deposited to the account

☐ Bank loans

☐ Refinancing proceeds deposited to the account

☐ Social Security or disability income

☐ Other nontaxable income (IRS tax refunds, certain lawsuit settlements, certain scholarships, etc.)

☐ Transfers between accounts

☐ Loans repaid to you by family or friends

☐ Refunds from stores for personal purchases

☐ Reimbursements from employers for your expense reports (be prepared to produce the reports)

---

ably do this when you have receipts that only belong in one expense category. But if the receipt or check needs to be split among several categories, what are you going to do? Think of credit cards. Each statement has auto expenses, office supplies, meals, travel, and entertainment. Unless you can make several photocopies of each statement to attach to each batch, you have a problem.

That's why it's important for you to do your bookkeeping *before* you go to an audit. Do it, even if you never bothered doing it before. (See Chapter 4 for more on record keeping.) Sure, your expenses might come out differently than they appear on the tax return. Don't worry. If your total expenses are the same, or similar, you'll be fine.

What If, after the Bookkeeping, Your Expenses Are Still Way Off?

You'll need to find the ways to come up with additional expenses—legally. Look here:

- **Credit cards.** Did you enter all the business expenses from each statement? From each credit card? Do you have a personal card that you sometimes used for business? Remember to include those business expenses. Did you

TABLE 13.3 Proof of Cash Spreadsheet

Deposits to All Accounts

	Note	Checking	Savings	Money Market	Total
January		3,345	250	650	4,245
February		3,345	50	650	4,045
March	1	3,815	250	150	4,215
April	2	5,345	250	1,950	7,545
May	3	3,545	250	1,115	4,910
June		3,345	250	1,115	4,710
July	4	45,345	250	41,115	86,710
August		3,345	250	1,115	4,710
September		3,345	250	1,115	4,710
October		3,345	250	1,115	4,710
November		3,345	250	1,115	4,710
December	5	4,345	250	2,115	6,710
Total Deposits		85,810	2,800	53,320	141,930

Less: Deduct all deposits that are not income

	Note	Checking	Savings	Money Market	
Advances	1	500			From credit card
Transfer	2	2,000			From money market
Advances	3	200			From credit card
Refi	4	42,000			Mortgage loan proceeds
Gift	5	1,000			From family
Transfers			2,800	53,320	From checking
Total nonincome		45,700	2,800	53,320	101,820
Actual income		**40,140**	0	0	**40,140**

Explanation of my cash flow:

All wages are deposited to the checking account.

Transfers are made each month to savings and money-market accounts.

The house was refinanced and the credit cards paid off in escrow.

The rest of the money from the refinance was transferred to the money-market account.

skip December's bill because it has a January date on it? Grab that bill. If the charges were in December, you may use them.

Did you have bad credit and have to use someone else's card? Get the other person's statements—and some of the receipts that show you signing for the charges. You may need some proof, but if you show the IRS examiner your really bad credit report, he or she might just smile and understand.

- **Cash.** Did you pay for things using cash in the normal course of the day but there are no receipts? Make reasonable estimates. Look back through your appointment book. If you traveled, make a list of the dates and places. List all the tips you gave out each day. List the cab fares, tolls, public transportation costs, and so on. Did you pay for parking, meters, pay phones? Using a spreadsheet, just list all the different out-of-pocket expenses. Be sure they don't add up to more than the cash you drew from your ATM or bank account.

For expenses where the IRS permits you to use standard amounts (auto, mileage, meals, and travel per diems), compare the actual costs with the standard rates. Often, I have been able to bypass a detailed scrutiny of the expenses via one of these methods. Tables with allowances for several years are available on the Internet. Chapter 6 tells you where to find them.

If you've pulled everything together and you still find discrepancies—call a tax professional. Find a tax pro with experience in audits, bookkeeping, and your industry. A professional may be able to read your mind and help you remember what you were thinking when you originally came up with the numbers on your tax return.

Unless, of course, you either simply made them up—or lied.

Still coming up short? You'll know before you go into the audit what you will lose. It won't be so intimidating when you already know the worst case.

What If You Don't Have Any Receipts?

The tax code operates on the "ordinary and necessary" principle. IRC §162 allows the deduction of ordinary and necessary expenses paid or incurred in carrying on a trade or business.[5] If it appears that an activity was entered into for profit, the rules of Section 162 are applied to each expense.

---

5. IRC §162, available at http://www.taxalmanac.org/index.php/Sec._162.

While the IRS is not always excited about the application of this principle, the courts have ensured that we taxpayers get the benefit of it. There's the old Cohan rule from 1930, when the appeals court decided in favor of entertainer George M. Cohan.[6] Cohan had deducted all his travel, meals, and business expenses without producing receipts. Can't you just see George M. riding around the country on rickety cars, buses, and trains, with his trunks full of vaudeville gear, costumes, props, and all, *and* dragging around another bag just for receipts and accounting records? Well, neither could the court. It determined that if the expenses make sense for your line of work, profession, or trade, you should be entitled to reasonable deductions in line with your industry—even if you don't have receipts.

Due to abuse of this provision, the courts have ruled that they will not allow *Cohan* if you have not made every reasonable attempt to re-create your records. If you make no attempt at all, don't count on *Cohan* to bail you out.

I tested the theory with a client who also happened to be an entertainer. Barry was audited a couple of years ago for his $50,000 worth of business expenses. Well, like good old George M., Barry had nary a receipt for all his travel, meals, and so on. Knowing we needed to provide proof of the travels and costs, I did a lot of work. Using various outside documents, like *TV Guide* and the postcards he sent me from the road each week, I was able to prove his travels. Using the IRS per diem rates, I established reasonable costs. The IRS accepted all the expenses, with no receipts, and better yet, no conflict. It was resolved at the auditor level, right in the office. Of course, it did take a little negotiating.

Negotiating

During an audit, you can negotiate, to some extent, on all levels. You must have a basis for your request. In George's case, discussed earlier, we were able to get the IRS to believe that $300,000 wasn't income because we were able to prove a pattern of behavior. In exchange for a letter from a banker, I was able to negotiate away $300,000.

Having a basis for your request may involve doing research on similar issues and being able to bring copies of those cases to the auditor. It may involve getting statements from objective third parties. It may involve agreeing to give up one set of expenses so that you can keep others that are more important to you in the future. For instance, I had a client whose tax return included an in-home office, while he was an employee, and $15,000 worth of garments he'd bought as samples. Alex was willing to give up the in-home office for that year, as long as the full amount of the

---

6. *Cohan v. Commissioner*, 39 F.2d 540 (1930).

garments was accepted. He needed those garments to support a Tax Court case. We didn't care about the employee office in home, because the following year he was a full-time independent contractor.

The IRS won't do it just because you ask. Not even if you're really cute.

TaxMama's Three Basic Rules of Tax Negotiating (KGB)

1. **Know.** Before you start negotiating, know exactly what you want to accomplish. (The IRS doesn't need to know that—but it's critical that you have it defined in your own mind.)
2. **Give up.** Have something to give up. (In exchange, be so thorough in your audit preparation that you find all expenses you overlooked. Look at missed itemized deductions—always a good source of errors in your favor!)
3. **Backup.** Give the auditor or appeals officer something tangible to put into the file to support your position. Providing backup documentation saves the auditor or officer time and makes the person look good to his or her superiors on review.

In George's audit, we weren't able to prove that the last $133,000 of deposits were transfers or loans. Since I was able to prove that there was a consistent pattern of behavior, I could negotiate with the IRS about the rest. The IRS would accept the logic and conclude the sum was not income in exchange for my preparing a worksheet with an explanation to provide the auditor for his file. It gave him an excuse to accept my position that the deposits probably were not income.

Office auditors have the discretion to decide what documentation is acceptable. They have to believe the information they see is adequate. Be sure to make an extra set of copies of all the schedules and work papers for the auditor's file. It provides documentation and makes him or her look better when superiors review the auditor's determination. Besides, the auditor can write notes on it, too.

Audit Reconsiderations, Appeals, and Tax Court: Some Brief Words

An audit reconsideration[7] is when the IRS agrees to reopen an audit that has already been completed and is past all the deadlines for protest on the local level. It is *not* an appeal. The audit goes back to the same level of examination, often the same

---

7. *Internal Revenue Manual*, Part 4, Chapter 13, "Audit Reconsideration"—Read the IRS's internal instructions, available at http://vur.me/taxmama/IRM_Part4.

office, which conducted the original audit. The IRS will not give you reconsideration if you have already signed off, agreeing to the original audit. You must have additional information that wasn't presented at the first audit. The IRS will also give you this opportunity if you didn't appear at the original audit. When you ask for the reconsideration, you'd better have at least 80 percent of your material ready. You generally get one shot to present your case. So prepare it well. While the IRS rarely agrees, you *can* get audit reconsiderations. First, you must have the audit report, which is on either Form 4549 or Form 1092-B. If you were working with an examiner, ask him or her for help. If you no longer have that contact information, call the IRS's main phone number at (800) 829-1040 and make the request. If you still have a contact name, ask the auditor's group manager for the reconsideration. If that doesn't work, here are your other options:

- Write to the branch chief.
- Have your tax professional contact the Practitioner Priority Service (PPS). (It's a special hotline at the tax pro community.) PPS has Form 3410, Request for Audit Reconsideration. Also ask for Forms 3411 and 3412.
- Contact the Taxpayers Advocate at (877) 777-4778.
- Make an appointment at an IRS Problem-Solving Day or Open House.
- Contact the Small Business/Self-Employed Operating Division.
- Contact the deputy director, Compliance Field Operations.
- Contact the director of the IRS.
- Contact your U.S. senator or representative—or all of them. Sometimes, the only thing that will work is political intervention.

Don't ever give up. There's always somewhere to go when you disagree with an audit. Decide if the cost to fight your battle is worth what you will win. Sometimes, it's cheaper just to give in to the IRS. But if it's really a matter of principle and all avenues fail, you may want to look for an advocacy group to take your case on. Sometimes what's happening to you is happening to enough other people that it's worth setting up a class action suit or rewriting legislation.

Should You Use Appeals Only as a Last Resort?

Some tax professionals find the appeals process is sometimes easier to deal with than the IRS's auditors. While all auditors must have college degrees, the degree does not necessarily have to be in accounting or taxation. Sometimes the auditors are not as well trained as we would like. With the IRS hiring thousands of new employees between 2009 and 2010, expect to see a lot of people new to auditing.

By the time the IRS agents get promoted to the appeals level, they have extensive field experience, education, training, and the ability to use and understand tax research and research tools. You are dealing with a seasoned professional who has more decision authority than the office auditor and many field auditors.

The goal of the Appeals Office is to settle cases without litigation. The appeals officers evaluate your case's strengths and weaknesses with an eye to how your case will stand up in court. They will pull the relevant court cases, decisions, and precedents (or at least the items the officers think are relevant). Ask them for their citations when you meet. Most important, have your own research ready. Give them a copy of your cases (not just the citations to cases) with your points highlighted. It will enhance their willingness to cooperate with you. You've done a big part of their job, and they have objective documentation, in your favor, to put into your IRS file.

Remember, generally, an appeal is not about supporting expenses. It is about tax law and precedents. If deductions were not substantiated during audit, expect the appeals officers to require supporting documents—or they might even kick the audit back to the original auditor to finish. If you couldn't resolve it at that level, do you really want to go there now?

Most tax professionals use the appeals process to their advantage. So can you. When confronted with a particularly troublesome auditor and a group manager who will not intervene, a tax pro would simply call a halt to the whole process. I'd tell the IRS to post its adjustments and walk away.

Then, I'd do one of two things:

1. Request fast-track mediation. This is handled by the Appeals Office. Fast-track mediation is rarely used, and the Appeals Office would like to see it used more often. The appeals officers will work intensely to reach a resolution at that meeting with you and the original examiner (and perhaps the auditor's manager). You can find more information about this program at http://vurl. bz/taxmama/IRS_Fast-Track.
2. Wait for the audit determination letter (30-day letter). When it comes, it tells you right on it that you can request an appeals hearing. If you haven't already, get a good tax professional involved. He or she will do a more efficient job at this level.

When writing the letter requesting the appeals hearing, briefly include specific areas where the auditor is incorrect and outline the documentation you are going to add for this hearing. *Do not* include a harangue of the auditor's bad qualities or what's wrong with the IRS or the system.

Meanwhile, get all your documentation together. This will include all the support for the unresolved income-expense issues. It will require that you do in-depth research on the tax law issues involved. This is where all that work you did on your business plan will pay off. If you have losses, the business plan will prove that wasn't your intention. But things do go wrong.

Getting Your Case to Tax Court

If you've missed your opportunity to go to appeals after the 30-day letter, wait for the 90-day letter (Notice of Deficiency). Owing less than $50,000 means you're eligible to file your petition as a small case. You'll find a Small Case Tax Petition Kit online at the U.S. Tax Court's Web site, http://www.ustaxcourt.gov/forms/Petition_Kit.pdf.

You may use an attorney, a CPA, or an enrolled agent (EA) to represent you. With a CPA or EA, you'll need to sign the petition yourself (in pro per). Once the case gets kicked back to appeals, your EA or CPA will handle the meeting for you. Tax Court cases usually get resolved at this level. I've resolved all my clients' Tax Court cases without ever going beyond appeals. In fact, reading many Tax Court decisions, it's clear some cases only went to Tax Court because the taxpayers were really rude or unpleasant to appeals—or their representative wanted to make some extra money. There are also those cases that look simple but were pushed up to Tax Court to establish a precedent.

Strategy: Use as much of the 90 days as you can to get your records as ready as possible. Send your petition in at least 10 days before the end of the 90 days. Enclose the $60 filing fee and mail to:

> The United States Tax Court
> 400 Second Street, NW
> Washington, DC 20217

Owing Taxes

All right, you've exhausted all logical ways to reduce your audit assessment. Or you filed a tax return and owe money. How do you go about paying it?

Naturally, if you have the money, send the check and get it over with. If you're not liquid right now, here are some ways to pay.

Credit Card

The first two companies listed below have contracts with the IRS and other government agencies. They have been processing millions of dollars' worth of government credit card payments for about a decade. (The EFTPS program is part of the IRS.) There are two advantages to using credit cards. The first is that you will have immediate proof of payment. The second is the bonus or mileage points you earn for those charges.

- **http://www.OfficialPayments.com.** Pay IRS, state, and local taxes online.
- **http://www.pay1040.com.** Make federal tax payments online.
- **http://www.eftps.gov.** Pay quarterly estimates, payroll taxes, and business taxes online.

When using these services, the tax agency doesn't pay the merchant fees—you do. (Merchant fees are the costs the merchants normally pay for accepting your credit card.) These fees will cost about 2.5 to 5 percent of the taxes you pay. (They're called "convenience" fees—that's for the convenience of the tax agency, not you.)

Suppose you'd like to use your credit cards but don't want to pay online. Here are two other ways to use your credit cards:

- **Alternative 1.** Use your credit card checks (you get all those things in the mail, daily, right?). Read the fine print. See what the company is going to charge you. Seen if you can get a no-transaction-fee check. Remember to ask for reduced interest or 0 percent interest on the transaction fee. Unfortunately, I have not seen any lately with transaction fees lower than 3 percent. You might still get your mileage or rewards points.
- **Alternative 2.** Call your credit card company and request a cash advance to be deposited into your bank account. It will take a week or 10 days, so do it now. If you cajole sweetly, you might get it without transaction fees— otherwise, expect to pay 2 to 3 percent of the amount charged. Look for a card that has a maximum fee. Beware. Most don't. Be sure to request low or 0 percent interest and ask about the mileage or reward points. *Note:* While these 0 percent rates used to be good for up to 18 months, most of them are now limited to 6 months. You will find the most current 0 percent cards at TaxMama's Credit Card Center—http://taxmama.com/quick-look-ups.

You Can't Afford to Pay Now, But Will Ultimately

If this is the case, there are three ways to go.

1. **File Form 9465, Installment Agreement Request.** This is the method the IRS suggests. Think twice before requesting an installment agreement (IA). There is a $105 fee for an IA, which you will have to pay again and again if you default on the agreement. (The fee is only $52 if payments are deducted directly from your bank account.) In addition, you give the IRS your bank account numbers and the right to attach your funds if you're late or miss a payment. In the past, the IRS levied the bank account immediately when you were late. These days, the kinder, friendlier IRS gives you a chance to make good. Or if your financial circumstances have changed, the IRS is willing to revise your IA. The fee to restructure an IA is $45. Anyone may get an installment agreement, as long as you're not in default on another balance.

2. **Don't file the Installment Agreement Request immediately.** Send the IRS whatever you can afford with the first balance due letter. Save up and send money every time the IRS sends you a balance due notice. If you expect to have enough money to pay the balance off in about six to nine months, this may be cheaper and less invasive than requesting the IA. You'll still be paying interest on the penalties and taxes, but the interest is in the 3–7 percent range these days—that's probably less than many credit cards.

3. **Borrow the money from family or friends.** If they love you and trust you— and you're really reliable about paying them back—it's the best option. When you're a few days late, they won't be attaching your bank account. If you're going to flake out on the loan, though, don't borrow the money in the first place. You will destroy valuable relationships and trust. There are still other options.

When the Balance Is Too Large to Pay Off

The balance is so large that you're just never going to have the money. You're elderly and are living on a fixed income. You're insolvent. You can't even afford a bankruptcy attorney. You're not hiding any assets or money. If this is the case, call the IRS and tell the truth. The IRS can put a special collections hold on your balance due for six months or a year and will contact you to review the situation for the next 10 years. If, during that time, you can never pay it, you're off the hook.

There is a 10-year limit for the IRS to collect money from you after a tax debt is recorded. Your state may have different limits or no limits at all.

Some actions can stop that clock, but it's best if you get a good tax professional to help you determine where you stand when you're in that situation. I always have a tax attorney perform those computations.

Request an Offer in Compromise

Suppose you aren't really insolvent, but the balance is just so unbearable that you feel beaten down by it. Perhaps you have a job or some sort of steady income from your business, but you'll never earn enough to pay all the taxes due.

You do have a way out. The Offer in Compromise (OIC) Program might be able to help you. When you file an offer in compromise, you're asking the IRS to accept a fraction of what you owe on your taxes—and to write off the rest of your debt. But don't get carried away. There is no promise that your tax debt of $50,000 will get cut to $3,000.

The OIC Myth WASHINGTON—The Internal Revenue Service today issued a consumer alert, advising taxpayers to beware of promoters' claims that tax debts can be settled for "pennies on the dollar" through the Offer in Compromise Program. Some promoters are inappropriately advising indebted taxpayers to file an Offer in Compromise (OIC) application with the IRS. This bad advice costs taxpayers money and time. An Offer in Compromise is an agreement between a taxpayer and the IRS that resolves the taxpayer's tax debt. The IRS has the authority to settle, or "compromise," federal tax liabilities by accepting less than full payment under certain circumstances.[8]

Qualifying for an Offer in Compromise

Late-night television, radio, and even some daytime television commercials fill your ears with promises of tax miracles. You're probably getting lots of e-mail, too. Since the IRS filed a tax lien against you, your mailbox is being filled with solicitations from certain tax firms promising you quick resolution of your problem. Be wary. The truth is most outfits will take far too much of your money— and not help you nearly as much as you'd expect. One promoter even offered a discounted price of $1,500 to give you a do-it-yourself kit, with instructions. That firm was shut down by the IRS, and some members did jail time. Only use

---

8. IRS Notice 2004-17, dated February 3, 2004, available at http://www.irs.gov/pub/irs-irbs/irb04-17.pdf.

firms when you can get a recommendation from someone you know who has used them successfully. Otherwise, go to your own tax professional for help or for a recommendation.

The IRS also offers a do-it-yourself kit. It's free. There's a Form 656 kit that can be downloaded from the IRS's Web site. The IRS even provides workshops on filling in these forms. Check the IRS Web site at http://www.irs.gov or call the agency at (800) 829-1040 to see if it is offering a workshop near you. But before you do all that, let's see if you qualify.

What if you don't qualify for an OIC? Don't waste your time applying if you don't meet the IRS standards for applying. Here are some general parameters—not the ones the IRS posts—but the reality it uses when considering your offers:

- Are you young, healthy, and able to work?
- Do you have a college education but are choosing not to pursue work in your own field because you'd rather follow your dream?
- Do you have a steady income?
- Do you have equity in your home? Or an IRA or other retirement account?
- Are you expecting a windfall? An inheritance? Or a great job about to start pouring money your way? Don't lie. That's tax fraud. It's one of the few reasons the IRS will send you to jail.

Look at your own earning capability over the next five years. Even though it may be tight, if there's enough left over, by living within your means or restructuring your lifestyle, the IRS will reject your offer. It won't wait while you pursue your dreams and live as a starving artist. It will simply reject your offer in compromise.

Suppose you do qualify and are ready to prepare an OIC. Be thorough. Attach legible copies of all forms, bank statements, and bills requested by the IRS. Enclose three months' worth. Read the information about how it all works on the IRS Web site (http://vur.me/taxmama/IRS_OIC). If you're not willing to provide the IRS with this much information, don't even start the process. The IRS now requires a fee of $150 be sent in with the application. So you're wasting your money if you don't follow through.

The IRS reports that more than 80 percent of applications for offers in compromise are rejected as incomplete. Another 10 percent are rejected because people don't respond. If you simply attach everything and enclose anything else the IRS wants, you're already in that small minority that might get accepted.

While I warn you away from unscrupulous representatives, I do recommend that you work with a competent tax professional who has a track record of getting OICs for his or her clients. It is a long, complicated process, and having a pro who has gone through it can help. Since you must provide all the documents anyway, you can save yourself dozens of hours of billable time if you gather them all and organize them yourself. I won't go into any more detail here; the application packet is remarkably self-explanatory.

Currently, the IRS is overloaded on offers in compromise applications. Expect the process to take about a year to a year and a half. Really. It's slow and nerve-racking.

The costs? Even if you hire an ethical tax professional to deal with the IRS on your behalf, expect to pay for at least 10 to 15 hours, if you're organized and cooperative. If you must be chased down and hounded to get documents or if you just dump all your records on the tax pro you hired and expect him or her to do all the work, you're up to 20 to 40 hours.

How about Filing Bankruptcy?

Perhaps you don't want to go through the misery of an OIC. You may not want to subject yourself to remarkable levels of stress and frustration, feeling you're at the mercy of an arbitrary system. You have one last alternative.

Look into bankruptcy. Discharging tax debt isn't easy. When you qualify, it is faster than an OIC, less intrusive—and much cheaper. Attorneys handling this will typically charge about $3,000.

To discharge your taxes in bankruptcy, you must qualify.

- All your returns have been filed.
- If filed, the taxes due were not based on fraud.
- If filed late, the return was filed two years or more before the bankruptcy petition.
- The tax return, with extensions, was due three years or more before filing of the bankruptcy petition.
- Tax liability was assessed more than 240 days before filing of the petition.

All those requirements must be met in order to qualify.

There are several complications about how the 240 days are counted or what stops the clock. As with all benefits, this one won't come too easily.

The biggest hurdle for many to overcome is the emotional one. There is an intense feeling of failure, of self-denigration when you're reduced to this. But if this is your only—or your best—option, take it. Trust me. I've seen the transformation in people who did. Many people spend years trying to resolve their tax debt through the IRS's channels and simply end up wasting 5 or 10 years feeling worthless, unable to sleep, and unable to maintain their relationships. Yes, taxes do destroy relationships.

Sometimes it's best to just clean the slate and start fresh. But if you do, make sure you don't get into trouble again. Please, don't use tax bankruptcy as part of your regular tax plan.

Summary of IRS Interactions

The information in this one chapter took me more than 20 years to learn. Much of it came through sheer stubbornness and the refusal to back down to my fear of the IRS. The rest of the information came through lots of audits and thousands of responses to notices. It helped that in the past few years, we really did get a kinder, gentler IRS.

Using the guidelines in this chapter, you'll never have to be afraid of the IRS or mystified by its confusing notices. You have everything you need in order to know how to respond to the usual notices—and audits.

Tax Notices, Audits, and Collection Notes Resources

Important Acronyms
- **FYTIN—form, year, TIN.** What you write on all checks to government agencies.
- **KGB—Know, give up, backup**. An audit negotiating tool.

Web Resources
- **List of IRS notices and explanations.** http://vur.me/taxmama/IRS-Notices.
- *Internal Revenue Manual*, **Part 4, Examining Process.** http://vur.me/taxmama/IRM_Part4.
- **Internal Revenue Service fast-track mediation process for audits and collections disputes.** http://vurl.bz/taxmama/IRS_Fast-Track.
- **Internal Revenue Service offer-in-compromise information.** http://vur.me/taxmama/IRS_OIC.
- **Form 433-A, Collection Information Statement for Wage Earners and Self-Employed Individuals.** http://www.irs.gov/pub/irs-pdf/f433a.pdf.
- **Form 433-B, Collection Information Statement for Business.** http://www.irs.gov/pub/irs-pdf/f433b.pdf.

- **Form 656, Offer in Compromise Application and Instruction Packet.** http://www.irs.gov/pub/irs-pdf/f656.pdf.
- **Form 2210, Underpayment of Estimated Taxes.** http://www.irs.gov/pub/irs-pdf/f2210.pdf.
- **Form 8822, Change of Address.** http://www.irs.gov/pub/irs-pdf/f8822.pdf.

Online Credit Card Payment Resources
- **Official Payments.** http://www.OfficialPayments.com: Lets you pay IRS, state, and local taxes online.
- **PAY1040.com.** http://www.pay1040.com: Make federal tax payments online.
- **EFTPS (Electronic Federal Tax Payment System).** http://www.eftps.gov. Pay quarterly estimates, payroll taxes, and business taxes online.

General Bankruptcy and Tax Bankruptcy Resources
- **TaxMama.** http://taxmama.com/tax-bankruptcy/bankruptcy-freedom.
- **U.S. Tax Court.** http://www.ustaxcourt.gov/forms/Petition_Kit.pdf. U.S. Tax Court Small Case Petition Kit.

Credit Resources
- **Ilyce Glink—credit and finance books.** http://www.thinkglink.com.
- **Liz Weston—credit guidance and resources.** http://asklizweston.com.

EPILOGUE

Some Final Words of Advice— and Resources to Rely On

If a man empties his purse into his head, no man can take it away from him. An investment in knowledge always pays the best interest.

—BENJAMIN FRANKLIN

All Good Things Must End

We've been together for so long now, I'm going to miss you. I have great confidence in your success. You've done everything right along the way. Your business plan is smashing. You worked out some of the kinks in the first few months of operations, so it's been rebalanced. Your tax pro has reviewed your accounting records, to high praise. Your customers love you.

Most of all, your home and family life has been enriched through your family's enthusiastic participation in shaping your legacy.

Let me leave you with this comment from my favorite writer and egotist, Isaac Asimov: "I am at least as intelligent as my tax advisor. So, I should have no trouble understanding the tax laws. But if I were to concentrate my energies towards learning everything I needed to know, the world would be deprived of many of my books."[1]

Follow Asimov's advice. Learn enough about taxes to build a strong foundation. Keep your trusted tax advisor handy, as well as your advisory team. Then concentrate your energies on what you do best—running your business.

---

1. For a history on the good doctor, his writings, his films, and his life, go to http://www.AsimovOnline.com.

Resources

You've been immersed in tax and business information throughout this book. You've learned so much more than you ever expected. There's so much to learn, to know, about tax law and strategy. This book was designed to be your guide—to lead you to more information. It was designed to open your mind to creative ways of thinking—to bring you perspectives you didn't have before and won't find anywhere else.

You've got power you never had. (Have I said this before? A dozen times perhaps? Oh my goodness, I've become my mother!) But, please, you're in business. Don't prepare your own tax returns. You have an advisory team. Use it. The team and the resources listed throughout the book will help keep you up to date. Most of the resources in these pages are available quickly and freely on the Internet.

Hang On to These Important Phone Numbers

- **IRS main phone number.** (800) TAX-1040 or (800) 829-1040
- **IRS forms and publications order line.** (800) TAX-FORM or (800) 829-3676
- **IRS e-help for EFTPS.** (800) 555-4477
- **Social Security Administration.** (800) 772-1213
- **Taxpayers Advocate Service.** (877) 777-4778
- **Your Business Bible.** http://www.yourbusinessbible.com. Look for worksheets and updates to this book.

For more resources, please check the end of each chapter and the wonderful index in this book. Thanks for letting me join you on your new business adventure!

Always leave them laughing when you say goodbye!

—George M. Cohan of the
Cohan rule fame[2]

---

2. Stacy A. Teicher, "No, your husband is not deductible . . . and other IRS tales," *Christian Science Monitor*, April 15, 2004: http://www.csmonitor.com/2004/0415/p01s04-wmgn.htm.

INDEX

ABOUT THE AUTHOR

Taking her first tax class in college, Eva Rosenberg declared she was avoiding this subject—for good. The information changes too much, too often. Who could ever keep up?

Intending to grow up to be vice president of international marketing for IBM, Eva took a brief detour, spending a couple of years with national CPA firms. Doing taxes temporarily, to earn a living while completing her MBA in international business, Eva kept running into companies and people with tax problems needing to be solved. Looking up, more than 20 years later, she finds herself the go-to gal for the tax community. CPAs, attorneys, and enrolled agents call her when their clients get audited or have tax problems that can't be resolved. Eva finds solutions that surprise even her—or she negotiates a fair resolution.

Not only does Eva help and advise tax professionals; she trains them. TaxMama's EA Exam Review Course helps prepare the tax professional community to pass the tough IRS examinations in order to gain the coveted *enrolled agent* designation. Never heard of enrolled agents or the Special Enrollment Examination (SEE)? Learn more about both at http://www.IRSExams.com.

Eva Rosenberg has written books, articles, tax columns, and even chapters of tax textbooks. An Internet pioneer and mentor to many, Eva founded the Internet's HelpDesk & WebReview in 1997 to provide a safe place to ask dumb questions about your business Web site. It lasted for nearly 10 years and inspired the Tax Mama.com Web site and persona.

Those years and experiences make Eva a popular resource for journalists. You'll find her quoted in publications as diverse as the *Wall Street Journal, Christian Science Monitor, Chicago Tribune, New York Times, Los Angeles Times, USA Today, Glamour, Woman's Day,* and *National Enquirer.* Her tips appear regularly in banking publications, including those of Wells Fargo, Guaranty Bank, and BankRate.com. Eva is still awed each time she sees her name in print.

An immigrant to America who has seen life as both a charity recipient and the donor, Eva has the refreshing ability to understand and address the needs of the rich and the poor, as well as the ESL and non-English-speaking community—and to cut through the sob stories. She recognizes just how easy it is, in America, to move your address from the back seat of your semi-demolished car to the deck of your 100-foot yacht, with your GPS and satellite-based Internet connection—and to lose it all. Or to live for free on the kindness of strangers.

Eva's frankness, sense of humor, and casual, stand-up tax delivery make her a popular talk show guest and speaker around the country. Her Dow Jones Market Watch.com tax columns are eagerly anticipated by readers, wondering just what IRS button she's going to push next. Eva proudly displays a framed copy of IRS Notice 2004-27 issued as a result of one of her MarketWatch.com articles.

New projects in 2010 include a weekly tax column for Equifax at http://www. Equifax.com and a weekly radio show on the Womens Radio network at http://www.WomensRadio.com.

Known as TaxMama for both her warmth and her nagging, Eva, an enrolled agent, is the publisher of the highly acclaimed TaxMama.com and author of the weekly, syndicated Ask TaxMama column and the daily TaxQuips podcast. The Tax Mama.com site is a free resource, warmly welcoming all taxpayers and tax professionals. Through the site, Eva provides articles, IRS news, links to tax forms for the IRS and all states, and free answers to visitors' tax questions . . . along with her own twist on pending and current legislation. Of course, Eva knows that people really come for the Money Funnies—the jokes pages.

Go to TaxMama.com for your free subscription and access to a continuing stream of tax advice, news, and tips—where taxes are fun.

Use this special sign-up address just for *Small Business Taxes Made Easy* readers, http://TaxMama.com/subscribeEASY, to get an autographed e-gift from your TaxMama. Be sure to visit Your Business Bible at http://www.yourbusinessbible.com to find worksheets and updates to this book.

After all, TaxMama is watching out for you!